Privacy and the Press

the rapid growth of mass media in the late nineteenth century, outlines the development of privacy law including recent decisions by the Supreme Court, and analyzes the impact of the law upon the news media.

Underscoring the whole of this study is a constant awareness of the crucial relationship between the right to privacy and the right of free speech guaranteed by the First Amendment. Because of his training and experience, the author confesses to favor the side of a free press, and he cites sound legal precedent to support his contention that freedom of expression is the foundation upon which all other freedoms are built.

PRIVACY AND THE PRESS is a book written for journalists and laymen, but with lawyers also in mind. It comes at a time when the right of privacy is at the forefront of public opinion.

DON R. PEMBER was for many years a practicing journalist, working on newspapers in Michigan. He is currently on the faculty of the School of Communications at the University of Washington.

PRIVACY
and the PRESS

The Law,
the Mass Media,
and the First Amendment

DON R. PEMBER

UNIVERSITY OF WASHINGTON PRESS

Seattle and London

Library of Congress Cataloging in Publication Data
Pember, Don R   1939–
    Privacy and the press.
    Bibliography: p.
    1. Privacy, Right of—U. S. I. Title.
KF1262.P4   342'.73'085   79-152335
                         ISBN 0-295-95152-4

For Diann

Preface

For years the study of the law of privacy has remained primarily the job of the lawyer or the legal scholar. Consequently, few persons outside the law know much about privacy: its history, its growth, and its imperatives. For most people this does not pose a problem—few of us are affected by the law of privacy. But the newsman is affected every day, many times a day, as he prepares his record of contemporary events. Each news story, each advertisement, and each picture poses the threat of a possible lawsuit.

I undertook this study in an attempt to help those members of society not directly involved with law to understand better the limitations and restrictions placed upon mass media by the law of privacy. Technical aspects of the law, problems on which law students spend many days of study, have been carefully excluded from this work, which concentrates on the substantive portions of the law. In some cases substantive problems have been reduced to terms which are undoubtedly alien to the lawyer, but which will be meaningful to the working newsman, magazine editor, or interested layman.

Privacy is a concept that touches varied aspects of human behavior. Consequently, a broad range of ideas is often included under the general heading, right of privacy. At one end of the spectrum is the anthropologists' amorphous concept of psychic space. Scientists such as Edward Hall [1] suggest that both human beings and other animals have a sense of psychic space, which varies from race to race, species to species, and culture to culture. Americans waiting for a bus will instinctively space themselves several feet apart; Arabs will cluster. When overpopulation or overcrowding diminishes the amount of psychic space available to a species, a crisis occurs, resulting in a drop in the birth rate or even death for many members of the species. And at the other end of the spectrum we see the pragmatic definitions of privacy, laid down in statute books in four states, which provide civil and criminal sanctions when an individual's identity is appropriated without consent for someone else's commercial gain.

In between these two definitions are arrayed a great many other explications of the concept of privacy. For example, many scholars agree that no less than five of the nine amendments of the Bill of Rights create a constitutional concept of privacy. The First Amendment's protections of expression, association, and religious conscience in a sense guard the individual privacy of a citizen. The Third Amendment guarantees to the individual that soldiers or militiamen cannot be quartered in his home during peacetime. The right to be free from an unreasonable search of the person or the home is established by the Fourth Amendment. The Fifth Amendment protects a person against being forced by any official body to incriminate himself, and the Seventh Amendment guarantees that no cruel or unusual punishment will be used to gain consent for an invasion of the individual's mind.

The development of a national data center, or an information warehouse, has often been labeled an invasion of privacy. Such a center, which could be filled with records covering a man's birth, schooling, military service, employment history, personality traits, credit status, and practically any other aspect of his life, would enable the government to assemble at the touch of a button all the information it might want about a particular individual.

Personality testing and the use of lie detectors constitute other kinds of invasion of privacy, according to many persons. The answering of personal questions which is often required of everyone applying for government as well as nongovernment jobs constitutes a trespass through his mind, an invasion of his private and personal life.

When measured alongside these numerous definitions of privacy, this study is very narrow. Its intent is to present a full discussion of one kind of privacy—that is, the law of privacy—and how it relates to the mass media in America.

The law of privacy differs from other kinds of privacy in specific ways. In the first place, the law of privacy is enforceable in a court of law or equity. An individual who feels that his privacy has been invaded can seek legal redress; an injunction, perhaps, to stop the invasion, or money damages to compensate for emotional distress. In addition, the law of privacy usually requires not only an intrusion or invasion, but some kind of publication of information about the injured party. Finally, the law of privacy protects an individual from the actions of other individuals, not from the actions of governments. Our constitutional right of privacy, if such a right does indeed exist, protects us only from action by the government. In general, provisions in declarations or bills of rights have been regarded as limitations upon the powers of government, rather than as sources of rights as between individuals. The outstanding exception is habeas corpus.

With these restrictions in mind, it can be readily seen that most of the kinds of privacy invasions discussed thus far will not be included in this study. There is no way, for example, to seek judicial assistance in maintaining psychic space, although many courts will entertain claims of a trespass on an individual's physical space. The concepts of personality testing and the gathering of data in a single national center are excluded for lack of a significant publication about the injured party. By concentrating on a single aspect of the broad range of privacy, this study will probe to a greater depth than has been reached in the past and explore a significant problem which has been largely ignored in the past—the basic conflict between the individual's right to enjoy his privacy and the freedom of the American press.

This study has several goals. I hope that the growth of the law of privacy as it relates to the media, particularly the news media, can be adequately traced. This has not been done previously, despite the volumes of research on privacy. Alan Westin, for example, in his widely acclaimed book, *Privacy and Freedom,* virtually ignored this aspect of privacy. Vance Packard and Myron Brenton, in their popular treatments of the subject, are guilty of the same omission.[2]

My second goal is to organize the law of privacy in such a fashion as to clarify its major principles and make them understandable to the informed layman who knows a little about both the law and the press. There is no intent to prepare an essay on "How to Avoid Privacy Litigation" for newsmen. Yet I cannot avoid hoping to offer some ideas to members of the press, many of whom have only a slight acquaintance with the law. Samuel Hofstader and George Horowitz, who have published a comprehensive volume on the right of privacy, failed in this respect. That book was designed primarily for legal scholars and lawyers.[3]

In fact, most of what has been published on the subject of privacy and the press has been written by attorneys for attorneys. Much of the available literature is therefore plaintiff-oriented—that is, directed at assisting the individual in fending off the snooping newsman through court action—and has resulted in an overemphasis in the literature on court decisions which favor the plaintiff. *Barber* v. *Time,* a suit brought by a woman with a rare disease who was plagued by newsmen in her hospital room, is one of the nation's best-known privacy decisions. In some respects Mrs. Barber's successful action against *Time* magazine has become a leading case. But when measured against the total body of privacy law, this case represents poor legal precedent. Persons who have been thrust into the public spotlight—either by choice or by chance—have rarely succeeded in privacy suits for news coverage about their plights. There are probably a dozen lesser known but similar cases in opposition to the *Barber* decision that reflect the true nature of the law. But because *Barber* has been heralded for many years in the literature, it stands out as an important precedent—which it is not. Hence, another of my goals is to offer a defense-oriented treatment of the law.

Finally, this study is designed to provide a theoretical and interpretive foundation for placing the law of privacy in its proper perspective to the First Amendment to the United States Constitution. With the exception of two or three law review articles, this has never been done. It is true that many attempts to lay a theoretical foundation lapse into what Judge Learned Hand once aptly called "shoveling smoke." This problem is acute when dealing with the common law, a body of ideas and principles which is itself amorphous. Yet, a proper framework can sometimes create order when only chaos has existed previously.

Anyone studying the law of privacy and the mass media soon encounters a basic philosophical problem, the same one with which courts have been faced throughout the history of privacy: Which is more important, the protection given to society by a free and unfettered press, or the peace of mind given the individual by rigid protection of the right to privacy? While I have attempted to remain objective in this study, there is little doubt that my training and experience as a newsman has placed me on the side of the free press. It is my belief that freedom of expression is the foundation upon which all other freedoms are built.

There are many persons without whose help this study could not have been completed. I owe a great deal of thanks to Professors William A. Hachten and Dwight L. Teeter of the School of Journalism, the University of Wisconsin. Without Professor Teeter's continued enthusiasm and Professor Hachten's scholarly guidance, this project would probably still be in the planning stage. Both gentlemen served beyond the call of duty on many occasions, and to them goes my warmest gratitude.

I also wish to thank Professor Harold L. Nelson, director of the University of Wisconsin School of Journalism, for his scholarly counsel and for his willingness to listen to my frequent "discoveries" and "problems." Thanks must also go to David Fellman, professor of political science at the University of Wisconsin, and Professors Samuel Mermin and Willard Hurst of the University of Wisconsin School of Law for their kind help.

My appreciation is also extended to Professor David Levy of the University of Oklahoma History Department, who took time from his work editing the letters of Louis Brandeis to help me locate correspondence between Samuel Warren and the late United States Supreme Court justice.

Finally, recognition must be given to the person who was chief typist, proofreader, and editor, my wife, Diann. Without her help this book would not have been written. For that reason it is dedicated to her.

D. R. P.

Seattle, Washington
October 1970

Contents

Privacy and the Press

I

The Roots of Privacy

If the jurisprudence of the last century has taught us anything, it is the necessity of recognizing that law cannot be static, unless a society is also static.

WILLIAM M. BEANEY [1]

As the last decade of the nineteenth century dawned in the United States, the nation began to awaken to what was perhaps the most profound social change that had ever occurred in man's life on this planet. Historian Henry Steele Commager called the decade the "watershed of American history":

On the one side lies an America predominantly agricultural; concerned with domestic problems; conforming, intellectually at least, to the political, economic, and moral principles inherited from the seventeenth and eighteenth centuries. . . . On the other side lies the modern America, predominately urban and industrial; . . . experiencing profound changes in population, social institutions, economy, and technology; and trying to accommodate its traditional institutions and habits of thought to conditions new and in part alien.[2]

The law of privacy was synthesized in the midst of this era. Its roots, both legal and social, lie in the agrarian eighteenth-century principles which were being left behind as the decade began. The forces that gave life to the law can undoubtedly be found somewhere in the years immediately preceding the opening of the decade. And, of course, the impact of the law on the American press and American society is inscribed upon the decades which followed.

To understand the synthesization of the law of privacy, it is first necessary to have at least an acquaintance with the changing human ecology of this nation in the late nineteenth century. "What history reveals to mankind about its past," Jacques Barzun wrote, "does not uncover the cause . . . of any event . . . but only the conditions . . . attending its emergence." [3] This chapter is an attempt to outline some of the societal and journalistic conditions which relate to the emergence of the law of privacy in 1890.

THE NEW NATION

The first colonies on the North American continent were founded and settled at least in part because of a lack of privacy in seventeenth-century England. Religious parishioners were not allowed the privacy of conscience to worship as they pleased, so they emigrated to the New World in search of the ecclesiastical solitude and repose they could not find in Great Britain; they desired the right "to be let alone." * Despite these desires, at least some of the new colonists found an even greater lack of privacy in the New World. In 1624, for example, in the investigation of a suspected plot against the leadership of Plymouth Plantation, Governor William Bradford intercepted the private mail of two plantation residents and read the letters before an assembly of all the people. Despite outraged protests from the two colonists, little could be done in their behalf.[4] The concept of

* The right "to be let alone" was first suggested by Thomas M. Cooley in his *A Treatise on the Law of Torts* (2nd ed.; Chicago: Callaghan, 1888), p. 29. Cooley discussed the idea under the heading "Personal Immunity" and suggested that the "right to one's person may be said to be a right of complete immunity: to be let alone." Cooley's phrase has been used frequently by authors to describe the right of privacy. As it will be seen, however, the modern right of privacy embraces both more and less than the simple concept of being "let alone."

privacy as a legal entity did not exist in North America in 1624, and it would not exist for at least another 266 years.

Despite the incident in Plymouth, recorded instances of invasions of privacy in the New World before the nineteenth century are unusual. America was a rural nation during, and for many decades after, the colonial period. Villages, farms, and other living units were usually far apart. And within villages there was generally great similarity in nationality, background, habits, and taste, providing little stimulation to spy into another person's beliefs, attitudes, or activities. The population of the nation was relatively small. In 1790, for example, the largest city was Philadelphia, with forty thousand inhabitants. By 1800 only 6 percent of the population lived in urban areas, and there were but three cities in the United States with more than twenty-five thousand inhabitants.[5]

Paradoxically, while considerable physical distance existed between villages and residences, little privacy was possible within most homes and in most places of public accommodation and work. While man had progressed a long way from caves and tentlike dwellings, homes with living, eating, and sleeping facilities in the same room were often the rule. In public inns, travelers shared many of the same facilities. If man could exalt his solitude, his isolation, his own little world in spacious colonial America, he might also regret on occasion his inability to find a place where he could withdraw within his own home.

The press of the late eighteenth and early nineteenth centuries was also significantly different than it would be in 1890. Politically oriented, the newspapers of the day were more interested in opinion and comment than in news. And the comment was directed at nothing as mundane as the private life of the average man; only political or public men were important and newsworthy. The press of this era was directed to an elite group— those who could read. Its content, therefore, reflected a higher standard than if it had been intended for a mass audience. In addition, the newspaper of this era was small both in size and in number. Few newspapers published more than four pages per edition, and most published weekly. In 1790 there were only eight daily newspapers in the United States, and seven of them were located either in New York or in Pennsylvania.[6] By 1800 the number of dailies had grown only to twenty-four.

THE CHANGING AMERICA

What occurred in the United States in the century between 1790 and 1890 is an incredible story. To reduce the account of this period to a few statistics on a few pages is a great injustice, but even with this scant account the significance of the one hundred years should be apparent.

The obvious focal point of the period is the American Civil War. Beginning with verbal skirmishes in the late eighteenth century, man's actions seemed to outrun his ability to control them. The four-year war tore the nation apart, leaving remnants of America's manhood and its eighteenth-century society strewn from the southeast coast to the western prairies of Texas. This war, which destroyed the planter dynasty of the South, also destroyed America's agrarian society. General Philip Sheridan's destruction of the fertile Shenandoah Valley and General William T. Sherman's devastation in his march through the deep South were overshadowed only by the fantastic industrial growth in the North. When Ulysses S. Grant and Robert E. Lee met at the courthouse at Appomattox, they marked not only the end of the rebellious Confederacy, but the end of the agrarian America of the yeoman farmer. The industrial age, and all that was good and bad about it, was arriving.

Beginning in the middle of the nineteenth century, the entire political, social, economic, and cultural structure of the United States underwent a marked change. Accelerated by the Civil War, this metamorphosis took place in all phases of life and was visible to all segments of society. Historian Henry Adams, returning with his family in 1868 after ten years abroad, wrote: "Had they been Tyrian traders of the year B.C. 1000, landing from a galley fresh from Gibraltar, they could hardly have been stranger on the shore of a world so changed from what it had been ten years before." By 1890 the transformation had nearly been completed, and there existed a nation of urban dwellers who not only desired more privacy but probably needed it as well. The industrial revolution brought more rural inhabitants to urban areas to find work. The development of water systems, indoor plumbing, mass transit, electricity, the telephone, and other "modern" conveniences made urban life more attractive. Many women, tired of the loneliness and drudgery of rural life, wanted neighbors, better education for their children, pretty clothes, and culture. The tendency was to move from the countryside to hamlets, from hamlets to towns, from towns to urban centers. All these factors added to the remarkable growth of the American city.[7]

In 1840, 1,845,000 persons, representing about 11 percent of the total population, lived in villages, towns, or cities of more than 2,500 inhabitants. By 1860 the portion of Americans living in urban places had jumped to nearly 20 percent. In 1880 nearly 15 million people—28 percent of the nation's population—lived in incorporated areas of more than 2,500. By 1890, 35 percent or 22 million people lived in urban areas. Even more significant, though, were the results of the 1890 census, in which for the first time the increase in urban population exceeded the increase in rural numbers: between 1881 and 1890 the population of rural America increased by 4,815,000, while the population of America's cities increased by 7,976,000. It would not be until 1920 that the nation would have more urban dwellers than rural, but clearly this trend in growth had significantly begun.

The growth of the immigrant population—most of whom came to American cities in answer to the demand for unskilled laborers—was even more startling. In 1820, 8,385 persons migrated to this nation from abroad. In 1890 more than 450,000 persons arrived on America's shores. In the ten-year period from the beginning of 1850 to the end of 1859, 2,814,554 immigrated to the United States. Between 1860 and 1869 the total dropped by more than 700,000 as a result of the Civil War. From 1870 to 1879 the total increased again to 2,742,157. But between 1880 and 1889, 5,248,568 persons immigrated to this nation—nearly double the highest ten-year total previously recorded.[8]

The tremendous influx into the cities caused the number and size of cities to increase. In 1840 there was only one American city with a population of more than 250,000, and only 12 cities had more than 25,000 inhabitants. By 1890 there were 11 American cities with more than 250,000 residents—three of these had a population of more than one million—and 124 cities had populations exceeding 25,000.

The year 1890 was the date when the United States Bureau of the Census officially declared the end of the American frontier. But it was more than that, as historian Thomas H. O'Connor has noted. "By that date it was abundantly clear that as a result of foreign immigration and Negro emancipation the nation had, and would continue to have, a population that was no longer homogeneous. . . . The new industrial centers spawned crowded cities, overcrowded tenements, and teeming slums whose close packed proletarian families bore little resemblance to the yeoman farmer of Jefferson's day." The ideals of rugged individualism and self-reliance began to fade in the great urban sprawls. Dependence on others for food, drink, housing, clothing, medical care, police and fire protection, and many other services was a part of city life. While these services were frequently less than adequate, the urban dweller was compelled to interact with society in order to survive. Add to this the close proximity in which families were forced to live in the overpopulated cities, and it should be apparent that physical privacy was difficult to attain. As O'Connor notes, "Curiosity, fascination, repugnance, fear, sympathy, greed, hostility, love, hate, and the thousand-and-one other conflicting emotions which affect people living in close association with one another—especially people of different races, creeds, nationalities, and economic levels—created a desire to know more and more about the intimate details of the lives, the actions, the habits, the customs, the thoughts, and the activities of those about them." [9]

THE GROWTH OF THE VALUE OF PRIVACY

While the new city life lacked the physical privacy which living in rural areas afforded, it did offer another kind of privacy. Sociologists report that city life freed men and women from what Edward Shils calls "the oppressive moral opinion of village and rural society." Living in an urban area increased the indifference of most residents to the behavior of their friends and neighbors. The urban environment was more exciting, with more things to do and see. Other activities—such as politics, art, music, theater, ambitions, and careers—drew attention "out of the narrow primordial sphere and turned it outward, toward public things." Author and critic Granville Hicks seemed to confirm Shils's thesis when in 1959, after living for several years in a small New England town, he wrote: "Our situation was the exact opposite of the situation of a family living in a New York city apartment. The city dweller is surrounded by multitudes of people, none of whom, as a rule, knows or cares to know anything about him. Of the kind of physical privacy that I enjoy he has none, but there is no doubt that he lives a more private life than I do." [10]

The growing feeling of indifference described by Shils applied to the upper sections of the working class, the middle class, and the elites, and was one of several factors contributing to the growth of privacy in the last half of the nineteenth century. He suggested that the emerging conception of respectability among the urban working classes made it imperative that "scandalous" behavior be avoided, or at least hushed. Hence there was a striving for familial privacy in the respectable working-class homes. The growth of individuality supported the belief, according to Shils, that one's actions and their history "belonged" to the self which generated them—a kind of privacy.

Whereas these and other factors fostered the concept of privacy within the middle and upper working classes, Shils argued that there was a large unskilled working class, immigrant and native, which did not share these beliefs or experiences. Living as they did, in the crowded tenement districts where the privacy of better neighborhoods was impossible, "awareness about the doings of one's neighbors, [and] the gratification of impulses of curiosity about . . . them [the neighbors], were perhaps among the main pleasures available" to this class of urban residents.[11]

Shils's interesting theory suggests that when urban dwellers gave up physical privacy to live in the city, they inherited "other kinds" of privacy. Until they enjoyed privacy its value could not be seen; and only when it became a valuable commodity did it merit protection. Shils may or may not be right. What is important is that the growth of urban America did play a role in the conceptualization of privacy as a legal entity. Whether growing, urban, industrial America caused the development of a legal right of privacy cannot be determined. There is little question, however, that it was a prominent condition which accompanied the synthesizing of the law.

THE GROWTH OF THE PRESS

The growth of the American press in the one hundred years after 1790 paralleled the development of the nation. The newspaper press experienced a small revolution in the 1830s when the development of the penny press increased circulation and placed a greater emphasis on content interesting to the common man. More people could buy and read newspapers that cost only a penny, and a kind of popular journalism emerged which featured more sensational, colorful, and, to the average reader, interesting news. Nevertheless, the circulation of the press was still limited to those who could read, and while this certainly was no longer merely the elite, it did not include "the masses."

The second revolution within American journalism occurred late in the nineteenth century, and by 1890 the results of this upheaval could be clearly seen. The number of American dailies increased almost one-hundredfold. Newspapers were larger, with larger circulations. Many changed their formats and added new kinds of content to appeal to the modern audiences.

The tremendous growth in the number of American newspapers did not begin until the Civil War had ended. In 1800 there were 24 dailies, and by 1860 this number had increased only to 387. But during the next 20 years the number of daily newspapers more than doubled, to a total of 971. Between 1880 and 1889 more than 625 new daily newspapers emerged. This was (and remains) the largest ten-year increase in the history of the American press. The growth in the daily press was matched by other mass media. Between 1880 and 1890 the number of weekly newspapers increased from 7,811 to 13,559. In 1880, 2,076 new books, or new editions of older works, appeared on the market; by 1890 this figure had jumped to a yearly total of 4,559.[12]

Finally, the circulation of the American daily press increased by nearly 1,100 percent between 1850 and 1890. At the mid-century point only 758,000 newspapers were circulated each day.

By 1870 this number had reached 2,607,000. In the next twenty years the daily press added nearly six million new readers, so that in 1890 the circulation of newspapers in the United States reached 8,387,000 copies daily. The increase in circulation was centered in the urban areas. For example, daily newspaper circulation in six cities—New York, Philadelphia, Chicago, Cleveland, Boston, and San Francisco—in 1880 was 1,823,508. By 1890 daily newspaper circulation in these cities was recorded at 6,164,093.[13]

The high growth rate of the press was probably stimulated by several conditions. Mass-production methods, themselves a product of the revolution in industry, meant that more and more businesses needed regional and national distribution of their goods. The result was not only new advertising techniques, but more advertising. A reader perusing the press of that era is struck by the increase in advertisements for department stores, railroads, patent medicines, breakfast foods, laundry soaps, baking powder, electricity or gas, the telephone companies, and book publishers. Classified advertising grew as well. The entire cycle of manufacturing, retailing, and buying meant more advertising dollars directed toward the mass media. The newspaper, of course, received the largest share of this increased revenue. In 1870 advertising in newspapers and periodicals totaled sixteen million dollars, according to one source.[14] By 1880 this figure had jumped to thirty-nine million dollars, of which newspapers received twenty-one million dollars. In 1890 advertising revenues in the print media reached seventy-one million dollars.[15]

With increased revenues newspapers could concentrate on turning out better products by taking advantage of the scores of innovations developed in the printing industry between 1870 and 1890. In addition, the fountain pen, the telephone, the typewriter, the bicycle, the trolley car, and the incandescent lamp all made their appearance between 1880 and 1900. Each of these devices, in its own way, aided in the gathering and preparation of news copy.

When the copy reached the composition room it was greeted by another host of new processes. By the turn of the century most large newspapers were using composing machines, which were developed between 1870 and 1890. Stereotyping, an inexpensive method of replacing bulky page forms containing thousands of lines of type with a single metal cast, was in general use by 1890. The use of stereotype plates not only led to new page design, but facilitated faster press runs, since there was no possibility of breaking open a form of raw type while the press was in operation. Printing presses themselves were vastly improved in the twenty years between 1870 and 1890, and by 1885 many newspapers owned automatic folders which could cut, fold, count, and sack twenty-four-page papers at press speed.

New photographic engraving processes gave publishers more freedom in their use of drawings and photographs. Thousands of artists were at work for newspapers and magazines preparing sketches and etchings to accompany news stories and advertisements. Finally, important improvements in papermaking made it possible to lower the price of newspapers. By 1892 the price of newsprint had dropped to three cents per pound, as compared with twelve cents per pound in 1872.

All these innovations meant that newspapers were able to package their news more attractively and get it to readers faster and cheaper than ever before. In its efforts to lower newspaper prices the press was aided by the United States government. The Postal Act of 1879 clearly defined second-class matter, and in 1885 a one-cent-a-pound rate for newspapers and magazines opened the way for inexpensive delivery of publications. Also, the Post Office Department established rural free delivery service in 1879, as well as extending free carrier service within cities.

Changes in production and physical appearance were not the only innovations in the press during this era. The people in the growing urban areas, bonded together in cultural and economic units, turned to the daily press for the story of their urban life and common interests. The result was what journalism historian Edwin Emery calls a "lusty new journalism." [16] Clever publishers and editors combined crime news and other sensational stories with sports, entertainment, and human interest features. The result was popular journalism which appealed strongly to the lower and middle classes of the "gilded age" and provided a means for vicarious excursions into other worlds.

The change in audience which partially caused the "new journalism" was the result of several societal developments. The first was a large influx of new residents into the city. The press became not only a source of information about the city, but was also a socializing influence, an interpreter of the new environment. It also provided a means for the city factory-workers to escape from the daily grind, for urbanites with small-town or farm backgrounds found city life to be drudgery after the varied and outdoor-oriented life of the rural areas.

The life of the average city resident, whether he worked in an office, a shop, or a factory, was stamped with a day-to-day sameness—arising at the same hour, going to the same place of work, doing the same job, returning to the same small apartment or room, and retiring at the same hour. The city worker longed for something new, something different, a change in his drab life. Many publishers, recognizing this need, selected stories not for their intellectual appeal or their significance as news, but rather for their excitement, humor, and entertainment value.

Another societal change affecting the contents of the press during this era was the emergence of the American woman from her traditional status as housekeeper and mother into a new role. In their newly acquired leisure hours, many American women began to read newspapers and magazines. They became consumers of ready-made foods, clothing, and other household items. A small number of women even found that they had time to become active socially, in clubs or in civic groups. Recognizing this new role of the American woman, advertisers began to address themselves to homemakers. To make their appeal successful, publishers laced their newspapers with stories designed for the new readers—"soft news," such as feature stories, pictures and drawings, humor, serialized fiction, and news of what other women were doing.

Leisure time, made possible for many women by new labor-saving devices, and the economic freedom enjoyed by many families gave birth to American "society." Arthur Schlesinger reports that by 1890 "every considerable city soon had its 'Four Hundred.'" While most American women did not belong to "high society," they derived vicarious pleasure from reading about America's newly rich society "as it built its great mansions, its country estates, its private art museums, and its marital alliances with European nobility."[17] Newspapers in many American cities vied with their New York contemporaries in giving prominence to society news.

But the influx of new city dwellers and the changing status of American women could not have affected newspaper readership if the educational system had not begun to have an impact upon the masses. At the time of the Civil War, free education, at least through high school, had become a strong part of the American tradition. By 1900 all states had compulsory attendance laws. Between 1860 and 1900 more and more American children attended elementary and high schools. School enrollment and expenditures for education increased vastly between 1870 and 1890. America had by no means reached the state of universal education, but schooling for children was the rule rather than the exception in the second half of the nineteenth century. By 1890 the average American had a fifth-grade education—more than enough to read and enjoy the "new journalism." [18]

Newspaper practices of the twilight years of the nineteenth century have been variously described as "popular journalism," "mass journalism," "sensationalism," and "yellow press." The terms "sensationalism" and "yellow press" carry a bad connotation, suggesting stories supposedly designed to stimulate unwholesome emotional responses in the reader—stories of crime and violence, sex and scandal, disasters and monstrosities. "Yellow press" derives either from the "colored" news copy used in the press (colored with respect to its emphasis on such things as crime and sex) [19] or from the "Yellow Kid," the first regular comic strip character to appear in American journalism. (The comic strips were another mark of the popular press.)

But to label the entire press of the late nineteenth century as sensational or yellow—a mold which has been cast by twentieth-century historians—is not correct. Many newspapers continued their calm, unemotional coverage of what their editors considered to be the news of the day. In addition, they presented long educational features, first-class reviews of books, concerts, and the theater, thoughtful, well-written editorials, and serialized versions of some of the period's great literature. Change, however, is more easily seen and recorded than continuity. Hence, the "yellow press" of the 1880s and 1890s became a symbol for the period, despite the fact that in some ways, such as those noted above, the era represented the "golden age" of American journalism, not the "yellow age" which is most often suggested.

PRIVACY AND THE NEW JOURNALISM

The new popular press in America, while attracting a large following of avid readers, also generated a number of critics. Intellectuals of the era scorned the sensationalism and poor taste of many of the big city daily newspapers. And for the first time there was widespread criticism that the methods and techniques of the newspaper press were being used to invade the individual's privacy.

Lawyer Louis Nizer, writing in the *Michigan Law Review* in 1941, suggested that it was only natural to expect such an outcry at this moment in history. "The social need which became crystallized in the right of privacy did not grow insistent until the age of great industrial expansion, when miraculous advances in transportation and communication threatened to annihilate time and space, when the press was going through the growing pains of 'yellow journalism,' when business first became big. . . . Its [the right of privacy as a legal entity] creation at that precise time was historically inevitable." Another writer, Edward N. Doan, wrote in 1937 that the demand for the judicial recognition of the right of privacy parallels almost exactly the rise of the modern metropolitan newspaper, "with all its chromatic shades." [20]

There is no way to determine whether Nizer and Doan are correct in their suggestions that the popular journalism was at least in part responsible for the development of the tort of privacy. Perhaps it is merely a historical accident that the two occurred simultaneously. Nevertheless, not until the last quarter of the nineteenth century were there significant public accusations that many methods used by the press constituted an invasion of privacy.

As early as 1873 the *Nation* magazine complained that the interviewing technique used by journalists was an affront to the men of importance. By interviewing leading public figures, the editors wrote, "newspaper correspondents are driving the public . . . into wondering that a sage can be such an ass." [21] The president of the United States, Grover Cleveland, at times also expressed frustration at and dislike of the popular press. Newsmen had been particularly insensitive to Cleveland's privacy when he was married in 1886, and had even followed the president and his bride on their honeymoon trip. A Washington newspaper correspondent detailed the scene at Deer Park, Maryland, on the day following the wedding:

When President Cleveland rose at 10 o'clock this morning and looked from the front windows of this cheerful little domicile upon the handsome vista of glade and green that stretched out before him, among the objects which met his astounded gaze was a small pavilion standing in the midst of a handsome cluster of tall trees, and in and around this pavilion lounged the flower of Washington journalism, somewhat battered by lack of sleep and wrestling with county telegraph operators, but still experiencing a lively interest in the Chief Executive and his whereabouts.

A few months after his honeymoon the president was moved to comment on the press while addressing a Harvard University audience. Cleveland denounced journalists as purveyors of "silly, mean, and cowardly lies that every day are found in the columns of certain newspapers which violate every instinct of American manliness, and in ghoulish glee desecrate every sacred relation of private life." [22]

The editor of the *Nation*, E. L. Godkin, wrote in *Scribner's Magazine* in July 1890 that the chief enemy of privacy in modern life was the curiosity shown by some people about the affairs of other people. "In all this, the advent of the newspaper, or rather of a particular class of newspaper, has made a great change. It has converted curiosity into what economists call an effectual demand, and gossip into a marketable commodity." [23]

This sampling of comments drawn from writings of the late nineteenth century demonstrates a growing concern about privacy and a disdain of anyone or anything which would diminish it. Some scholars, looking back on American journalism in the 1880s and 1890s, similarly deplored the techniques used by the press. Arthur Schlesinger said in 1933: "Undoubtedly prying sensationalism robbed American life of much of its privacy to the gain chiefly of morbid curiosity." Legal scholar Elbridge L. Adams wrote in 1905: "It will probably not be seriously questioned that the American newspaper press, with a few honorable exceptions, has far overstepped the bounds of decency and propriety in its betrayal by word and picture of the private life of individuals." Finally, Frank Luther Mott, in his lengthy history of the American press, notes that invasion of privacy by prying reporters was a trademark of that journalistic era. "The prevalence of gossip and scandal stories, in which innocent persons were frequently dragged into the columns of newspapers, produced a kind of 'keyhole journalism' which was no less indecent; yet it was a part of the formula upon which the great circulations were based." [24]

While criticism of this kind is not uncommon, it is in some respects unjust. The writers have taken the worst aspects of one era of American journalism and suggested that it is representative of all newspapers published during the period. In reality, careful study of the press of 1890 reveals that "keyhole journalism" and sex and scandal were the exception rather than the rule. Indeed, after reading many of the newspapers of 1890 one comes away substantially in agreement with Joseph E. Chamberlain, a Boston newspaper editor during the era, who wrote in 1930, "In a marked sense, the Eighties represented the best achievement of the journalism of the nineteenth century." [25]

Whether the criticism of the press was just or unjust, the fact remains that such criticism was prevalent during the ten years preceding 1890. It would have been strange, indeed, if this criticism had not affected the thought of legal scholars in their consideration of the individual's right of privacy. Gossip about the private affairs of other people had existed before the development and growth of the new journalism. The curiosity of the American people was a fact of nature long before the first printing press was imported onto the continent. But the whispered word over the back fence is not as cold or impersonal as ink on newsprint. And, as legal scholar Edward J. Bloustein noted, "A newspaper report . . . assumes an imperious and unyielding influence . . . [and] tends to be treated as the very fount of truth and authenticity." [26] Hence, the excesses of the newspaper press became one of the pillars upon which the right of privacy was to be constructed.

THE BACKWASH OF EXCESSES

As the Gay Nineties opened, the American people still did not have a legally enforceable right of privacy. Courts in both England and the United States had granted individual rights which were on the periphery of privacy, but no court had ever stopped the kind of "Paul Pry" journalism which was described earlier on the ground that it was an invasion of privacy.

Yet, according to the commentators of the era, the nation was ready for the recognition of such a right. The country had changed greatly since its inception as a small, agrarian nation of yeoman farmers. Both the social environment and the newspaper press had undergone a drastic transformation. The changes in these two particular areas combined to create a rather urgent need for legal recognition of the right of privacy.

When recognition was finally achieved, it was done in a quiet, scholarly way which made little immediate impact. Two Boston lawyers, Samuel D. Warren and Louis D. Brandeis, both less than fifteen years out of law school, published in the *Harvard Law Review* a plea for the legal protection of the right of privacy. It took many years for the fruits of this labor to ripen, but time and a growing awareness of the rights of the individual in a society worked in their favor. Today, the results of this modest beginning are virtually legend. The seeds sown in Cambridge in 1890 in the fertile field of the common law have brought forth not only a new tort law, but a tort law highly responsive to hybrid variations.

The law of privacy, which has grown vigorously in the past seventy years, did not emerge from a vacuum. All law is a reflection of the society which creates it, and the law of privacy was no exception. The lusty, urban society of the last quarter of the nineteenth century is in many ways responsible for the development of the law of privacy. While a direct cause-and-effect relationship can never be established, the conditions which existed at this time in our national history—the crowded cities; the newly literate masses; the popular press seeking new readers;

the affluent, society-minded upper classes—shaped the development of American law during the period. It was in the backwash of this era, by all accounts an era of excesses, that the doctrine of privacy was formulated.

II

The Law of Privacy Is Synthesized

The common law has always recognized a man's house as his castle, impregnable, often, even to its own officers engaged in the execution of its commands. Shall the courts thus close the front entrance to constituted authority, and open wide the back door to idle or prurient curiosity?

SAMUEL D. WARREN AND LOUIS D. BRANDEIS [1]

The first day of December 1890 dawned frigid in Boston. A cold wave swept into the Boston Bay area shortly after midnight on gusty northwest winds, pushing the temperature downward to a crisp twenty degrees as the sun rose along the frosty coast. Light snow was forecast for the city. The arrival of the last month of the year brought with it the usual preholiday spirit. Newspaper columnists noted that the social calendar was beginning to fill.[2] Soon Christmas decorations would appear on homes and store fronts in the busy seaport city as residents prepared to celebrate the holiday season and usher in the second twelve months of the new decade.

That first year of what we now sentimentally remember as the Gay Nineties was not a particularly noteworthy one for Boston. The Democrats gained new strength in the state and captured the statehouse in the November election. The influenza epidemic, which struck many of the nation's cities in the early months of the year, passed without serious consequences in Boston. The murder trial of Isaac Sawtell for the killing and mutilation of his brother Hiram was front-page news throughout the year. And the Boston Leaguers won the championship in the Players Baseball League, while the local team could muster only a fifth-place finish in the older and stronger National League.

The month of December would, however, be remembered at least by legal scholars, for during that month the *Harvard Law Review* featured an article entitled "The Right to Privacy." Written by two young Boston lawyers in their office on the third floor of a small frame building on Devonshire Street, the article is the common starting point for any discussion of the legal right to privacy in the United States. The authors, Samuel D. Warren and Louis D. Brandeis, had collaborated previously on journal articles, but their efforts had attracted little attention. On this occasion, however, the pair boldly proposed the recognition of an entirely new branch of tort law,* the right of privacy. Their proposal would leave its marks not only in the December issue of the *Harvard Law Review*, but upon the pages of American legal history as well.

WARREN AND BRANDEIS

Samuel Dennis Warren II and Louis Dembitz Brandeis became acquainted while studying law at Harvard University in the mid-1870s. Brandeis had journeyed to Cambridge from Louisville, Kentucky, where his immigrant family owned a small mercantile shop. Warren, on the other hand, was Boston-born and -bred, the son of a wealthy paper manufacturer, a product of Brahmin stock. Their friendship at Harvard was the direct result of Brandeis' poor eyesight. After diagnosing the problem as muscular and prescribing exercises to strengthen the eyes, the doctor told the young student he could not continue in law school unless he could find friends willing to read his law assignments aloud to him. Several of Brandeis' friends took on the task, but Samuel Warren carried the greatest share of the burden.

---

* The law of torts, a part of the common law, provides legal remedy for civil wrongs such as trespass, assault, or defamation.

At graduation in 1877 Samuel Warren finished law school second in his class—to Louis Brandeis. The future United States Supreme Court justice returned to his home in Louisville, but found the atmosphere uninspiring after Cambridge. In 1879, when Warren suggested the formation of a law partnership in Boston, Brandeis left Louisville to make his home permanently in the East. The young lawyers began their practice in a one-room, third-floor office, handling at first only the business generated by Warren family paper mill interests. Later, new clients were acquired in Boston and New York, often through friendships begun during their years at Harvard. The Warren family was socially active, and before long Brandeis was in the thick of Boston social life. In the early years of the partnership Warren and Brandeis frequently spent hours at a tavern near the Parker House discussing legal and other matters with Oliver Wendell Holmes, Jr., who at that time was practicing law and teaching at Harvard and the Lowell Institute. These afternoon chats lasted until Holmes was elevated to the Supreme Judicial Court of Massachusetts in 1882.

In 1883 Warren married Mabel Bayard, daughter of Senator Thomas F. Bayard of Delaware, a future United States secretary of state. The friendship between the two lawyers did not diminish, however, and frequently the Warrens and Brandeis spent summer week ends at the Warren family summer home in Beverly, Massachusetts. Brandeis, in addition to developing new social interests since his return to the Boston area, was frequently asked to lecture to Harvard Law School classes. In 1887 Brandeis joined with a group of legal scholars to found the *Harvard Law Review*. A year later he and Warren collaborated in writing "The Watuppa Pond Cases," which was published in the second volume of the review. In 1889 the pair again coauthored an article entitled "The Law of Ponds," which appeared in Volume 3 of the law review.

During that same year Samuel Warren's father died, and the younger Warren dissolved his partnership with Brandeis to take over the family paper mill interests. Although the partnership ended, the friendship between these two men lasted to the end of Warren's life in 1910. Brandeis was then retained to arrange the transfer of the mill to a family trusteeship—a piece of business which would return to haunt him in 1916 when the United States Senate considered his name for appointment to the Supreme Court of the United States.*

It was sometime during 1890, probably early autumn, that Warren and Brandeis prepared their now-famous proposal for the recognition of a right of privacy. There has been much speculation about why the article was written at all. Because the article itself exhibits the authors' great dissatisfaction with the popular newspaper press of the day, this is often assumed to be the reason for the article. For example, Brandeis' biographer, Alpheus T. Mason, wrote that Samuel and Mabel Warren entertained elaborately, and "*The Saturday Evening Gazette* which specialized in 'blue blood items' reported their activities in lurid detail. This annoyed Warren who took the matter up with Brandeis. The privacy article was the result." [3]

Other writers have suggested other motives. Stanford law professor Marc A. Franklin proposed that the article echoed the prevalent desire of social leaders to elevate the standards of the masses. Warren and Brandeis, according to Franklin, reflected the position taken by Andrew Carnegie in his famous *Gospel of Wealth,* which made the distribution of wealth for the moral elevation of the poor an obligation of the wealthy, the "rich man's burden." [4]

While the article did reflect a certain concern for the reading habits of the community, the likelihood that this was the motive for its publication is slim. The Warren-Brandeis proposal was essentially a rich man's plea to the press to stop its gossiping and snooping, not an argument for an improvement of general journalistic standards. If an upgrading of the press was the purpose of the piece, the thrust of the article should have been directed at this goal. In fact, the authors used the comments about the press to demonstrate the need for the new tort remedy, and the thrust of the article was a proposal of this remedy.

Law professor William L. Prosser has suggested that press cov-

* Samuel Warren's brother Edward was unhappy with the way Sam ran the family business after his father's death. When Woodrow Wilson appointed Brandeis to the high court, one of the charges made against the justice-designate during the Senate confirmation hearings was that he had favored Sam's interests in the business to the detriment of other members of the family. Brandeis, and others, denied the allegation. For the complete story, see A. L. Todd, *Justice on Trial: The Case of Louis D. Brandeis* (New York: McGraw-Hill, 1964).

erage of the wedding of one of the Warren daughters prompted the article. Prosser said that although both men shared a dissatisfaction with the popular journalism, the wedding incident provided the spark.[5] But there is no basis in fact for this contention, since the first Warren daughter to be wed, Mabel Bayard Warren, was married to J. G. Bradley on 4 November 1905, nearly fifteen years after the publication of the law review article. Prosser's eminence among legal scholars has given credence to the wedding tale, which has been spread far and wide, so that today it is undoubtedly the most popular explanation for the Warren-Brandeis article.

Finally, several authors have advanced the idea that the two lawyers were moved by an article by *Nation* editor E. L. Godkin which appeared in *Scribner's Magazine* in July 1890. Godkin concluded his dramatic plea for the recognition of a right of privacy with the assertion that a legal remedy was not a likely solution, since "press laws, more than any others, have to be supported by the manners of the community," and the American people were not sensitive to such things as invasion of privacy.[6]

In 1905 lawyer Elbridge Adams published a long article on the right to privacy in the *American Law Review,* suggesting that the Godkin piece probably stimulated Warren and Brandeis to write "The Right to Privacy." Brandeis saw the piece and sent it to Warren in April of the same year. He included a letter in which he noted: "My own recollection is that it was not Godkin's article but a specific suggestion of yours, as well as your deep-seated abhorrence of the invasions of social privacy, which led to our taking up the inquiry." When Warren received the letter, he made this notation at the bottom with reference to Brandeis' comment: "You are right of course about the genesis of the article." Warren later wrote the same comment in a letter to Brandeis dated 10 April 1905. The explanation in this exchange of letters is supported by the recollections of Warren's grandson, Samuel Warren IV. "My impression," he wrote, "is that the social news gathered in many of the papers in the '80's included lists of guests and scraps of talk at private houses on minor social occasions that were in no sense infected with a public interest. This, my grandfather felt, was wrong and consequently he discussed it with Mr. Brandeis, his close friend and law partner." [7]

This is undoubtedly the true story behind the publication of 'The Right to Privacy." Its genesis lay in Warren's Boston social life, disturbed, as it were, by gossiping reporters. The hand of Brandeis was brought into the task of drafting the proposal through his friendship with Warren. Biographer Mason quotes Brandeis as writing many years afterward, "This, like so many of my public activities, I did not volunteer to do." [8] But he did do it, and his work with Warren has become legend in legal circles. While the importance of the article perhaps has been overstated in light of the law today, the proposal was nevertheless an auspicious beginning for the law of privacy.

THE SACRED PRECINCTS

"The Right to Privacy" was twenty-eight pages long, with three distinct sections. The first section established the need for the legal recognition of the right of privacy by giving reasons largely centering around the reporting techniques of the newspaper press. Once this need had been substantiated, Warren and Brandeis then asserted that certain analogous common law and equity remedies might be expanded to protect the right of privacy. Finally, the limits of the right were suggested in the final seven pages.

Warren and Brandeis began with the premise that man's spiritual nature, his feelings, and his intellect were given legal recognition through the development of a series of remedies, from assault and nuisance laws to libel and copyright. But this was no longer enough. "Instantaneous photographs and newspaper enterprise have invaded the sacred precincts of private and domestic life; and numerous mechanical devices threaten to make good the prediction that 'what is whispered in the closet shall be proclaimed from the house-tops.' " [9] A legal remedy was needed to secure for the individual the protection of the person, the right to be let alone.

The authors then detailed their charges against the press. "The press is overstepping in every direction the obvious bounds of propriety and decency. Gossip is no longer the resource of the idle and of the vicious, but has become a trade, which is pursued with industry as well as effrontery. To satisfy a prurient taste the details of sexual relations are spread broadcast in the columns of the daily papers. To occupy the indolent, column upon column is filled with idle gossip, which can only be procured by intrusion upon the domestic circle." Because of the invasions of privacy by the press, individuals were being subjected to mental pain and distress far greater than could be inflicted by mere bodily injury, the two lawyers asserted. The gossip which was spread both belittled and perverted the relative importance of things, dwarfing the "thoughts and aspirations of people. . . . Easy of comprehension, appealing to that weak side of human nature which is never wholly cast down by the misfortunes and frailties of our neighbors, no one can be surprised that it usurps the place of interest in brains capable of other things. Triviality destroys at once robustness of thought and delicacy of feeling. No enthusiasm can flourish, no generous impulse can survive under its blighting influence" (p. 195).

PROTECTION OF THE RIGHT OF PRIVACY

From this indictment of the press and its effects upon the average man, it was but a short step to the consideration of a remedy for the situation. And this, undoubtedly, was the weakest link in the entire article. Strangely, while some scholars have challenged the legal aspects of the Warren-Brandeis argument, no one has taken exception to their portrayal of the press of 1890, the "evil" for which the remedy was needed (see Chap. 3).

Warren and Brandeis then turned to the search for the legal principle needed for protection against invasion of privacy. They found such a principle in the doctrine of common law copyright, which invests in an author or artist the exclusive right to make copies of his work for a limited period of time; it is automatic and lasts indefinitely, as long as no publication occurs. However, once publication is made, the author must apply for statutory copyright protection. In both Great Britain and the United States, provisions were made through statutes for the protection of an individual intellectual or artistic work after it had been published.

From as early as the middle years of the eighteenth century there are recorded instances of British courts protecting the right of an individual to control the use of materials such as unpublished manuscripts, diaries, or letters.[10] At first this protection was extended only to those items incorporating true artistic or literary merit; but courts of equity in Great Britain and the United States later ruled that almost any unpublished works, valuable or not, were to be protected.[11] In some ways these later rulings marked a slight shift in emphasis from a position firmly based on property rights to one based on the right of the individual to control the communication of his thoughts, sentiments, and emotions, as expressed in his writings or other works. Nevertheless, courts continued to base their decisions almost exclusively in concepts of property rights.

After a brief summation of the common law of copyright, Warren and Brandeis suggested that

. . . these considerations lead us to the conclusion that the protection afforded to thoughts, sentiments, and emotions, expressed through the medium of writing or of the arts, so far as it consists in preventing publication, is merely an instance of the enforcement of the more general right of the individual to be let alone. . . . The principle which protects personal productions, not against theft and physical appropriation, but against publication in any form, is in reality not the principle of private property, but that of an inviolate personality (p. 205).

The Boston lawyers then took the next step in their "theoretical" proposal. "If, then, the decisions [in common law copyright] indicate a general right to privacy for thoughts, emotions, and sensations, these should receive the same protection, whether expressed in writing, or in conduct, in conversation, in attitudes, or in facial expressions" (p. 206). In this fashion they neatly established what they called "the right to one's personality."

Obviously, a key to the Warren-Brandeis argument is their conclusion that the protection given the individual under common law copyright is part of the larger right to be let alone. Within this assertion rests the cornerstone of their legal argument. If accepted, the conclusion provides a simple and logical means of extending the right of privacy from a substantial root growth in the past. If the conclusion is rejected, however, it is difficult to sustain the remainder of the legal proposal.

But before the Warren-Brandeis tort could safely be said to

cover the broad spectrum of the right of privacy, another series of cases had to be dealt with. Beginning as early as 1825 English courts had ruled that the publication of unpublished lectures or of a series of unpublished etchings or the copying and sale of a photographic portrait constituted a breach of an implied contract or trust between the author of the lectures or the subject of the portrait and the individual who sought to publish the work.[12] Again, the property-right concept was at the core of most of these rulings.

In an effort to include these kinds of civil wrongs under the heading of invasion of privacy, Warren and Brandeis challenged the efficacy of the remedy in dealing with the problem. "The narrower doctrine may have satisfied the demands of society at a time when the abuse to be guarded against could rarely have arisen without violating a contract or a special confidence; but now that modern devices afford abundant opportunities for the perpetuation of such wrongs without any participation by the injured party, the protection granted by the law must be placed on a broader foundation." The pair cited recent developments in photography to support their argument. "[In the past] the state of photographic art was such that one's picture could seldom be taken without his consciously 'sitting' for the purpose; but since the latest advances in photographic art have rendered it possible to take pictures surreptitiously, the doctrines of contract and of trust are inadequate to support the required protection . . ." (p. 211).

Warren and Brandeis found it difficult to conceive of a theory of the law under which the casual recipient of a letter, who proceeds to publish it, is guilty of a breach of contract, express or implied. "He opens it, and reads. Surely, he has not made any contract; he has not accepted any trust," they said (p. 211). Warren and Brandeis concluded, then, that these rights, which in the past had been protected under contract law, were in fact rights which should be protected under the principles of a right of privacy. "The principle which protects personal writings and any other productions of the intellect or of emotions, is the right to privacy, and the law has no new principle to formulate when it extends this protection to the personal appearance, sayings, acts, and to personal relations, domestic or otherwise" (p. 213).

LIMITS OF THE LAW

After suggesting the new remedy, Warren and Brandeis set out the limitations of the proposed right. First, the right of privacy did not prohibit the publication of any matter of public or general interest. The authors defined "public or general interest" by equating it with material which would be protected by qualified privilege under the law of libel and slander. In later chapters it will become clear that the definition of "public interest" has remained a cause for legal dispute since the article was published. Even today it is possible to put together only an outline of what the concept "public or general interest" means in the law of privacy.

The right of privacy, according to the authors, did not prohibit the publication of any matter—even private affairs—under circumstances which would render it a privileged communication according to the law of libel or slander. This would include publications made in meetings of public bodies or in courts or associations which are infected with a public purpose. The law of privacy did not redress any wrong suffered by oral publication of private matter, Warren and Brandeis wrote. The injury did not become substantial enough until a large-scale communication of the information was undertaken. Also, the right of privacy ceased when the individual published the facts himself, or consented to their publication.

Truth, long a defense in libel actions, did not afford a defense for a privacy suit, according to the authors. "It is not for injury to the individual's character that redress or prevention is sought, but for injury to the right of privacy" (p. 218). Finally, the absence of malice did not afford a defense. Warren and Brandeis argued that the individual must be held responsible for the consequences of his intentional acts, whether or not the consequences were foreseen.

Two elements of the tort remained. First, a definition of the legal injury caused by an invasion of privacy; or, in other words, for what damage would the plaintiff be compensated? The law of libel, for example, protects an individual's reputation, and when libeled the plaintiff seeks compensation to redress injury to his reputation. In other torts, such as battery, the plaintiff is compensated for physical injury. Warren and Brandeis argued that an invasion of privacy caused the plaintiff to suffer mentally, and that this mental suffering should be the basis for the lawsuit. The authors, however, offered little explanation of how this mental suffering might be measured so as to provide fair compensation for the injured party.

Finally, Warren and Brandeis suggested that there were at least two legal remedies for individuals whose privacy was invaded. Damage suits would provide monetary compensation for any injury to the plaintiff's feelings or suffering. Also, they suggested that injunctive relief be granted in some cases. Injunctive relief, gained through a court of equity, is only effective to stop an invasion of privacy and provides no compensation for damage already incurred.* For example, an individual may seek a court injunction to stop a newspaper from running his photograph in an advertisement. Usually, the individual seeking the permanent injunction of the defendant's conduct must demonstrate that the publication will cause him to suffer irremediable damage—damage which cannot be remedied in a lawsuit after the action has occurred. Warren and Brandeis did not elaborate on what kinds of cases might require injunctive relief.

The authors also hinted strongly that criminal action might be appropriate in some cases to punish those individuals who invaded the privacy of others. Indeed, at about the same time that the article was being prepared, a Boston attorney, William H. Dunbar, proposed state legislation which called for five-year im-

---

* Equity is a separate system of jurisprudence, which supplements the common law and provides judicial relief in those cases not within the jurisdiction of the common-law courts. The system of equity has its roots in old English law. It was developed because of the rigidity of the common law, which forced judges to turn away many litigants who presented morally, if not legally, valid claims. Litigants began appealing to the king for justice, and by the fourteenth century these requests were being turned over to the king's chancellor for resolution. Over the centuries this system of law became institutionalized and grew up parallel to the older common law. Procedure was less ritualized, remedies were more flexible, and precedent—the heart of the common law—was often overlooked rather than strictly followed. The courts of equity, or chancery as they are often called, were bound more by the ideas and philosophies of the judge than by strict notions of justice. Today, common law and equity courts are no longer separate; the two jurisdictions are usually joined in a single tribunal. However, to invoke the more flexible equity jurisdiction, the litigant must show the court that he lacks a remedy at law.

prisonment and a fine of one thousand dollars for certain invasions of privacy.[13] While this extreme penalty would have been limited to cases in which a newspaper or magazine published statements about the private affairs of an individual after being asked to refrain from such action, the law, nevertheless, would have been a potent weapon. The measure was never approved.

THE FUTURE IMPACT

In the years following 1890 legal scholars found that Warren and Brandeis' plea for the recognition of a right of privacy had a strong impact upon initial growth of the tort. After Brandeis was elevated to the United States Supreme Court, the association of his name with the *Harvard Law Review* article added even more weight to the proposal. Although Brandeis was probably drafted into working on the project, he apparently shared Warren's sensitive feelings about privacy. In 1928, for example, when the Supreme Court handed down its important decision regarding the use at a criminal trial of evidence obtained by illegal wiretapping, Brandeis dissented from the majority opinion that approved the use of such material. His comments bear a striking resemblance to passages from his 1890 proposal.

> The makers of our Constitution undertook to secure conditions favorable to the pursuit of happiness. They recognized the significance of man's spiritual nature, of his feelings, and of his intellect. They knew that only a part of the pain, pleasure and satisfaction of life are to be found in material things. They sought to protect Americans in their beliefs, their thoughts, their emotions and their sensations. They conferred, as against the Government, the right to be let alone—the most comprehensive of rights and the right most valued by civilized men.[14]

The importance of the Warren-Brandeis article is that other legal scholars—judges, lawyers, educators—began looking at old problems in a new light. In this sense, the two young Boston attorneys did succeed in synthesizing a new legal concept. That the law did not develop exactly as they suggested does not detract from their achievement. As legal scholar Harry Kalven wrote quite aptly, "The impact of the article resides not so much in the power of its argument as in the social status it gave to the tort. In the vernacular of the sports page, it lent it 'class.' "[15]

The strength and vitality which Warren and Brandeis gave to the law of privacy rests in their proposal for legal recognition of such a right. As will be seen in following chapters, American courts have been reluctant to restrict the press in the manner suggested in the law review article. Instead, other varieties of "invasion of privacy" suits have developed and flourished in the past eighty-two years, varieties probably not envisioned by Warren and Brandeis. But the seeds for these hybrids were sown in 1890 by two attorneys bold enough to argue in print that the law was wrong and young enough to try to change it.

III

Warren and Brandeis' "The Right to Privacy": An Evaluation of the Argument

---

The biggest interviewing enterprise of the century begins next week, when Uncle Samuel's census takers will swarm forth and pump us all dry. The census taker of 1890 has a prodigious nose, and he is authorized to poke into everybody's business with a vengeance. . . . There never was such a Paul Pry sent out by the government before. . . . The question arises—Has an American freeman any private rights and privileges which his government is bound to respect? It seems not.

Boston Globe [1]

THE PRESS

Oliver Wendell Holmes, writing in 1912 as a member of the United States Supreme Court, remarked: "It is one of the misfortunes of the law that ideas become encysted in phrases and thereafter for a long time cease to provoke further analysis." [2] One need only look to the body of constitutional law surrounding the First Amendment to find unmistakable examples of Holmes's assertion. "Clear and present danger" and "preferred position" are just two of scores of such encysted concepts. The same assertion can be made about other aspects of the law as well. Many of the ideas in "The Right to Privacy" by Samuel Warren and Louis Brandeis, for example, have become locked in molded phrases and have never undergone the scrutiny of the doubting scholar. Most of the few attempts to examine closely the Warren-

Brandeis proposal came before 1910, and since then many of the assertions and assumptions presented by the authors have taken on the status of fact, if not revealed truth. As a result, most contemporary writers who deal with the subject of privacy base their historical treatment on what Warren and Brandeis wrote nearly eighty-two years ago.

There has been no known public challenge to the portrait of the Boston press presented by Warren and Brandeis. Few writers have questioned any of the basic legal propositions in the proposal. Whereas during the thirty years following publication of the piece, judges and courts were often reluctant to accept the Warren-Brandeis argument, few, if any, attempted to challenge the authors' reading of more than one hundred years of legal history. And today it is difficult to find any writer—scholar or layman—who does not accept the basic conclusion reached by the two young Boston lawyers: that the legal right of privacy was merely a short, logical extension of what was accepted common-law doctrine in 1890.[3]

The questions asked in this chapter should have been asked before the doctrine of a right of privacy received widespread acceptance. Had this been done, it is quite possible that the profile of the tort would be different than it is today. The inspection begins with an examination of the charges leveled against the press by Warren and Brandeis. Their characterization of the media, it will be recalled, was quite graphic: "The press is overstepping . . . the obvious bounds of propriety and decency. Gossip . . . has become a trade. . . . The details of sexual relations are spread broadcast in the columns of the daily papers. . . . Column upon column is filled with idle gossip. . . ."[4] But was this an accurate representation of the Boston press in 1890?

THE BOSTON PRESS

Boston was second only to New York in commercial importance as the final decade of the eighteenth century opened. Its deep harbor made the city a natural port and business center of the East. Since the Civil War, Boston had grown greatly, and as the 1890s began the city was a mixture of old and new. Tradition, dating back to the early days of the American colonial era, was being nudged aside as the borders of metropolitan areas strained with the influx of newcomers from small towns and farms who came to the city to find work in the factories and shops. In addition, immigrants from Ireland, Germany, and other parts of Europe filled residential districts along the narrow Boston streets. The markets crackled as the multitude of foreign tongues mixed with proper Bostonian English. For all its eighteenth-century tradition and history, Boston was making a different kind of history in 1890 as it kept in step with the rise of the cities in the East.

There were eight English-language daily newspapers in Boston as the decade opened. In addition, there were at least twenty weekly newspapers of general circulation and numerous specialized journals. Frank Luther Mott noted that Boston was not as lively a newspaper city as "any one of half a dozen others." Another historian, Sidney Kobre, wrote that the Boston press mirrored the varied economic and cultural interests of the city. The established newspapers founded in the era of the penny press continued to be solid and respectable, but new dailies arose to respond to the changing wants and needs of the city.[5]

Two Boston journalists of the era have given similar descriptions of the city's press. Edwin Bacon, managing editor of the *Boston Daily Advertiser,* wrote in 1886: "The journalistic profession here includes a large number of liberally educated people; and the 'Bohemian,' thanks to the better influences prevailing in American journalism, is now a rarity in Boston. Boston has reason to plume herself a trifle on the cleanliness and tone of her periodical literature." [6] *Boston Transcript* editor Joseph E. Chamberlain wrote in 1930 about the press of the late nineteenth century: "In a marked sense, the eighties [1880's] represented the best achievement of the journalism of the nineteenth century. The achievement was less strenuous, less voluminous, but rather more intellectual, than the current production of the twentieth century." [7]

While it had its own personality, the Boston press nevertheless also displayed the good and the bad of American journalism of the era. The typical daily newspaper in the city was eight pages of small, hard-to-read type. There were few pictures, drawings, or sketches in the news columns, but simple line drawings appeared frequently in advertisements. Most headlines were only one column wide, but often four or five headlines or decks appeared above a major story.

There was an unusually high proportion (compared to standards in 1971) of crime and disaster news in the Boston press of 1890. Murders, suicides, executions, and accidental deaths received full coverage, leaving little to the readers' imaginations. Shipwrecks, natural calamities such as tornadoes and severe winter storms, epidemics, business failures, and other disasters received equally broad newspaper coverage.

Despite the high percentage of "bad" news, reports on the affairs of government were the staple item in the city's press. While practices varied among the many newspapers, most gave extensive coverage to all levels of government. It was not unusual, for example, for a newspaper to run the complete text of an important speech of the president or the governor. Daily reports from Washington could be found on the front page of each newspaper.

After reading the first and last pages of his newspaper (where most of the serious news was presented), a Bostonian could turn to inside pages and find a wide variety of other news and features. Each daily paper reported sports news, including reports on prize fighting and horse racing in the bolder, more sensational *Boston Globe,* and most gave extensive coverage of the business and financial situation. There were usually four to six meaty, well-written editorials on page 4 or 6. And while there was little of what is today called women's news, recipes and home remedies appeared sporadically in most newspapers.

Many columns were devoted to the coverage of theater, music, and dance, as well as the more popular entertainment events, such as vaudeville and the circus. In the larger Saturday or Sunday editions readers would be treated to the serialized fiction of contemporary authors such as Jules Verne and C. Rider Haggard. Multitudes of long feature articles on wide-ranging topics also filled the columns of these editions. While the editor of 1890 had fewer pages to work with, he also had more room for news on each page since the ratio of advertising to news rarely rose above the 30 percent level and never reached the normal 60 percent advertising, 40 percent news common in many daily newspapers of the 1970s.[8]

The Boston newspaper editor of 1890, while scarcely faultless, seemed aware of the shortcomings within his profession. In February of that year most of the Boston papers reported a speech by Harvard President Charles W. Eliot in which the educator branded many members of the Boston press as "drunkards, thieves, deadbeats, and bummers." [9] Eliot later denied making the statement, but also noted that he had not been aware that reporters were present during his speech. Later that year, the *Boston Morning Journal* reprinted a *New York Sun* editorial entitled "Should Reporters Be Gentlemen?" The *Journal* editors said that they abhorred the kind of shameless fake reporter in favor with the fraudulent press. The *Sun* editorial defined him in these terms:

He cannot be too depraved to suit the use of his employer. He must possess the arts of the confidence man, the furtive keeness [*sic*] of the practiced thief, and be endowed with all the malodorous gifts of the professional imposter. To glue his ear to a crack in a door, to consort with blacklegs [a swindler, especially in horse racing or gambling] and burglars, to entice and provoke to crime for the sake of possible exposure, to master the acrobatics of chimneys and the bedroom window, and to penetrate and violate the sanctity of the jury room—these are the qualifications.

In commenting on the *Sun* editorial, the *Journal* noted:

The liberty of one man ends at the point where it interferes with the liberty of another, and the malodorous must find this out if it wishes to provide for its own safety. Interference with private life, except for the perfectly justifiable report and gossip which can do no harm, is only pardonable in the newspaper when men and women are brought to the bar of justice or of public opinion, by some grave misdemeanor or emergency in their careers.[10]

The candid admission by the *Journal* editors that members of the journalistic trade cared little about the individual privacy of the citizens of Boston lends credence to the charges made by Warren and Brandeis against the press. Other journalists in Boston, while using perhaps softer words, echoed the remarks in the *Journal*. "We are all fond of reading of the private life and personal habits of people of note, and especially of those who have become famous through their writing," noted a columnist in the *Boston Daily Advertiser* in March 1890. A *Boston Evening Transcript* columnist wrote that he had read the Sunday papers for a change (the *Transcript* did not publish a Sunday edition) and found them "abounding in the customary and sarcastic remarks about society, intermingled with more or less feeble and inaccurate attempts to tell what society is doing." He lamented this kind of reporting and then noted: "There is a great deal of vanity, humbug, false pretense and even cruelty about 'society' beyond a doubt; but more than half these disagreeable things, at the lowest calculation, come from the relations of one limited set with another set that is jealous of it. . . . So long as society is written about by the people who can't get into it, or who have been thrust out of it for good reasons, we may expect few but bitter and envious things to be said about it." [11]

While these statements suggest the existence of the kind of journalism deplored by Warren and Brandeis, they also demonstrate a sensitivity to the right of privacy on the part of at least some members of the press. Indeed, members of the Boston daily press instituted one of their biggest editorial campaigns of 1890 against the United States Census Bureau and the 1890 Decennial Census. The excerpt from the *Boston Globe* printed at the beginning of this chapter was perhaps the sharpest attack against the "national invasion of privacy," but other newspapers were also highly critical of the questions asked in the census. The *Boston Evening Transcript* reported on 2 June 1890 that such questions as those regarding a family's financial condition and those relating to physical ailments or defects of family members "have elicited such a storm of disapprobation from all quarters that the superintendent of the census has modified his orders so that enumerators will simply report to the Census Bureau a refusal to answer them." The *Transcript* added that *The Medical Journal* and other publications "denounce the questions as atrocious and likely to cause great suffering in families" (p. 4). The *New York Sun* claimed that these kinds of questions were unconstitutional. The approximately forty questions in the 1890 census were the kind that most Americans answer today without a twinge of feeling; the most objectionable were designed to obtain information on illness and disease within families, and to determine whether dwellings were owned, mortgaged, or rented.

GOSSIP AND THE PRESS

At this point the Boston press seems to present a paradoxical image. I have cited secondary sources which both praise and condemn the city's newspapers, and the press of the late nineteenth century in general. Also, the comments by members of the press, such as those cited above, suggest that at least some persons within the profession were acutely sensitive to the right of individual privacy. In an attempt to attain a more comprehensive appraisal of the Boston press in 1890, I analyzed four of the city's eight daily newspapers—the *Boston Globe*, the *Boston Journal*, the *Boston Daily Advertiser*, and the *Boston Evening Transcript*.[12]

Of the four, the *Globe* had the largest circulation, and it was also the most audacious. The *Globe* could most easily be labeled "sensational," for it represented the lusty new journalism described in the first chapter. There were sensational headlines, and great stress was placed on news of crime and other mayhem. *Globe* editors followed the lead of New York's Charles A. Dana and published news that was interesting, but not necessarily important. The *Globe* had the only real gossip column of any of the four newspapers. It appeared each Sunday under the heading "Table Gossip," but was petty gossip and largely inoffensive when measured by mid-twentieth-century standards. During 1890 the Samuel Warren family was mentioned once, when it was reported that Mr. and Mrs. S. D. Warren gave a "handsome wedding breakfast" after the marriage of Katherine H. Clarke and Mr. Watson.[13]

The *Boston Journal* was probably a typical newspaper of the era, tending toward sensationalism but still respectable enough to be read in the better homes in the city. While it avoided the extremes of the *Globe*, the *Journal* also stressed news of crime and disaster. Its staple item was news of government—national, state, and local—and there was some business news. The newspaper did not publish a local gossip column.

The *Boston Evening Transcript* might be described as a literary journal rather than a newspaper. It was the "Bible" of proper Bostonians during the late nineteenth century, despite its small circulation. While it provided adequate coverage of the news of the day—including some sensational accounts of crime and other disasters—scores of book reviews and stories on the theater, concerts, and recitals made up the heart of each issue. In addition, poems, capsule summaries of articles from leading magazines, serialized fiction, and well-written feature articles about conservation, finance, and wildlife were also liberally spread throughout the newspaper.

The *Daily Advertiser*, oldest of the Boston dailies, was the city's business review. While placing heavy emphasis on news of Boston cultural life, as well as standard news items, the newspaper's strength was its coverage of business and finance. Many columns in each edition were devoted to maritime and shipping reports, and at least two full pages of each issue were filled with Boston business news and reports from the major American stock exchanges.

The analysis of the four Boston newspapers revealed instances of poor journalism, bad taste, some sensationalism, and even gossip. The examination failed to uncover, however, any instances in which the press was "overstepping in every direction the obvious bounds of propriety and decency." It did not appear that gossip had become a trade, "pursued with industry as well as effrontery," and there was no evidence that "the details of sexual relations are spread broadcast in the columns of the daily papers." These were the charges made by Warren and Brandeis, but the facts do not seem to support these broad assertions. Nor does the evidence realistically support Warren and Brandeis' incredible lists of "effects" which the Boston press supposedly had upon readers. "No one can be surprised," they wrote, "that it usurps the place of interest in brains capable of other things. Triviality destroys at once robustness of thought and delicacy of feeling. No enthusiasm can flourish, no generous impulse can survive under its blighting influence." [14] In reality, certain Boston dailies represented high literary standards—readers of the era were treated to a caliber of feature story and serialized fiction that would make their counterparts of today envious.

It is of course possible that the four newspapers examined were not typical of the 1890 press, that they were more virtuous than most. This is possible, but not probable. It could also be true that Warren and Brandeis directed their criticism at the weekly press—the *Saturday Evening Gazette,* for example. Brandeis' biographer, Alpheus T. Mason, mentioned the *Gazette* as being particularly offensive. I attempted to locate copies of that newspaper, but they are almost nonexistent today.[15] The *Gazette* was sold during 1890, and comments about it in the daily press give some clue to its nature. It published one of the most widely read social columns, but reportedly was always edited "with good judgment and good taste." The new stockholders in the corporation which owned the newspaper were prominent and successful businessmen.[16]

THE BOUNDS OF PROPRIETY

It is difficult for a contemporary man to evaluate the press of the 1890s. Mores and values have changed in the intervening years, and what was considered to be outrageous then might be accepted practice today. But Warren and Brandeis did not use vague adjectives such as "outrageous" or "sensational"; they were quite specific in their charges. The evidence just does not support their indictment. Even allowing for the possibility that the four newspapers I examined were atypical, and that the *Saturday Evening Gazette* was indeed a social snooper, Warren and Brandeis were still guilty of verbal overkill. Their characterization of the Boston press was less than accurate.

This erroneous portrait of the press is unfortunate for at least two reasons. First, most legal scholars have adopted the Warren-Brandeis characterization, and as a result law journals and other legal periodicals have published a good deal of information that is at least incomplete, if not inaccurate. The press of Boston deserves a better fate. More important, however, the two lawyers built their argument upon this incomplete picture. The fact that the judicial community never really accepted their proposal might be due in part to an absence of the kind of journalistic excesses which they described.

All the material necessary to make a comprehensive evaluation of the Boston press in 1890 has not been examined. That which has does not support Warren and Brandeis. But until all the source material can be examined, and unless a contemporary scholar can somehow evaluate this material from the viewpoint of nineteenth-century man, a comprehensive appraisal will not be possible.

A LOOK AT THE LAW

Warren and Brandeis followed up their evaluation of the substantive evil, the press, with an outline of the pre-1890 law which they believed led naturally to the recognition of a legal right of privacy. The key to their argument, as noted previously, was the willingness to accept a few broad assumptions or to take a few long jumps from settled law to proposed law. To appreciate the importance of these assumptions and jumps, it is necessary to understand the law in 1890.

PRIVACY AND ANCIENT LIGHTS

Anglo-American law was slow to develop a legal interest in the personality of the individual. Before medieval times the Romans recognized the importance of the sanctity of the individual's identity and afforded a legal remedy for mental suffering resulting from humiliating treatment or insult. While property rights received early recognition in the common law, it was not until the fourteenth century that personal rights began to develop. The first recoveries for civil assault—an attempt at bodily harm —were recorded in 1348.[17] Slowly, other personal rights emerged. The first known judgment for defamation was recorded in 1356; recoveries for nuisances, noises, odors, dust, and smoke soon followed. In 1745 the first known recovery for alienation of affection was granted in an English court.[18]

But throughout this period of the extension of personal rights, courts in both Great Britain and the United States more often than not sought the violation of some property right as the basis for any recovery. Their tendency was understandable. The violation of a property right was much easier to demonstrate than the violation of a personal right. Also, it was simpler to determine value in the payment of damages when property rights were involved. How does one measure, for example, the damage resulting to a parent from the seduction of a daughter? It was fairly easy to estimate her worth to her parents as a servant and housekeeper—and courts were prone to take this tack. It was difficult to fix a financial value on the mental suffering experienced by the parents. A good example of this kind of judicial hesitancy can be seen in a line of cases, beginning in the early eighteenth century, involving ancient lights or windows, which is perhaps the earliest assertion of a legal right of privacy. These cases, none of which were cited by Warren and Brandeis, graphically demonstrate how British courts would uphold property rights over personal rights—even if an invasion of privacy had occurred.

The legal principle involved was a simple one: B owned a dwelling abutting A's property. Windows on the side of B's dwelling looked out onto A's garden. A, who found it difficult to enjoy the privacy of his garden when B was peering out his windows, built a wall to block the view from the house. B went to court to force A to remove the wall, arguing that A's wall obstructed the light and air which should flow into the house through the windows. A argued that he had a right to protect the privacy of his garden by building a wall on his own property. The court almost consistently ruled in B's favor and made A remove the wall. The theory behind the decision was that B enjoyed a property right in the windows and A could not obstruct the flow of light and air into the house. Two contingent circumstances must be noted, however. B's windows had to exist before A's garden, they must be *"ancient lights"* or windows. Also, if B added a window after A had constructed his garden, A would have the right to obstruct the view from this added window, so long as the others, the ancient windows, remained unobstructed.

Perhaps the first recorded case in which this principle was established was *Cherrington* v. *Abney,* decided in 1709 in the British High Court of Chancery.[19] In this case the dwelling owner attempted to increase the number of windows on the side of his building from six to eight. The court ruled that the building owner had, by increasing the number of windows, changed the existing relationship to the prejudice of the abutting property. The dimensions or the number of windows may not be increased, even when a new building is constructed.

Following *Cherrington,* British courts reinforced the ancient-lights principle in a series of cases.[20] In these decisions British chancellors ruled consistently that the right of privacy did not exist—at least legally. In 1811 Justice Coram Le Blanc said, "Although an action for opening a window to disturb the plaintiff's privacy was to be read of in books, I have never known such an action maintained."[21]

In *Turner* v. *Spooner,* fifty years later, the chancellors ruled that an intrusion upon a neighbor's privacy was not a ground for interference at law or in equity. "With regard to the question of privacy, no doubt the owner of a house would prefer that a neighbor should not have the right of looking into his windows or yard, but neither this court nor a court of law will interfere on the mere ground of invasion of privacy . . ." (p. 803). In 1865 Lord Westbury, the chancellor, noted in *Tapling* v. *Jones* that invasion of privacy was often used as an argument in the ancient-lights cases, but that invasion of privacy "is not treated by the law as a wrong for which a remedy is given" (p. 304).

The ancient-lights cases are included in this discussion to demonstrate the prominence of property rights over personal rights in this era of British law. In addition, these cases are the first known instances in which the plea of invasion of privacy was heard in Anglo-American courts, and, as it has been shown, it was rejected rather brusquely.

LITERARY PROPERTY

The concept of property, a greatly revered legal entity, was expanded in the eighteenth and nineteenth centuries to include not only physical, tangible things, but also the incorporeal rights surrounding those things, and even products and processes of the mind. A law of literary property developed, and it was in the expansion of these concepts that Warren and Brandeis found the most adaptable pillar to support their contention that a legally enforceable right of privacy already existed, though it was not recognized as such.

The first major recorded case dealing with the problem of literary property and common law copyright occurred in 1741. Plaintiff Alexander Pope sought an injunction to stop the sale of a book which included personal letters he had written to various friends. The court ruled that the writer retained a property right in a letter and that it could not be published without his permission. The receiver of the letter had a special property right, perhaps ownership of the paper upon which the letter was written, but the writer owned the thoughts and words. This principle was still applicable despite the lack of any literary value in the letters themselves. Lord Chancellor Hardwicke enjoined bookseller Curl from vending the volume, *Letters from Swift, Pope and Others.*[22]

In 1758 the British court of chancery stopped the publication of Lord Clarendon's *History of the Reign of Charles the Second from the Restoration to the Year 1667.* Henry, former Earl of Clarendon and author of the work, gave a copy of the manuscript to a friend. Henry died thirty-three years later without ever publishing the book, at which time the friend attempted to publish the manuscript. The court ruled that Henry's giving away a copy of the manuscript did not involve giving the recipient of the gift the right to publish it. This case established that an author had a property right in an unpublished work, independent of any copyright statute.[23]

Eleven years later, in the case of *Millar v. Taylor* (which was quoted from extensively in the Warren and Brandeis article), Lord Mansfield ruled that at common law the author of any book or literary composition has the sole right of first printing and publishing his work. Warren and Brandeis chose to cite dicta * by Justice Yates that every man has a right to keep his sentiments to himself, or to make them public. It is important to remember that the case was decided on the basis of the prop-

---

* Obiter dicta (singular, dictum) are statements or comments made by a judge or justice in a legal opinion which concern some rule of law or proposition that is peripheral to the determination of the case at hand. The strength of dicta was most aptly described by New York Judge Irving G. Vann in Colonial City Transit Co. v. Kingston City Railroad Co., 154 N.Y. 493 (1897), at 495. "If, as sometimes happens, broader statements were made by way of argument or otherwise than were essential to the decision of the questions presented, they are the dicta of the writer or the opinion and not the decision of the court. A judicial opinion, like evidence, is only binding so far as it is relevant, and when it wanders from the point at issue, it no longer has force as an official utterance." Dictum is opposed to the rule of the case, or the ratio decidendi. Obviously, it does not carry the precedent value of a rule. Nevertheless, dicta from important courts, such as the United States Supreme Court, take on a greater value than those from lower courts.

erty right of an author in his works, and that Yates's comments were somewhat off the point.[24]

While the British courts reinforced this principle in a long series of cases dating from the end of the eighteenth century to the middle of the nineteenth century, certain modifications were added along the way. In 1813, for example, Vice-Chancellor Thomas Plumer ruled in *Perceval* v. *Phipps* that a receiver may publish the contents of a letter when it is necessary to vindicate his character from false imputations cast upon him by the writer. Plumer did not stop even at this point, but added that he did not believe that every private letter upon any subject was a literary work, to be protected under the principle of copyright. In other words, Plumer argued that unless a letter or work had some literary value, it would not be protected.[25]

This narrowing of the doctrine of literary property did not stand long, as it was overruled five years later in *Gee* v. *Pritchard.* Again, the court enjoined the publication of private letters by the receiver, despite his claim that publication was required to vindicate his character. Lord Eldon stressed that the writer's claim to the words and thoughts in the letters was a property claim. Plaintiff's counsel attempted to sustain the injunction on the grounds that the publication of the letters would be painful to the plaintiff's feelings. The chancellor interrupted the argument with this interjection—"I will relieve you from that argument. The question will be whether the bill [of complaint] has stated facts of which this court can take notice, as a case of civil property, which it is bound to protect." [26]

The growth of the British law on the subject seemed to climax in 1849 in *Prince Albert* v. *Strange,*[27] a *cause célèbre* because the participants included Queen Victoria and Prince Consort Albert. The queen and Albert made drawings and etchings which they kept for their own use. The man who printed the works for the couple retained copies of the drawings, which he later gave to William Strange, who planned to exhibit them and publish a catalogue describing them. The British chancellors stopped both actions, ruling that there was a property right in the works which belonged to Victoria and Albert. The chancellors also ruled that there was a breach of contract by the printer, and that the plaintiff was entitled to protection in the enjoyment of what was his. The holding or the rule in the case followed established legal principles. However, in dicta, Lord Cottenham referred to a right of privacy and argued that this was a right which a court of equity could protect by injunction. Vice-Chancellor Bruce commented in much the same vein that the common law "shelters the privacy and seclusion of thought and sentiments committed to writing, and desired by the author to remain not generally known." [28]

This case has been cited many times as one root of the law of privacy. Warren and Brandeis relied on it heavily in their argument. But despite what was said in dicta, the case was decided on the basis of property rights, not a right of privacy. The nature of the case led the chancellors to make loose remarks concerning the sacredness of the home and the need to censure those who, through mercenary desires, invade the repose and seclusion of private life. But the decision itself rests squarely on the well-established grounds of property rights.

Counsel for Queen Victoria and Prince Albert expressly said: "The interference of this court is not asked for on the grounds of decorum or good taste, but upon the general principle that this court will protect every person in the free and innocent use of his own property and will prevent anyone from interfering with that use to the injury of the owner." This was the only available right for the plaintiffs to plead in 1849. The argument that the right protected was in fact a right of privacy came after the decision, primarily from Warren and Brandeis, using dicta from the chancellors to support their position. As Herbert Spencer Hadley said shortly after the publication of the Warren and Brandeis proposal, "It is to be remembered that no position, however extreme, can want for support and justification in the dicta of decisions." [29]

While definitive, the *Prince Albert* decision was not the last ruling on the subject. There was one more important case in Britain before 1890 which dealt with the concept of literary property or common law copyright: *Mayhall* v. *Higbey*.[30] A photographer lent ninety photographic portraits of famous persons to the proprietor of *The Illustrated News of the World*. When the newspaper became insolvent, the pictures were sold at auction to the defendant, who subsequently copied, published, and sold them. The court of the exchequer awarded the plaintiff photographer damages and enjoined the defendant from selling any more copies of the photographs. "The nature of the right of an author in his works is analogous to the rights of ownership in other personal property," the court ruled. "He may prevent publication." The *Mayhall* case was one of the first instances in which a plaintiff received money damages. Usually the claim was brought in equity court, and an injunction to stop the defendant's action was the only remedy available.

While the law of literary property was growing in Great Britain, it was also developing in the United States. One of the earliest cases occurred in 1811 in Louisiana Territory, and surprisingly Warren and Brandeis either missed or ignored it.[31] The defendant obtained a copy of a letter the plaintiff had written to a third party. He threatened to publish it, but was stopped by an injunction obtained by the plaintiff. The defendant then advertised that he had posted a copy of the letter on the wall of his printing shop for public inspection. The plaintiff went back to court and attempted to get the defendant's copies of the letter, and to have the printer found in contempt of court for disobeying the injunction.

At this stage of the action Judge Francis-Xavier Martin ruled that a letter was an object of property and could not be published without the writer's consent. The defendant argued that the court injunction was in violation of the First Amendment guarantee of freedom of the press, the first recorded instance of this defense being used in a literary property case.* But it failed to carry the day. Judge Martin wrote: "If this article can be invoked to support the defendant, in the right of printing the work of another, or violating the secrets of his correspondence, it will protect the propagation of any slander or libel. Neither Congress, nor the Circuit Court of the United States, seems to have ever considered this article as susceptible of so strange a construction" (p. 315).

This decision was the forerunner of a long series of similar rulings in American courts, most of which were pronounced in New York State chancery courts. In 1839, in *Brandreth* v. *Lance*,[32]

---

* Louisiana, a federal territory in 1811, was subject to the provisions of the Bill of Rights, while states were not.

New York Chancellor Reuben H. Walworth refused to enjoin the publication of a book entitled *The Life, Exploits, Comical Adventures and Amorous Intrigues of Benjamin Brandling M.D.U.P.L.U.S., a Distinguished Pill Vender* [*sic.*], *Written by Himself; Interspersed with Racy Descriptions of Scenes of Life in London and New York.* The plaintiff, Brandreth, said that the book was supposedly his biography, which had been written by a disgruntled former employee, Lance, and he argued that it was libelous. Walworth said that if he stopped publication of a book on the grounds that it might be libelous, he would be infringing upon the liberty of the press. If the book were indeed libelous, Brandreth could institute a civil suit after publication. The important statement by Walworth came in dicta—that an injunction could only be granted where the publication would interfere with the plaintiff's right of literary or other property.

Three years later, in *Wetmore* v. *Scovell*,[33] Vice-Chancellor William T. McCoun modified the literary property rule in much the same way that Vice-Chancellor Plumer had in *Perceval* v. *Phipps.* McCoun said that a letter must possess the attributes of a literary composition before its publication could be stopped under copyright law: "Publication should not be forbidden merely and solely because it may disturb the peace of families and outrage the feelings of the authors of such letters." In addition, McCoun asserted that there was no interference with freedom of the press when publication was limited in a case of legitimate common law copyright infringement.

Chancellor Walworth reinforced the *Wetmore* decision in 1848 in *Hoyt* v. *MacKenzie,* when he said: "No one, it is true, whose moral sense is not depraved, can justify the purloining of private letters, and publishing them for the purpose of wounding the feelings of individuals, or of gratifying a perverted public taste. . . . But this court has no jurisdiction to restrain and punish crime, or to enforce the performance of moral duties, except so far as they are connected with the rights of property."[34]

The *Wetmore-Hoyt* rule remained the law for seven years before it was overruled in *Woolsey* v. *Judd,* perhaps the leading United States case on the subject. In *Woolsey,* Justice John Duer of the New York Superior Court ruled that the *Wetmore* and *Hoyt* decisions were a departure from the law to the extent that the plaintiff was required to demonstrate that the property in question possessed the requisites of literary composition. "The writers of letters," Duer wrote, "whether they are literary compositions, or familiar letters, or letters of business, possesses the sole and exclusive right of publishing the same. . . ." [35]

Duer added that the receiver may only justify his publication of a letter when he can show that the publication was necessary to the vindication of his own rights or conduct against unjust imputations. In his definitive opinion Duer made comments worthy of extensive quotation. He called the unauthorized publication of letters

. . . one of the most odious breaches of private confidence, or social duty, and of honorable feelings which can well be imagined. It strikes at the root of that free interchange of advice, opinions and sentiments, which seems essential to the well-being of society, and may involve whole families in great distress from the public display of facts and circumstances which were reposed in the bosom of others, in the fullest and most affecting confidence that they should remain forever inviolable secrets.

But, Duer added, jurisdiction of a court cannot be justified on these grounds alone; the court is not the general guardian of society's morals. "We fully admit that an injunction can never be granted, unless it appears that the personal legal rights of the party who seeks the aid of the court are in danger of violation" (p. 383). The one ground upon which relief can be granted, Duer said, is an invasion of an exclusive right of property which remains in the writer—even after the letters have been sent.

This was the law in 1855 in the United States. It was also the law in 1890. It seems strange that Warren and Brandeis placed such great emphasis on dicta from a British case, *Prince Albert* v. *Strange,* but ignored the rule in the leading American case, *Woolsey* v. *Judd.* There were other American decisions in the general area of common law copyright and literary property. All reinforce the principle laid down in *Woolsey* v. *Judd.*[36] In *Grigsby* v. *Breckenridge,* Kentucky Court of Appeals Judge George Robertson spoke broadly that a production of the mind is property in every essential sense in which a production of the hands is the producer's property. Robertson said that the sender has a qualified property right in a letter, which gives him and only him the right to publish its contents.

In a dissent Judge Rufus K. Williams insisted that the sender enjoyed a general property right—that is, he owned the words, the thoughts, and the paper on which they were written. Williams called the "secret privacy of the family relationship" sacred (p. 512). Despite their differences on what kind of a property right was involved, both judges agreed that the sender's right to control the publication of a letter was based on a property right.

Before moving into other aspects of the law discussed by Warren and Brandeis, let us consider one of the key theoretical links made by the two scholars with reference to literary property and privacy: "The principle which protects personal productions, not against theft and physical appropriation, but against publication in any form, is in reality not the principle of private property, but that of an inviolate personality." [37] A thorough reading of eighteenth- and nineteenth-century case law on literary property makes it difficult to arrive at the same conclusion reached by the two authors. If there was one point agreed upon by the courts in the United States and England in their *rulings*, it was that a property right was essential in any consideration of a judicial remedy to stop the unauthorized publication of letters, manuscripts, photographs, or any other so-called product of the mind. It is true that in certain cases judges and justices did speak of privacy and the right to enjoy private relationships. But in every instance this was dicta, judicial philosophy. And while it may have been good philosophy, in the nineteenth century it was not good law.

Warren and Brandeis were not pleading a case at the bar. Their ideas regarding literary property were essentially theoretical rather than factual statements. Their conclusion, quoted above, represents at most a statement of "what should be," not "what is." Acceptance of this conclusion, despite its faults, provides a comfortable if somewhat shaky bridge between the law of literary property and privacy.

The common law is constructed of many bridges such as this one, some more secure than others. Because it is "discovered" law rather than legislation, the common law must always seek roots in the past. For example, for Warren and Brandeis to have announced merely that the "yellow press" necessitated a law of privacy and that they were outlining their conception of the law would have been unthinkable. They had to find some tie, however tenuous, with the past. This method of "discovery" does not necessarily provide a neat, well-constructed, and logical growth of the common law, but it certainly makes this growth interesting.

A BREACH OF CONTRACT

In addition to the law of literary property, Warren and Brandeis used a series of British and American cases involving breach of contract as a support for their proposal. Cases of this nature [38] established the legal doctrine that an implied contract existed between certain parties which, if broken, entitled the injured party to seek remedy by injunction. A British court ruled in 1820 that there was an implied contract between a doctor and his assistant, and that if, after the employment was terminated, the assistant sold recipes for medicines which he had copied while working for the doctor, he broke this contract. Another ruling established that there was an implied contract between a student and a lecturer, and that the student could not make a copy of the lecture and sell it for profit. In 1884 British chancellors decided that when an audience was admitted to a lecture, they agreed to an implied contract not to publish the lecture for profit.[39]

Perhaps the leading case in the series is *Pollard* v. *The Photographic Co.*, decided in a British court of chancery in 1888. The plaintiff was a young lady who had employed a photographer to make her portrait. The photographer kept a copy of the picture and exhibited it in his shop window three months later as a Christmas card. The court stopped him from exhibiting the picture or selling copies of it because it was a breach of an implied contract between the photographer and his subject. Justice Ford North wrote: "The customer who sits for the negative thus puts the power of reproducing the object in the hands of the photographer; and in my opinion the photographer who uses the negative to produce other copies for his own use, without authority, is abusing the power confidentially placed in his hands merely for the purpose of supplying the customer. . . ."[40]

In the past these kinds of decisions were at least partially based on the idea that there was some kind of property right held by the plaintiff, be he lecturer, doctor, or author. The court in *Pollard* refused to concede that there was not property right in the individual features of the photographer's subject. But Justice North did say that whether a property right was at stake was not important, since "the Court of Chancery has always had . . . jurisdiction to prevent what that court considered and treated as a wrong, whether arising from a violation of an unquestionable right, or from a breach of contract . . ." (p. 255).

Warren and Brandeis argued that breach of contract was too narrow a doctrine on which to base decisions in situations such as these. In the past, they argued, an individual had to "sit" to have a photograph taken. "But since the latest advances in photographic art have rendered it possible to take pictures surreptitiously," a new legal doctrine had to be formulated. There was no contract involved in a situation such as this, they argued. The doctrines which in the past had been under contract law should, in fact, be protected under a right of privacy. "The principle which protects personal writings and any other productions of the intellect or of emotions, is the right to privacy, and the law has no new principle to formulate when it extends this protection to the personal appearance, sayings, acts, and to personal relations, domestic or otherwise." [41]

Again, if one is prepared to cross the semantic bridge constructed by the two legal scholars, acceptance of their argument is an easy matter. But this bridge and the one between the law of literary property and privacy are built of speculation, ideas, and words. Warren and Brandeis were obviously convinced that these bridges were strong enough to support a logical extension of the common law. A great majority of the legal profession apparently agreed, because these two bodies of law—contract and literary property—have been adopted as the derivative basis of the right of privacy by practically all the courts in which the right has been upheld. But despite this fact it should be clear that, as in their description of the Boston press, Warren and Brandeis probably overstated their case; there is a certain tenuous quality about the connections between literary property and breach of contract and the law of privacy.

MENTAL SUFFERING AND DAMAGES

After establishing their case for a law of privacy, Warren and Brandeis turned to the dual problems of injury and damages. Just what kind of injury did an invasion of the right of privacy create? They did not labor the point, but stated simply that the injury was mental suffering caused by the wrongful act. In later years some judges were to comment that mental suffering was too nebulous an injury for which to provide compensation. How is mental suffering measured?

Whether or not it could be measured, some American and British courts had been providing monetary compensation for mental suffering for many years prior to the Warren-Brandeis suggestion. Recognition of mental suffering as an injury came primarily in alienation of affection and seduction suits dating back to 1745, when a plaintiff was awarded damages for the loss of the comfort and society of his wife.[42] In later decisions courts explicitly granted damages for mental suffering by the parents or the spouse.[43] In *Phillips* v. *Hoyle,* for example, the Massachusetts Supreme Judicial Court ruled that "in an action for seduction, injury to the plaintiff's feelings is an element in computing the damages, as being a natural consequence of the principal injury."[44]

There was at least one other instance of damages being awarded for emotional harm before 1890. In an unusual trespass case in Vermont in 1880 a plaintiff was awarded compensation because an emotional disturbance had injured her health. The plaintiff was a blind music teacher who gave lessons each week to the defendant's daughter. After the lesson the plaintiff stayed overnight in a private room at the defendant's home. One night the defendant came into her room, sat on her bed, and "made repeated solicitations to her for sexual intimacy—which she repelled." She sued and collected damages for her injured health, which she said was caused by the emotional shock of the trespass. Justice Timothy Redfield said, "Her right of quiet occupancy and privacy was absolute and exclusive."[45]

But rulings such as these were exceptional; in most cases, courts refused to grant redress for mere emotional injuries. In negligence cases, for example, recovery was continually denied. In Massachusetts in 1848 a plaintiff sought damages from the city of Williamstown for the terror and mental suffering he experienced when a bridge he was riding on collapsed. The court ruled that damages could be awarded for any mental suffering attendant to physical injury, but that the town was not liable for mental suffering due to risk, peril, or fright.[46]

In two cases involving the death of children in railroad or streetcar accidents, courts in Louisiana and Kentucky ruled that damages could not be awarded for the mental suffering experienced by the parents due to the loss of their children. "Damages for the mental suffering of one person on account of a physical injury to another are too remote to be given by court or jury," the Kentucky judge ruled.[47]

In light of the state of the law, it is not surprising that the Warren-Brandeis proposition of mental suffering as a basis for damages in a privacy suit received much criticism from other legal scholars. Some questioned how mental suffering could be calculated in a dollar amount. Other critics charged that recovery was awarded for emotional disturbance without showing that any emotional disturbance occurred. Courts have been reluctant to recognize the tort of privacy on the basis of these two criticisms alone.[48] Also, as legal scholar Harry Kalven points out, if inflicting emotional harm in this special way is now actionable on the grounds of underlying principle, why should not all intentional infliction of emotional harm be recognized? [49]

PERIPHERAL CASES

Two additional cases need to be mentioned before moving to an examination of the growth of the law of privacy. The first, *Demay* v. *Roberts*,[50] decided in 1881, was perhaps the first real privacy case. The defendant was a doctor who had taken an untrained assistant to aid him in the delivery of a child at the expectant mother's home. The plaintiffs, the parents, believed that the assistant was a medical man and made no objection to his presence at the birth. Later, when they discovered the real identity of the assistant, they sued the doctor. The Michigan Supreme Court ruled in their favor because the young, untrained assistant had "intruded upon the privacy of the plaintiff." The occasion of the child's birth was a sacred one, Chief Justice Isaac Marston said. "The plaintiff had a legal right to the privacy of her apartment at such a time, and the law secures to her this right by requiring others to observe it. . . ." Recovery in this case was granted on the ground of invasion of privacy, not trespass or any other tort.

The second case was *Manola* v. *Stevens,* an unreported New York decision which was announced in the summer of 1890. Opera star Marion Manola was appearing in *Castles in the Air* at the Broadway Theater in New York City. In one scene she was required to appear onstage wearing tights. The manager of the production, Benjamin Stevens, tried to persuade the actress to be photographed in costume for a poster, advertising the production. She refused. Stevens hired photographer Harry Myers to snap a flash picture of the opera star while she was performing. After the picture was taken Miss Manola sought and obtained a court injunction prohibiting Stevens from using the flash picture. Judge George L. Ingraham of the New York Supreme Court made the injunction permanent when no one appeared to oppose the order.[51]

Demay and *Manola* are important cases because they are cited in later years as two initial privacy decisions. In *Demay,* courts have seen an obvious intrusion on the private life of an expectant mother. In *Manola,* legal scholars note the first case in which an individual stopped the display or publication of his photograph without resorting to the breach of contract argument.

A CONCLUDING WORD

"The Right to Privacy" by Warren and Brandeis, despite its inherent weaknesses, today remains what Brandeis once called it, "a vital force" behind the growth of the law of privacy.[52] But in many respects its significance has been exaggerated. Courts have never seen fit, for example, to restrict publication of the news to the extremes advocated by the two Boston attorneys. And, in reality, it took nearly forty years for the tort to gain a foothold in a respectable number of American jurisdictions.

But the Warren-Brandeis article, while perhaps not *the* major factor in shaping the growth of the law of privacy, nevertheless gave early impetus to the tort. In the decades following its publication, few scholars found fault with the proposal. Harry Kalven suggests why: "I suspect that fascination with the great Brandeis trade mark, excitement over the law at a point of growth, and appreciation of privacy as a key value have combined to dull the normal critical sense of judges and commentators and have caused them not to see the pettiness of the tort they have sponsored." [53] Kalven has probably captured the essence of what occurred in the years following 1890 with regard to the proposal by Warren and Brandeis. While courts in many jurisdictions refused to accept the semantic bridges between the property rights of common law copyright and the "inviolate personality," others accepted the argument, noting the classic style of the article, the eminence of one of its authors, and the fascinating aspects of the tort.

Few critics noted that Warren and Brandeis failed to give any consideration to the concept of freedom of the press. In the past this has been frequently written off as being typical of the times; it was contended, for example, that freedom of the press was not an important idea in this stage of our legal development. But this is not true. As will be shown in the next chapter, in the first twenty years following the publication of the article, many courts rejected the tort because it interfered with freedom of the press. The fact that the two authors failed to distinguish the news-gathering and information role of the press from its advertising and trade aspects resulted in the failure of the law to develop in the manner they suggested. Newsworthy material was granted immunity from lawsuits, and society news has generally been considered newsworthy.

One paradox remains in the history of the growth of the law of privacy. Warren and Brandeis based much of their legal argument on British common-law doctrine regarding literary property and breach of contract. Yet today there is no tort remedy for an invasion of privacy in Great Britain. The law has not developed there—in fact, it has been rejected.[54] This paradoxical situation suggests that the connection between the British case law and the right of an inviolate personality was not so strong as Warren and Brandeis argued.

IV

The Development Begins: 1890-1910

Indeed, one can logically argue that the concept of a right of privacy was never required in the first place, and that its whole history is an illustration of how well-meaning but impatient academicians can upset the normal development of the law by pushing it too hard.

FREDERICK DAVIS [1]

The development of the law of privacy in the first twenty years following the proposal of the tort by Samuel Warren and Louis Brandeis must be characterized as sporadic at best. The common-law recognition of the law occurred in only five states—Georgia, Indiana, New Jersey, Kentucky, and Louisiana; statutes creating a right of privacy were approved in four states—California, New York, Utah, and Virginia; and the legal recognition of the tort was specifically denied in two states—Michigan and Rhode Island. In Massachusetts, the home of the two young lawyers, a federal court refused to enjoin the publication of a biography on the grounds that it constituted an invasion of privacy. In addition, from 1890 to 1910 at least eight law journal articles were published on the subject, some arguing for, others arguing against the recognition of the right.*

* While this book is confined to a study of privacy and the press, many states

The greatest growth of the law came in New York, where, following judicial refusal to recognize the common law right of privacy, a statutory measure gave citizens a limited protection. Much case law followed. In some jurisdictions courts refused recognition of the right because it infringed upon the constitutional freedoms of speech and press. While many of the major decisions reinforcing freedom of the press would not be handed down for several years, "the idea that a broadly defined freedom of the press was essential to the maintenance of a viable political system and an open society was widely held." [2] Other courts argued that Warren and Brandeis were essentially wrong because unless a property right of some kind was at stake, no judicial remedy was available.

But despite the uneven nature of the beginning, there was a beginning. Gradually, courts in a few jurisdictions accepted the idea that the privacy of the individual was a right worthy and deserving of legal protection. While the law did not develop in the exact manner proposed by Warren and Brandeis, their article played a significant part in promoting the growth of the tort.

THE PHILANTHROPIST AND THE LAW

One of the first major court decisions involving privacy was made a few years after the appearance of "The Right to Privacy." Fifteen years after the death of Mrs. Mary Hamilton Schuyler in 1877, the Woman's Memorial Fund Association of New York revealed plans to exhibit a life-size statue of the great philanthropist at the World's Columbian Exposition opening in Chicago in 1893. The statue of Mrs. Schuyler was to be labeled "The Typical Philanthropist" and displayed next to a statue of Susan B. Anthony, "The Typical Reformer."

Members of the Schuyler family objected to this display on the grounds that it constituted an invasion of privacy. The plaintiffs argued that Mary Schuyler had never been a public character, either as an artist or as a candidate for office, and consequently her personality was not public property. A lower court

recognized the existence of a legally enforceable right of privacy in cases not involving the mass media. These cases are included to demonstrate the growth of the law across the nation.

in New York granted an injunction stopping the display, despite the defendant's contention that if indeed anyone's privacy had been invaded, it was not the plaintiffs', Mary Schuyler's stepson and nephew, but the dead woman's. Presiding Judge Charles H. Van Brunt argued that "it cannot be that by death all protection to the reputation of the dead, and the feelings of the living in connection with the dead, has absolutely been lost." [3]

Defendant Ernest Curtis appealed the ruling to the court of appeals. Judge Rufus W. Peckham reversed the lower-court decision and permitted the display. Noting that the suit was a test case seeking judicial enforcement of the right of privacy, Peckham said that the plaintiffs had picked the wrong case for such a test. It was unnecessary to rule on the existence of a right of privacy, Peckham said, for this case involved no question of that right in Mrs. Schuyler's lifetime. The relatives of the deceased philanthropist could not maintain an action based on Mary Schuyler's right of privacy "because whatever right of privacy Mrs. Schuyler had died with her," Peckham announced. [4]

The doctrine that the right of privacy dies with the individual, first established in this case, has been reinforced many times in New York and in other jurisdictions. It remains today as one of the key defenses in a privacy action and has been used successfully on several occasions by mass media defendants. [5]

After the lower-court decision in *Schuyler*, but before the reversal by the court of appeals, another privacy suit began to make its way through the New York courts. For the first time a newspaper was involved as the defendant. Joseph Jaffa, editor of *Der Wachter*, a New York City publication, planned to conduct a popularity contest between two actors—Rudolph Marks, the plaintiff, who was also a part-time law student, and an actor named Mogulesko—by publishing the pictures of both men and letting the readers vote on their respective popularity. Marks refused to consent to the use of his picture, but Jaffa used it anyway. A lawsuit resulted, and an injunction was granted prohibiting the use of Marks's picture in *Der Wachter*.

Judge David McAdam, basing his decision on the lower-court rulings in *Schuyler* v. *Curtis* (the reversal did not occur until 1895), wrote:

If a person can be compelled to submit to have his name and profile put up in this manner for public criticism to test his popularity with certain people, he could be required to submit to the same test as to his honesty, or morality, or any other virtue or vice selected, or be declared inferior to his competitor—a comparison which might prove most odious. . . . Such a wrong is not without its remedy. No newspaper or institution, no matter how worthy, has the right to use the name or picture of any one for such a purpose without his consent.

McAdam wrote that when individuals transgress the law, invoke its aid, or put themselves up as candidates for public favor, "they warrant criticism, and ought not to complain of it. . . ." But, "where they are content with the privacy of their homes, they are entitled to peace of mind, and cannot be suspended over the press heated gridiron of excited rivalry. . . ." [6]

Two questions come to mind after reading McAdam's decision. Would the case have been decided differently if McAdam had had the benefit of the final disposition of *Schuyler?* Probably not, since the rule in *Schuyler* was narrow with regard to the expiration of the right of privacy. But as an actor, did Rudolph Marks not put himself up for public criticism? It certainly appeared that he did, although Judge McAdam did not agree.

A year after the *Marks* decision Judge Henry Bischoff, Jr., of the New York Supreme Court ruled that parents may not sue to enjoin the publication of a portrait of an infant daughter. "It is fundamental to the jurisdiction of the court in any case where it is applied to for an injunction," Bischoff said, "that some property right *belonging to the party seeking relief* is in jeopardy . . ." (emphasis added). Only the child could sue, he added, and then he was not certain that the case would stand. [7] This rule has been slightly modified in the past seventy-five years, as subsequent chapters will show.

PRIVACY AND THE INVENTOR

The first right of privacy suit filed in a federal court received a stormy welcome. Emily A. Corliss, wife of the deceased inventor George H. Corliss, sought to stop the publication of a biography and picture of her late husband. Mrs. Corliss argued that her husband was a private character and the publication of his biography constituted an invasion of the right of privacy. Judge LeBaron B. Colt of the First United States Circuit Court, Massachusetts, disagreed and dissolved the injunction instituted by the district court. Judge Colt said that Corliss was a public man, in the same sense as authors or artists are public men. "It would be a remarkable exception to the liberty of the press if the lives of great inventors could not be given to the public without their own consent while living, or the approval of their family when dead." The jurist then noted that in reality the matter of consent, and whether the subject was living or dead, was unimportant.

Freedom of speech and of the press is secured by the constitution of the United States and the constitutions of most of the states. This constitutional privilege implies a right to freely utter and publish whatever the citizen may please, and to be protected from any responsibility for so doing, except so far as such publication, by reason of its blasphemy, obscenity, or scandalous character, may be a public offense, or by its falsehood and malice, may injuriously affect the standing, reputation, or pecuniary interests of individuals. In other words, under our laws, one can speak and publish what he desires, provided he commits no offense against public morals or private reputation.[8]

Colt argued that there could be no right of privacy if this right interfered with the freedom of expression—which he believed it clearly did in this case.

Colt used principles other than freedom of the press to protect distribution of Corliss' picture. A man who asks for public recognition, the judge said, surrenders his right of privacy to the public. "When any one obtains a picture or photograph of such a person, and there is no breach of contract or violation of confidence in the method by which it was obtained, he has the right to reproduce it, whether in a newspaper, magazine or a book." [9] Corliss, Colt said, was a public man, and the distribution of his picture was thus protected.

The *Corliss* case was the first instance in which a defendant was sued for publishing what was clearly news or information— not advertising or publicity matter. Colt's argument, while seemingly applicable across the board to any kind of publication, has been limited somewhat in the intervening years. Nevertheless, the philosophy that society is built and served by the free exchange of information has been used time and again to protect the news media, and other media as well.

In Michigan, for example, five years later, the supreme court refused to prohibit use of the name and likeness of the late John Atkinson, well-known attorney and politician, on the label of a cigar. At least part of Justice Frank A. Hooker's reluctance to recognize the right of privacy was based on his strong belief that such a remedy might restrict the press. The court, in response to a suit by Atkinson's widow, ruled that "so long as such use does not amount to a libel, we are of the opinion that Colonel John Atkinson would himself be remediless, were he alive, and the same is true of his friends who survive." [10]

Hooker's opinion, which was representative of one school of judicial thinking in the 1890s, attacked many of the arguments supporting a law of privacy. He curtly dismissed the Warren-Brandeis article, noting that "an examination of the article will show that authoritative decisions which support the theory advocated are wanting" (p. 375). With similar brevity Hooker dismissed the threat to an individual's privacy posed by the candid photographer: "If we admit the impertinence of the act, it must also be admitted that there are many impertinences which are not actionable, and which courts of equity will not restrain" (pp. 381–82). The Michigan Supreme Court justice argued that men differed in their feelings and emotions and that it was impractical to make a right of action depend upon the sensitivities of a man.

> The wisdom of the law has been vindicated by experience. This "law of privacy" seems to have obtained a foothold at one time in the history of our jurisprudence—not by that name it is true, but in effect. It is evidenced by the old maxim, "The greater the truth, the greater the libel," and the result has been the emphatic expression of public disapproval, by the emancipation of the press, and the establishment of freedom of speech, and the abolition in most of our States of the maxim quoted by constitutional provisions. . . . [P. 383]

Hooker's legal history may have been a bit weak,* but his idea was unusual and was widely quoted during the era. While

---

* The analogy between the old libel maxim and privacy is a bit strained. When the state restricted the publication of a libel, it did so *originally* to protect the public peace. In privacy it is not the public peace which is at stake, but the feelings and emotions of the plaintiff.

freedom of expression had little to do with cigar labels, the Michigan justice nevertheless spoke for many when he refused to recognize the legal right of privacy. *Atkinson* marked the first clear refutation of the right of privacy in any jurisdiction, and this opinion remained law in Michigan until 1948.

The last state to consider the recognition of privacy before the end of the century was California. In 1899 the legislature approved an amendment to the criminal libel statute which made it a misdemeanor to publish the portrait of any person in a newspaper or book or on a handbill or poster without the individual's consent. Two categories of individuals were excepted from this restrictive measure—the holders of public office and convicted criminals. All participants in the publishing process were equally liable—owner, editor, manager, engraver—and a conviction brought a fine of from one hundred dollars to five hundred dollars and up to six months in jail. There were no reported instances of prosecution under the statute, and the law remained a dead letter until 1915, when it was repealed. Nevertheless, this was the nation's first privacy statute, preceding the more famous New York law by four years.

As the nineteenth century ended, the law of privacy had barely gained a toehold in contemporary American law. The Michigan Supreme Court had refused to recognize the right, a federal court in Massachusetts had reacted in similar fashion, and the New York courts had been less than hospitable in two of the three decisions which reached the appellate level. Things would change, however, as the twentieth century began.

ABIGAIL ROBERSON—"FLOUR OF THE FAMILY"

The case of *Roberson* v. *Rochester Folding Box Co.* reached the New York Court of Appeals, the highest court in the state, in 1902. The case had been in the courts since early 1900,[11] when Miss Abigail Roberson first sought legal action to stop the publication of her portrait on posters advertising Franklin Mills Flour. The posters—about twenty-five thousand copies—were displayed in stores, warehouses, saloons, and other public places. Beneath her picture were the words, "Flour of the Family." The likeness on the posters was quite good, but Miss Roberson nevertheless argued that she was humiliated and caused to suffer greatly by this commercial exposure, and that her privacy had been invaded. She sought fifteen thousand dollars in damages and an injunction to stop distribution of the posters. The decision of the New York Supreme Court overruling the defendant's demurrer * was affirmed by the appellate division.[12] The court of appeals, however, overruled the appellate division and sustained the demurrer, stating that there was no such thing as a legal right of privacy in New York.

Chief Judge Alton B. Parker spoke for the four-member majority of the court when he said, "An examination of the authorities leads us to the conclusion that the so-called 'right of privacy' has not yet found an abiding place in our jurisprudence, and, as we view it, the doctrine cannot now be incorporated without doing violence to settled principles of law by which the profession and the public have long been guided." [13] Parker said that the court was being asked to create a broad right—a right which would go beyond the case in point, to include such things as photographs snapped in public. But before such a right could be established, many problems had to be solved. How can the distinction between a private and a public character be drawn? Should writing and speaking be included as well as pictures? Problems like these, he said, suggest "the absolute impossibility of dealing with this subject save by legislative enactment, by which may be drawn arbitrary distinctions which no court should promulgate as a part of general jurisprudence" (p. 555). Parker was joined in his opinion by Judges Denis O'Brien, Edgar M. Cullen, and William E. Werner.

Judge John C. Gray, joined by Judges Albert Haight and Edward T. Bartlett, registered a vigorous dissent. Gray argued that the right of privacy was certainly within the field of accepted legal principles and was not opposed by any New York court decision. There should be a recognition of this right, the dissenters argued.

The decision in the case created a controversy rarely seen fol-

---

* A demurrer is a plea made by the defendant at the beginning of a lawsuit in which he says that even if all the allegations made by the plaintiff are true,

lowing a court ruling. Newspapers, prompted by the outrageous facts in the case, chastised the court and Judge Parker. *The New York Times* editorialized on 23 August 1902: "Several glaring illustrations have of late been furnished of the amazing opinion of Judge Parker of the Court of Appeals of this State, that the right of privacy is not a right which in the State of New York anybody is bound to respect, or which the courts will lend their aid to enforce. We happen to know that the decision excited as much amazement among lawyers and jurists as among the promiscuous lay public." The *Times* editorial writer noted the problems which beset President Theodore Roosevelt and financier J. Pierpont Morgan as they attempted to live their lives in relative solitude. "If there be, as Judge Parker says there is, no law now to cover these savage and horrible practices, practices incompatible with the claims of the community in which they are allowed to be committed with impunity to be called a civilized community, then the decent people will say that it is high time that there were such a law."

The fury of the attack by the press and others prompted one of the members of the four-man majority, Judge Denis O'Brien, to answer the critics in print. O'Brien's forum was the *Columbia Law Review*, from which he argued forcefully that invasion of privacy was one of the penalties the famous must pay when they reach "the pinnacle of their earthly ambitions." O'Brien reminded the critics that

. . . it is only a short time since a bill was introduced into the Senate of this state and passed for the very purpose of prohibiting the use of pictures and photographs without the consent of the person represented. That bill would have covered every case referred to in the above article, but it was the most unpopular bill that had made its appearance in the legislature for many years. The opposition of the press not only defeated the bill, but went so far as to demand the retirement of its author to private life.

O'Brien said that he was not even certain that legislation was the best way to attack the problem, asserting that when courts or legislators attempted to meddle in matters such as a right of privacy, "it often happens that they do more harm than good." [14]

---

this does not constitute a legal wrong. If the demurrer is sustained, the lawsuit ends. If the demurrer is overruled, the plaintiff then sets out to show that his allegations are true.

THE NEW YORK PRIVACY STATUTE

The result of the uproar created by the *Roberson* decision was passage by the New York legislature of a privacy statute—much like the one described by O'Brien—on 7 April 1903. The measure, which went into effect on 1 September 1903, limited court action to those instances in which an individual's name or likeness was used without consent for advertising and trade purposes.[15] Violation of the act, which became an amendment to the state's Civil Rights Law, was a misdemeanor. The second section provided a civil remedy for the complaining party, permitting him to seek both injunctive relief and money damages.

This law, while limited in scope, nevertheless has grown to encompass a wide range of problems. As will be seen in subsequent chapters, the New York measure is responsible for about one-half of all the reported privacy decisions in the United States since 1903. The tough judicial problems of defining "purposes of trade" and "advertising," construing such terms as "use," "name," and "portrait," and generally determining the scope of the act, its nature (is it a penal statute or a remedial statute?), and its purpose have provided much grist for the legal mills.

The constitutionality of the statute was tested in two cases five years after its enactment. In the first, *Wyatt* v. *James Mc-Creery Co.*,[16] the plaintiff, Helen Wyatt, sued a photographer for the unauthorized circulation and sale of her picture. The defendant had photographed the plaintiff for a reduced price and claimed that she had relinquished her rights to the picture when she orally authorized him to do what he wanted with it. In court, defendant McCreery argued that it was unconstitutional for the legislature arbitrarily to deprive an individual of his property rights. Justice George Ingraham disagreed and said that the legislature had the right and the power to stop the unauthorized use of an individual's portrait. There could be no constitutional objection to the law on these grounds.

At about the same time Aida T. Rhodes brought a similar suit against the Sperry and Hutchinson Company for exhibiting her picture to advertise the benefits of its trading stamps. Again the defendant complained that it was deprived of liberty and property without due process. The trading-stamp vendor also argued that the statute violated the United States Constitution because it impaired the obligation of contract. The latter argument was based on the premise that an oral agreement between a photographer and a subject, made before the law was passed, would now be invalid. The court of appeals refused to accept these arguments. There was no interference with a contract, the court said, because the act was prospective and did not apply to pictures taken or acquired before it became law. The Sperry and Hutchinson Company appealed to the United States Supreme Court, but the judgment of the state court was affirmed.[17]

The enactment of the New York statute gave individuals protection in the use of their name in connection with commercial enterprise. Was such a law really needed? To be sure, the court of appeals in *Roberson* had been clear enough in ruling that only the state legislature could create a right of privacy. But eleven years earlier, in a suit similar to the *Roberson* case, a British throat specialist had won both an injunction and damages in a New York court for the unauthorized use of his name by a pharmaceutical firm in advertisements for its throat lozenges.[18] In his complaint Dr. Morell MacKenzie did not even mention the right of privacy; he merely argued that his name was being used without his permission. The supreme court granted the injunction because, it said, the continued use of the doctor's name would cause him to suffer professional damage and was an infringement of his right to the sole use of his name. Whether Abigail Roberson could have successfully sued on these grounds rather than on the broader right of privacy is an interesting question, but one without an answer.

WHAT ARE TRADE PURPOSES?

One of the first questions New York courts were asked to answer was: What are trade purposes? Is the use of an individual's name or picture in a news story a trade purpose? Many years were needed to settle this question, but generally courts ruled that such use was not a trade purpose. The first case which posed this question was litigated in 1908.

On 27 April 1907 the *New York World* published a picture

and news story on John Moser, who claimed that the story, which was rather unpleasant, was untrue. But instead of suing for libel he brought an action under the privacy statute, claiming that the sale of the newspaper constituted a trade purpose. The New York Supreme Court disagreed. Justice James A. Betts ruled that the statute was passed to remedy situations such as befell Abigail Roberson, who found her picture on advertising posters scattered throughout the state. Justice Betts continued:

> While it may be that this statute is in terms broad enough to give a cause of action to a person whose portrait was unauthorizedly published or used in a newspaper continuously, day after day, or week after week, in connection with the advertisement with some patent medicine or some other commodity which the advertiser was interested in selling, and for the purpose of trade on his own part; yet I do not think it was ever intended by the Legislature that under the guise of this statute a newspaper publication could be prohibited from using or publishing the name or portrait in a single issue of a person without his consent having first been obtained. . . . If the publication of a portrait can under this statute be prohibited in a daily newspaper, the publication of a name could also be prohibited . . . , so that the publication of a daily newspaper in this state showing and giving an accurate account of occurrences throughout the civilized world would be an impossibility. . . .[19]

Betts concluded that the statute was not intended to apply to the kind of publications of which Moser complained.

Two years later a similar case again reached the supreme court, this time involving prize fighter Jim Jeffries. Jeffries had written an autobiography which was on sale in bookstores throughout New York. At about the same time the *New York Evening Journal* began to publish a serialized biography of the boxer which was written by one of its staff reporters. Jeffries sought to restrain publication of the *Journal* biography and claimed twenty-five thousand dollars in damages. He argued that by using his picture and name in its news columns the newspaper was attempting to effect an increase in its circulation, which would in turn increase the value of the newspaper as an advertising medium.

Justice Edward B. Whitney said that the plaintiff's argument was based on a faulty reading of the law, which "stretches the language of the statute ad absurdum." Whitney continued: "In my opinion a picture is not used 'for advertising purposes' within its [the statute's] meaning unless the picture is part of an advertisement, while 'trade' refers to 'commerce or traffic,' not to dissemination of information. According to the plaintiff's construction the picture of a pugilist or president would bring the case within the statute where that of an obscure and quiet citizen would probably not. . . ." [20] Whitney denied the injunction and dismissed the damage suit.

The *Moser* and *Jeffries* cases laid the legal groundwork for one of the key defenses the press has used in defeating invasion-of-privacy suits. But the question of whether the publication of a newspaper or magazine constituted a trade purpose was by no means settled. Indeed, sixty years later the United States Supreme Court had to scold a New York court for its ruling that the use of a picture in a feature story in a news magazine constituted a trade purpose.[21] But these two cases, decided in what was the dawn of the era of privacy, made the going a good deal easier as more and more jurisdictions began to recognize the tort.

COMMON-LAW RECOGNITION

While the New York privacy statute was being adopted and construed between 1903 and 1910, privacy decisions were being made in other parts of the nation. For the first time the invasion of privacy was recognized as a legal wrong for which a remedy at common law was available. This recognition occurred clearly in Georgia, Indiana, and Kentucky, and was strongly hinted at in New Jersey and Louisiana. In addition, Rhode Island refused to recognize the right in a strongly worded decision in 1909.

The most important lawsuit during the decade was between Paolo Pavesich and the New England Mutual Life Insurance Company.[22] Pavesich was a well-known artist. One day, while reading a copy of the *Atlanta Constitution,* he found his picture in an advertisement for life insurance. Pavesich's photograph, which had been taken from a negative held by an Atlanta photographer named J. Q. Adams, was placed next to a sickly looking, ill-dressed individual. Above the portrait of the artist were the words, "Do It Now. The Man Who Did." Above the other photograph were the words, "Do It While You Can. The Man Who Didn't." Beneath the picture of Pavesich was this testimonial:

"In my healthy and productive period of my life I bought insurance in the New England Mutual Life Insurance Co., of Boston, Mass., and to-day my family is protected and I am drawing an annual dividend on my paid-up policies."

Pavesich sought damages totaling twenty-five thousand dollars, but the lower court agreed with the defendant that no legal wrong had occurred. The Georgia Supreme Court, however, unanimously overruled this decision. Pavesich sued for both invasion of privacy and libel, something which was and is fairly common. The uncertain nature of privacy law probably prompted many plaintiffs to use libel, an established cause of action, to bolster the new idea of a right of privacy.* Justice Andrew J. Cobb wrote the opinion for the court, which ruled that both counts presented by the plaintiff—libel and privacy—set out causes of action.

Cobb argued that the right of privacy was derived from natural law and had not been recognized previously only because of the "conservatism of the judiciary." In addition, it was a right recognized by the principles of municipal law and guaranteed to persons by both the United States and the Georgia constitutional provisions, which declared that no person could be deprived of liberty except by due process of law. The right might be waived, Cobb said, by seeking an occupation or position which called for the approval or patronage of the public; but he did not accept the argument that the constitutional freedoms of speech and press prohibited legal enforcement of the right. Cobb then quoted Lord Mansfield, a British jurist who was at his best presiding at seditious libel trials in the late eighteenth century: "The liberty of the press consists in printing without any previous license, subject to the consequences of the law" (p. 203). Cobb said that he would compromise in some respects: "To make intelligent, forceful, and effective expression of opinion it may be necessary to refer to the life, conduct, and character of a person; and so

---

* As noted in the text, lawsuits for both invasion of privacy and libel were commonly filed jointly. Today, a similar practice exists. Rules of pleading vary from state to state, and in some instances it is difficult to base two actions on a single set of circumstances. Throughout this study the fact that both a libel and a privacy action were filed in a case will be mentioned only when it has a significant impact upon the court's ruling. For further information on joint libel-privacy suits, see John W. Wade, "Defamation and the Right of Privacy," *Vanderbilt Law Review* 15 (October 1962): 1093–1125.

long as the truth is adhered to, the right of privacy of another cannot be said to have been invaded . . . provided the reference to such person and the manner in which he is referred to is reasonably and legitimately proper . . ." (pp. 203–4).

Cobb added that the law considered the welfare of the public better served by maintaining the liberty of the press than by allowing individuals to assert their right of privacy in such a way as to interfere with the free expression of sentiment and ideas in which the public might be legitimately interested. But this was not the situation in the case of Pavesich. There was "not the slightest semblance of an expression of an idea, a thought, or an opinion, within the meaning of the constitutional provision" (p. 219). "The form and features of the plaintiff are his own. The defendant insurance company and its agents had no more authority to display them in public for the purpose of advertising the business in which they were engaged than they would have had to compel the plaintiff to place himself upon exhibition for this purpose" (p. 217). The mercenary motives and advertising purposes mitigated any right to freedom of the press which existed; this was a clear case of an invasion of privacy. Then Cobb prophesied: "We venture to predict that the day will come when the American bar will marvel that a contrary view [that no legal right of privacy existed] was ever entertained by judges of eminence and ability" (p. 220).

I have discussed the *Pavesich* case extensively not only because it was the first nonstatutory recognition of the right of privacy, but also because it was typical of what occurred in many jurisdictions in similar cases. The case became the leading precedent for many years and provided the legal foundation for similar rulings in many other jurisdictions. The decision pleased many persons, including Brandeis. Less than a month after the ruling he wrote Justice Cobb and complimented him on his "comprehensive and forceful opinion, which will go far toward establishing the right of privacy as an existing right." [23]

The right of privacy was first recognized in Indiana in 1908 in the little-known decision of *Pritchett* v. *Knox County Board of Commissioners.*[24] The plaintiff owned property adjoining the site of a newly constructed jail. She complained that the prisoners could look out their windows into her residence. Judge Daniel W. Comstock ordered the jail to cover the windows facing the plaintiff's property on the grounds that they constituted a nuisance. But in dicta Comstock said that the right of privacy, an argument used by the plaintiff, was "well recognized" and cited the *Pavesich* decision to support the contention.

A year later in Kentucky the court of appeals granted legal recognition to the right of privacy in a case which presented facts similar to the *Pavesich* case. The plaintiff, Senator Jack P. Chinn, sued the defendant pharmaceutical firm when it published a testimonial letter signed by a Senator J. P. Chinn. The letter appeared in Doan's Directory, a booklet used by the defendant to advertise its Doan's kidney pills. Justice J. P. Hobson said that it would be up to a jury to decide whether the publication was libelous, but that the phony letter certainly constituted an invasion of privacy. "We concur with those holding that a person is entitled to the right of privacy as to his picture, and that the publication of the picture of a person without his consent, as a part of an advertisement for the purpose of exploiting the publisher's business, is a violation of a right of privacy and entitles him to recover without proof of special damages." [25] Hobson said that it was customary for the press to publish the pictures of prominent public men. But, he said, it was a very different thing for a manufacturer to use a man's picture to advertise goods in connection with a forged letter endorsing the goods.

LOUISIANA AND NEW JERSEY: TACIT RECOGNITION

Recognition of the right of privacy was hinted at in two Louisiana decisions before the decade ended.[26] The circumstances in both were similar. The plaintiffs were criminal suspects who had been photographed when they were jailed to await trial. In both cases the pictures were put in police files. After the suspects were acquitted, they demanded the return of these photographs. When the police refused, they brought suit against the New Orleans police. In both cases the court ordered the photographs returned, stating that the pictures should be taken only after conviction. Privacy is not specifically mentioned in the decisions, but in the syllabus * at the beginning of the Schulman opinion these words were printed: "Actions—Civil Remedies. . . . The Civil District Court has jurisdiction of a complaint if it relates to a personal right—the right to be left alone." Most authorities and, more importantly, the Louisiana courts cite these two cases as constituting recognition of the right of privacy in the state.

The same kind of quasi recognition occurred in New Jersey in 1907. This time the suit involved an attempt by plaintiff John Vanderbilt to cancel a fraudulent birth record. The plaintiff's wife had a child by another man, but told hospital officials that Vanderbilt was the child's father, so that his name appeared on the birth certificate. The lower court ruled against Vanderbilt on the ground that because no property right was involved, there was no basis for a suit. The appellate court, however, reversed the ruling, stating that an individual had rights other than property rights which could be enforced in a court of equity.[27] In his opinion Judge James B. Dill announced that the court rejected the ruling made in *Roberson* v. *Rochester Folding Box Co.*, and instead adopted Judge Gray's dissent in the case. Most authorities, as well as the New Jersey courts, agree that the *Vanderbilt* case constituted legal recognition of a right of privacy in New Jersey.

Finally, in June 1909 recognition of the right of privacy was vigorously denied by the Rhode Island Supreme Court in the case of *Henry* v. *Cherry and Webb*. The defendants, who owned a dry goods store in Providence, had published an advertisement in the *Providence Evening Bulletin* that included a picture of the plaintiff sitting in an automobile wearing a new auto coat. Henry sued both for invasion of privacy and for libel, and lost on both counts. Chief Justice Edward C. Dubois said that the picture was not defamatory in any way, and then attacked the proposal of a legal right of privacy. Dubois said that he failed to see the analogy between property rights and the right of privacy. He also asserted that mental suffering alone was not an injury of which the law should take cognizance. After a long review of the case law to date, he concluded, quoting from the *Roberson* decision, "the so-called 'right of privacy' has not as yet

* The syllabus is a summary of the points of law discussed in the decision.

found an abiding place in our jurisprudence, and, as we view it, the doctrine cannot now be incorporated without doing violence to settled principles of law." [28]

STATUTORY PROTECTIONS

New York was not the only state to enact privacy legislation during the first decade of the twentieth century. Pennsylvania, Virginia, and Utah all followed suit in one way or another. The Pennsylvania law, approved in 1903, was not really a privacy statute, but authorized civil actions for the recovery of damages arising from negligent but nondefamatory newspaper publications.[29] Nevertheless, many of the evils aimed at were the kind outlined by Warren and Brandeis in 1890. Governor Samuel W. Pennypacker, in comments appended to his signature on the measure, said the law was needed to protect the citizen whose conduct constituted "no part of the right of the public to information. . . . The woman whose domestic griefs have been unfeelingly paraded, . . . the quiet citizen whose peace of mind has been destroyed by the publication of evil gossip," persons such as these must have the right to recover damages, he added. The law, however, remained virtually unused until it was repealed in 1907.[30]

In 1904, less than a year after the passage of both the New York and the Pennsylvania laws, the Virginia legislature approved a privacy statute.[31] This statute, still on the books, is similar to the New York law, limiting privacy actions to cases in which pictures or names have been used for trade or advertising purposes. There are, however, a few minor differences between the two statutes. Under Virginia law surviving relatives retain a right to action against an individual who exploits the name or likeness of a dead relative. This is not possible in New York. Also, only Virginia residents can institute an action under the law, while in New York any person can take advantage of the statutory provisions. The common law of privacy was denied in Virginia in 1905 in the unreported decision, *Cyrus* v. *Boston Chemical Co.*,[32] and there have been no decisions since 1904 which construe the statute.

Finally, in 1909 Utah passed a privacy statute modeled after

Article 5 of the New York Civil Rights Law. Again minor differences existed. Relatives and heirs were given the right to
bring suit in Utah, as in Virginia. Also, in 1963 the Utah statute
was amended to give corporations as well as persons a right of
privacy. Utah is the only state giving business enterprises this
protection. Only one case has been brought under the Utah statute since 1909, and it resulted in a very narrow construction of
the law.[33] This case will be fully discussed in Chapter 8.

THE FIRST TWENTY YEARS

Between 1891 and 1911 the law of privacy took its first few
hesitant steps forward. Its recognition, by statute and common
law, in nine states—though California's statute would be short-
lived—represented a modest but secure beginning. Despite the
refusal of courts in Michigan and Rhode Island to recognize a
legal right of privacy, Warren saw his idea begin to grow before
he died in 1910.

But the amount of growth in the first twenty years is not
nearly so important as the kind of growth that occurred. Certain
boundaries began to appear, some of which were perhaps a bit
distasteful to Warren and Brandeis. It will be recalled that
while the two attorneys agreed that the right of privacy should
not prohibit the publication of matter in the general interest,
they keyed this qualification to "who" rather than "what." Public
characters, men such as artists and politicians who have dedicated their lives to the public, do not enjoy the same right of
privacy as those who attempted to screen their lives from public
scrutiny. "Since the propriety of publishing the very same facts
may depend wholly upon the person concerning whom they are
published, no fixed formula can be used to prohibit obnoxious
publications." [34]

The differentiation between public and private characters
can be found in many of the reported cases between 1891 and
1911. A more important consideration, though, was the nature
of the publication. Was it an advertisement or a news story? Was
it published for a trade purpose or to inform? Did the defendant
use the plaintiff's name or picture for his own financial gain or
to benefit the public? Courts were willing to find an invasion of

privacy if the use was spurred by mercenary motives, but re-fused to recognize such an invasion if the publication was in a news story or feature report. Of course, the New York privacy statute had a good deal to do with the emergence of this pattern, since it was designed to remedy invasions of privacy that were made to enrich the defendant. This distinction was adopted in other states as they groped to shape the law.

Another important factor in the early development of the law was the judicial recognition and enunciation of what might be called a First Amendment philosophy, that is, an understanding and appreciation of the ideas and doctrines which shaped both federal and state constitutional guarantees of freedom of press and speech. There was no reported case in which a constitutional provision regarding freedom of the press was invoked in the *rule* to defeat a privacy suit. This would not happen in federal courts until 1967.[35] Most important opinions, however, indicated an awareness of the importance of a free press.

Judge Colt placed freedom of the press above the rights of the individual in *Corliss* v. *Walker*. Michigan Supreme Court Justice Hooker in *Atkinson* v. *Doherty* asserted that the nation had many years earlier rejected the use of truthful reports as the basis for lawsuits. Even Justice Cobb agreed in his forceful opinion in *Pavesich* v. *New England Mutual Life Ins. Co.* that in many cases publicity was absolutely essential to the welfare of the public. These opinions and many more are recognition that at certain times the rights of the individual must be made secondary to the broad public right manifested in part in the policy of an unfettered press. This kind of philosophy permeated the growth of the law of privacy. While hard-pressed to point to specific decisions in which freedom of the press was the actual basis of a ruling against an invasion of privacy complaint, it is fairly simple to cite numerous cases in which the First Amendment philosophy is used in consideration of the claim.

The growth of the law of privacy in the next sixty years would be far-ranging and rapid. But the press, aided by a strong judicial commitment to liberty of expression, would be able to shape this growth in such a way as to protect the vital function of news dissemination from serious encroachment.

V

Press Protection Expands: 1911-30

Times have changed since Brandeis wrote in 1890. Seeing how society dames and damsels sell their faces for cash in connection with cosmetics, cameras, and cars, one suspects that the right to publicity is more highly valued than any right to privacy. . . . I recommend that respect for privacy be left to public opinion and the conscience of owners and editors.

ZECHARIAH CHAFEE, JR. [1]

In the second and third decades of the twentieth century the use of the right of privacy as a cause of action in a lawsuit increased little. The common-law right was recognized in two states, Kansas and Missouri, and in the federal territory of Alaska. New media of communication, primarily motion pictures, caused some courts to redefine doctrines developed during the preceding twenty years. But by 1930, forty years after the publication of Samuel Warren and Louis Brandeis' "The Right to Privacy," the growth of the law could only be termed disappointing. Legal scholars were still debating even the existence of such a right. In 1937, in a review of tort development during the preceding half century, Francis Bohlen wrote: "Fifty years ago the right which every normal and decent person feels in living his life to himself appeared likely to be protected by a legal recognition of a right to privacy. Unfortunately the campaign for its recognition, brilliantly begun by the article written by Justice Brandeis and published in the *Harvard Law Review has almost completely failed"* (emphasis added).[2]

While the growth of the law was unspectacular between 1911 and 1930, the protection for the publication of news and information expanded. In New York the privacy statute received further definition in a series of cases which added significantly to the understanding of the law and to the protection of the press. Cases in Washington, Alaska, and Kentucky also strengthened the idea that the press was exempt from privacy actions when reporting facts of general interest. Again, the First Amendment philosophy pervaded many key opinions and added to the growing foundation of precedent to support the press's claim of immunity from liability.

INCREASED RECOGNITION

When the family of five-year-old Onel Munden opened their local newspaper one day in 1910, they saw a picture of their son—advertising Elgin watches for a local jewelry store. The Harris-Goar Jewelry Company used the young man's picture as a part of an advertisement which read: "Papa is going to buy mama an Elgin watch for a present, and someone (I mustn't tell who) is going to buy my sister a diamond ring. So don't you think you ought to buy me something? The payments are so easy, you'll never miss the money if you get it of Harris-Goar Co., 1207 Grand Ave., Kansas City, Mo. Gifts for Everybody, Everywhere in their Free Catalogue." [3] Onel's family filed a lawsuit in Missouri state court against the jeweler, charging both libel and invasion of privacy. Defendant P. S. Harris demurred, arguing that there was no such thing as an invasion of privacy and that the advertisement was not defamatory. The court ruled that both complaints were sufficient—that it was up to a jury to decide if there had been a libel, and that certainly there was a right of privacy.

But Judge James Ellison presented a rationale a little different from what had appeared in the past. Rather than arguing that the plaintiff had suffered mental distress from having his picture spread throughout the city in an advertisement, Judge Ellison took an economic point of view. The defendant had no right to use the plaintiff's picture because that is a right which the plaintiff may wish to exercise himself, for his own profit, the judge said. "If there is value in it [the plaintiff's appearance], why is it not the property of him who gives it the value and from whom the value springs?" (p. 659). The judge concluded that an individual had an exclusive right to his picture because it was a property right of material profit.

Seven years later, on the other side of the Missouri River, the state of Kansas recognized a legal right of privacy.[4] While Stella Kunz was shopping in a dry goods store, owners W. H. Allen and Charles H. Bayne secretly took movies of her. The film was made into an advertisement for the store and was shown at the neighborhood theater. Justice Silas W. Porter, speaking for the Kansas Supreme Court, ruled that the exhibition in a theater of the photograph of a person, taken without her consent, for the purpose of exploiting the publisher's business was an invasion of the right of privacy.

The only other jurisdiction to recognize a legal right of privacy before 1931 was Alaska, in the case of *Smith* v. *Suratt*. The story began in Detroit, where the plaintiff organized a private expedition to fly over the North Pole, giving picture rights for the adventure to Pathé News Service. While arrangements were under way in Nenana, Alaska, Richard Suratt, a photographer for International News Service, took pictures of the preparations. In addition, Suratt announced his intention to follow the expedition and take pictures all along the way. The plaintiff went to court to stop Suratt, arguing that the expedition was a business and that the pictures taken by the INS photographer would render the Pathé film valueless.

Federal District Judge Cecil H. Clegg refused to accept the plaintiff's contention, calling the expedition a heroic adventure rather than a business. "Ever since the ill-fated expedition of Sir John Franklin to discover a Northwest Passage on this continent, such attempts have been surrounded and clothed with a remarkable public interest. . . . As such, as a public enterprise in which everybody is interested . . . it cannot claim any right of privacy."[5] Clegg said that Suratt had a right to photograph and gather news about the expedition, that there could be no right of privacy adhering to an enterprise of this public character, even though it was financed by private individuals. While recognizing the existence of a right of privacy, Clegg refused to label the photographer's actions an invasion of that right.

This case remains a strange precedent in that there was no assertion that an individual's right of privacy had been violated; rather, it was contended that there was a property right in a public event, a right which could be sold. As such, perhaps the right of privacy was the wrong basis for the suit. Having granted film rights to Pathé, the Arctic explorers could hardly argue that publicity about the expedition would cause them grave mental suffering; it was obvious that they were seeking publicity—in fact, they were trying to sell it. They were actually complaining about an infringement upon their right of publicity. The legal concept of a right of publicity did not emerge until the 1950s, however, about thirty years too late for the plaintiffs in this case.[6]

THE REALTOR AND THE SENATOR

The right of privacy was first advanced as a cause of action in Washington State in 1911 by young Bessie Hillman and her millionaire father, C. D. Hillman. Hillman was indicted by a federal grand jury in August 1910 for mail fraud in connection with a large-scale real estate operation he was conducting. The *Seattle Star* indictment story carried the headline, "Hillman Accused of Fraud, Warrant for Big Real Estate Shark, Federal Officials Are Hot on His Trail." Parts of the story told readers that the United States government had charged Hillman with attempting one of the biggest swindles in the history of the Northwest.

> The specific charge laid against Hillman today is based on a new real estate deal Hillman is now engaged in, ten miles from Everett. Hillman has acquired title to about 12,000 acres of logged-off lands at Port Susan. . . . He was offering parcels of this land for sale at $100 and more. Prospectuses and blind advertisements were sent out by Hillman, it is charged, giving glowing accounts of the future of Birmingham [the development]. A sawmill and charcoal factory were all to be established there Hillman claimed. All these things, according to the federal officers, were untrue and without foundation.[7]

The story continued, relating that Hillman had been convicted on a similar charge in 1905, but that the Washington Supreme

Court had ordered a new hearing because the trial court had failed to grant a change of venue (moving the trial to a different part of the state). The second trial was never held. With the story, the *Star* published a photograph of Hillman and the other members of his family, including his daughter, Bessie. Hillman, in behalf of his daughter, brought a suit for both libel and invasion of privacy.

The court said that the photograph of Bessie was not offensive in itself, and that, since the little girl was not mentioned in the article, there was no libel. Judge Stephen J. Chadwick frankly admitted that the court believed that the little girl had been wronged. "Yet we find that plaintiff's case does not fall within any of the rules so far recognized by the courts, permitting a recovery for an invasion of privacy," he added (p. 695). Chadwick said that the difficulty in recognizing the right lay in the determination of a fixed line between public and private characters. "This case presents a subject for legislation, and to the legislative body an appeal might be so framed that in the future, the names of the innocent and unoffending, as well as their likenesses, shall not be linked with those whose relations to the public have made them and their reputations, in a sense, the common property of men" (p. 696).

While unable to find a remedy for Bessie Hillman, the Washington Supreme Court did manage to find the means to protect the name of another, more important individual thirteen years later. This was Senator Robert La Follette of Wisconsin, at that time the Progressive party candidate for president of the United States. La Follette was seeking a writ of mandamus * to prohibit the secretary of state from certifying the names of persons nominated by the La Follette State party to fill various state offices. According to La Follette, he had not given the party officials permission to use his name, and he believed that if the certification took place and the party was listed on the ballot, people would be misled into thinking that a vote for the La Follette party candidates would be a vote for the presidential electors pledged to support the Wisconsin senator. This would not be

---

* A writ of mandamus is a command or order, written or oral, which a court may issue, requiring an individual to take or refrain from taking a specific action. In some states "mandate" has been substituted for mandamus as the formal title of the writ.

the case, since La Follette was a candidate of the Progressive party.

Judge J. B. Bridges ruled that a man's name belongs to him and that others cannot use it without his permission. "We have no hesitancy in holding that those organizing and creating the La Follette State Party had no right to use Mr. La Follette's name in that connection against his wishes." [8] Bridges ordered the name changed to "the State Party." Right of privacy was not mentioned in the decision; however, there can be little doubt that the basic considerations behind the ruling were similar to those behind the right of privacy—a right which could not be enforced thirteen years earlier. Today, however, Washington still does not recognize the right of privacy.

The other Washington, the District of Columbia, also had its first encounter with the law of privacy between 1911 and 1930. Mrs. Louise Peed, who had become a subject of public interest after she was found near death in a North Capitol Street rooming house, sued the *Washington Herald* when the newspaper stole a copy of a picture from her home and published it in their 5 February 1926 edition. The *Herald* reported that while the plaintiff was visiting a friend she was nearly asphyxiated when a gas jet was carelessly left open.

Justice Siddons of the District of Columbia Supreme Court ruled that the publication was actionable. "If the right to one's person is a right of complete immunity: 'to be let alone,' then it would be seriously impaired if, without consent, a picture of his person could be obtained by another and published in a newspaper," he wrote. Despite the strong stand in favor of a legally enforceable right of privacy, Siddons' opinion—which was never officially reported—was not considered a recognition of the tort in the District of Columbia. It was not until twenty-one years later that the residents of the nation's capital gained such protection officially.[9]

PRIVACY IN NEW YORK

The most interesting developments in the law of privacy between 1911 and 1930 took place in the State of New York. In a series of cases spanning the twenty-year period, courts endeavored to chart further the boundaries of the state's statute. The result was a small, but important, enlargement of the area of protected expression.

IN MOTION PICTURES

In 1909 America's fledgling motion picture industry was getting off to a slow start. Films were shown primarily in motion picture machines in arcades around major cities. One of the experimental film-making ideas of the era was a re-enactment of important news events, a kind of replay of the week's top stories, with a new cast. Actors were used in the newsmakers' roles.

On 23 January 1909 two steamships, the *Florida* and the *S.S. Republic,* collided in Long Island Sound. The wireless operator on the *Republic,* John R. Binns, immediately began sending out the C.Q.D. distress call, and his actions resulted in the rescue of all but six of the seventeen hundred passengers before the ship sank. This was the first time the wireless had been used in such a rescue operation, and Binns became a national hero, cited for his gallantry by nations, governments, and the press. His picture was published extensively with accounts of the collision and rescue, and he received countless offers to exhibit himself as a hero —offers which he declined.

The Vitagraph Company of America prepared a re-enactment of the *Republic* disaster which was exhibited in motion picture machines around New York. Binns's part was played by an actor, but his name was used throughout the film. One of the scenes which offended Binns depicted the wireless operator smiling, smoking casually, and winking at passengers at the time of the collision. Binns sued for both libel and invasion of privacy.

The appellate division of the New York Supreme Court ruled that the film was libelous, but denied recovery for invasion of privacy, arguing that a double recovery on the basis of a single act by the defendant could not be allowed. The Court of Appeals sustained the libel judgment, but overruled the lower court's dismissal of the privacy suit. To the defendant's argument that Binns's photograph had not been used, since an actor played his part, Judge Emory Chase answered: "A picture within the meaning of the statute is not necessarily a photograph of the living person, but includes any representation of such person." Chase said that the defendant had used Binn's name and picture as a matter of business and profit, contrary to the prohibition of the statute.[10]

Two other documentary motion pictures resulted in privacy suits before 1930. In 1915, August G. Merle sued for invasion of privacy when producers of the motion picture, *The Inside of White Slave Traffic*, filmed his factory and building as places where the white-slavers plied their trade. Both buildings had Merle's name on them, but neither was ever used in connection with white-slave traffic.

The New York Supreme Court ruled that in order to collect libel damages Merle would have to plead special damages * (which he did not do) because there was not enough in the film to imply that he was involved in the white-slave business. As for an invasion of privacy, the court ruled that the name was not used for purposes of trade merely because it appeared on a building photographed. "Certainly where a man places a sign upon the outside of a building he cannot claim that a person who would otherwise have a right to photograph the building is precluded from using that picture because the sign also appears in the picture." [11] The sign was an incidental part of the photograph of the building and could not be presumed to add to the trade value of the motion picture, the court ruled.

Four years later a New York attorney filed suit against the Universal Film Manufacturing Company for the use of her photograph and name in their weekly film review of current events. The films were newsreels, not re-enactments or photoplays, of Grace Humiston as she aided police in solving a baffling mystery surrounding the disappearance of young Ruth Cruger. The film showed the plaintiff as she led police to the body of the girl, which had been buried under the floor in the back room of a New York City shop. Miss Humiston argued that her name and photograph were used for trade purposes.

Justice Walter L. Smith, speaking for the appellate division of the New York Supreme Court, agreed that movie production was

* Generally speaking, to prove special damages a plaintiff must demonstrate that he incurred a financial loss because of the publication of the libel.

surely a trade—but not a trade in the sense the legislature considered trade when the privacy statute was enacted. "Waiving for the moment the question of the constitutional right . . . the reasonable and necessary inference is not only that the statute does not apply to the publication of a newspaper in a single issue, but also the statute does not apply to the publication of a picture or a name in a single set of films of actual events, issued at one time for distribution in different parts of the country before different audiences as a matter of current news." Justice Smith said that it did not matter what motivated the film makers to produce the motion pictures. "The fact that this publication is so markedly different from the publication which is recognized as the inspiration of the passage of the law in question, in itself furnishes a strong probability that it is not within the prohibitive act. . . ." [12]

The plaintiff also argued that even if the film itself did not come within the reach of the statute, advertisements for the motion picture which used the plaintiff's name should be forbidden. Again the court disagreed. Justice Smith said that if the name could not be used in the advertisements, then the films could not be advertised at all, since the motion pitcures were about people. Smith called the use of the plaintiff's name in the advertisements a use "incidental to the exhibition of the film itself."

These three motion picture cases helped establish rules which lasted for many years. Time and again the courts would be asked whether newsreels and filmed re-enactments of newsworthy events were protected. Over the long run, courts placed within the protected area *any* filmed report of a news event. The only factor which diminished this protection was fictionalization of the account. Some decisions ruled against the film makers, but they were exceptions to the general trend.

IN MAGAZINES, BOOKS, AND NEWSPAPERS

In 1913 the *National Police Gazette*, forerunner of today's weekly publication of the same name, was considered a sporting journal, for barbershop reading. The 18 January issue of that year featured a full-page picture layout of five female entertainers, one of whom was May Colyer, a professional high diver. The *Gazette* somehow obtained the picture of Miss Colyer, taken while she was in costume, and published it with the photographs of four other women above the caption, "Five of a Kind on This Page. Most of Them Adorn the Burlesque Stage, All of Them Favorites with the Bald-Headed Boys." Miss Colyer was identified as May Collier, "A Great Trick Diver."

The diver brought suit against the *Gazette* for invasion of privacy. She argued that the magazine was a mere advertising sheet and that every one of its pictures and illustrations were used for advertising or trade purposes. The appellate division of the New York Supreme Court refused to accept this argument, asserting that the statute had a broader meaning. "Applied as the appellant would desire," Justice William J. Carr wrote, "it would cover nearly every issue of our newspapers and especially our great number of monthly magazines, in which advertising matter is in great bulk, and oftentimes, as interesting as the letter-press." [13] The court argued that the statute must be interpreted in light of the evil at which it was aimed. Justice Carr wrote that even in 1903, when the law was adopted, the custom of putting an individual's picture in the newspaper was common; if the legislature had wanted to stop this, it could have said so.

Fourteen years later a similar claim was made against the book publisher Doubleday, Doran and Company, and author Edna Ferber, who wrote *Show Boat*. Wayne Damron, the plaintiff, complained that his name was used at one point in the book, a scene in Catlettsburg, Kentucky, for a character in the story, and that this violated his right of privacy. Justice Edward J. Gavegan refused to give Damron's claim serious consideration. "The law was not passed with the idea of interfering with the circulation of newspapers or the publication of books within proper limits," he said. "In defining whether a name or likeness is used primarily for advertising or trade, we may have to weigh the circumstances, the extent, degree, or character of the use. . . . The single appearance of plaintiff's name in this book [398 pages long] is clearly not a use prohibited by the statute." [14] In later cases New York courts faced the problem of multiple uses of a name in single publications, but the single-use rule stood as stated above.

In the last important New York case between 1911 and 1930 the plaintiff, Stephen J. McNulty, who was an artist's model, complained that H. T. Webster, a cartoonist for the *New York World*, had prepared a cartoon which contained his photographic likeness. The drawing was entitled "The Boy Who Made Good" and depicted two cartoon characters looking at a magazine, which contained McNulty's picture. The dialogue between the two characters was:

Paw, it's th' livin' breathin' image of Elmer! An' don't he look han'some in his new golf suit! My stars and body!

A boy's get tew be purty prominent tew git his pitcher printed in a magazine. I knowed Elmer would make good when he got up tew th' city. Gee Whillikers!

The cartoon was not only printed in the *World*, but was sold as a syndicated feature to other newspapers. McNulty sued for both libel and invasion of privacy. The supreme court ruled that while the cartoon contained his picture, the dialogue did not refer to him, and in the absence of an allegation connecting the words with the picture, there was no libel.

The invasion of privacy action was a different matter. Justice John L. Walsh admitted that while the statute did not prohibit the use of the name or picture of an individual in a single issue of a newspaper or magazine, the fact that the cartoon was sold to other newspapers for profit constituted an invasion of privacy. Publication of the cartoon in the *World* was protected against a lawsuit. But the syndication of the cartoon created a trade purpose, and the newspaper was liable for damages.[15]

The *McNulty* decision illustrates one of the basic differences between invasion of privacy and libel. A libel is generally a libel, wherever it is printed. If John Smith was a good, respected American and someone falsely called him a Communist, it would not matter whether the statement appeared in an advertisement, a news story, a syndicated column, or on a billboard. It would still be libelous, and the source of the statement would be liable for damages. Where or how the statement was used, in other words, is usually not important. But when it is a question of the right of privacy, how or where the picture or name was used is important. Use of a picture in an advertisement could result in a successful suit; use of the same picture in a news story probably would not. This reveals something about the true nature of the tort. In most cases the individual is not really being compensated for any suffering he experienced; he is being compensated because another person was able to make a financial gain from his property—his name or face—a gain in which the plaintiff should at least have shared.

Although other privacy suits were decided in New York between 1911 and 1930, only two had significance for the development of the law. In 1911 the supreme court ruled that under the statute the right of privacy was a personal right and died with the individual. This was, and is, the general rule in common-law jurisdictions as well. Nine years later the appellate division of the supreme court ruled that even a drawing made from a picture constituted the appropriation of a likeness and was actionable. Justice Frank C. Laughlin wrote: "If the wholesome provisions of the Civil Rights Law upon which this action is based, can be thwarted by using a portrait or picture without consent, provided some slight change in the pose is made by enlargement of the picture or otherwise, the statute will be of little use. . . ." [16]

THE INVOLUNTARY PUBLIC FIGURE

The most important privacy decision of the two-decade period was made in Kentucky, the second state to recognize the common-law right of privacy. The story behind the case began in Louisville in 1928. Lillian Jones and her husband Thomas were walking on Chestnut Street when two men attacked Mr. Jones with knives and stabbed him to death. During the struggle Mrs. Jones fought fiercely to protect her husband, but was unable to subdue the attackers. The following day, in a story about the street killing, the *Louisville Herald Post* quoted Mrs. Jones as saying: "I would have killed them. I tried. I fought with them. I struck the tall man, but they got away. A woman hasn't got a chance against brutes. But if I could have killed them I would have done so. I will revenge him someday." [17] Accompanying the story were pictures of Mr. and Mrs. Jones.

Mrs. Jones sued, asserting that the photographs were published without her consent, that she had been misquoted, and that since she was not a public character she had a right to live a quiet, unpublicized life. The Kentucky Supreme Court refused Mrs. Jones's plea for two thousand dollars damages. Judge William Rogers Clay wrote the court's opinion, which has since been widely quoted. In a key paragraph Clay described the right of privacy as "the right to live one's life in seclusion, without being subjected to unwarranted and undesired publicity. In short it is the right to be let alone. . . . There are times, however, when one, whether willing or not, becomes an actor in an occurrence of public or general interest. When this takes place he emerges from his seclusion, and it is not an invasion of his right of privacy to publish his photograph with an account of such occurrence" (p. 229). Judge Clay reminded the plaintiff that the incident took place on a public street, and that the language attributed to her was certainly not uncomplimentary. There was no invasion of her right of privacy, the judge asserted, because Mrs. Jones became "an innocent actor in a great tragedy in which the public had a deep concern" (p. 229).

The so-called involuntary public figure rule, while suggested in other decisions, was first clearly stated in this case. It will be recalled that Warren and Brandeis themselves suggested that genuine public figures who choose a life in the public eye—actors, artists, public office holders—would not enjoy the same right of privacy as the private citizen. The Kentucky Supreme Court ruling significantly expanded this privilege to include those who came into public view not only by choice but by circumstance.

It should also be pointed out that the Kentucky ruling really was based on a consideration entirely foreign to the previously described New York decisions. New York courts spent most of their time defining purposes of trade. A newsworthy individual in New York who found his picture in the newspaper was often faced with this dilemma: the court would agree that his right of privacy was abused, but no cause for legal action existed since the abuse was not for purposes of trade. The Kentucky court, in the same situation, was now bound to a doctrine that refused to acknowledge that there was an invasion of privacy; the newsworthy individual did not enjoy such a right, at least with respect to events surrounding his newsworthiness. These differences, while perhaps subtle, are important and result from the growth of the law of privacy from a statutory base in New York and from a common-law base in Kentucky. In the four decades following the *Jones* case the involuntary public figure rule was expanded, as will be seen in forthcoming chapters, and became a durable bulwark in the press's battle for freedom to report the newsworthy.

At about the same time that the *Jones* case was being litigated in Kentucky, the supreme court of eastern Georgia was considering the plea of George W. Bazemore that an invasion of his privacy had occurred when the *Savannah Press* published a picture of his dead, deformed newborn son.[18] The child was born in Glenville, Georgia, on 29 May 1928, with his heart outside his body. After an operation failed to save the child's life, the hospital allowed a private photographer to take a picture of the deformed baby. The photographer, George R. Foltz, sold several copies of the picture, including one to the *Savannah Press*, which published it with a story.

Bazemore brought suit against the hospital, Foltz, and the newspaper. At first glance it appeared that there were two factors militating against the suit. First, the baby was dead and the right of privacy was regarded as a personal right, expiring with the death of the individual. But eighteen years earlier, in Kentucky, the supreme court had sustained a cause of action by parents in a similar suit when a photographer made extra copies of a picture of a dead baby.[19] In that case the court said that when the photographer made more than the agreed upon number of pictures, he invaded the rights of the parents. Chief Justice J. P. Hobson wrote that it was impossible to distinguish the case from one involving a living person.

The second factor which appeared to work against the Bazemores' suit, at least that portion of it brought against the *Savannah Press*, was that the child's picture was used in a news story, not an advertisement. Experience to this point in all jurisdictions exempted legitimate news from the scope of a privacy action. But in this case neither the death of the baby nor the use as a news item served to defeat the suit. In a short, uninformative opinion, Judge Peter W. Meldrim sustained the cause of action against all three defendants.

The question comes to mind, was the decision the signal of a change in doctrine in privacy law, or was it merely one of those unexplainable decisions that come along now and then, completely out of line with both past and future law? That the Bazemores were able to win a suit based on the publication of their baby's photograph did signal a minor change in policy in the common law. Since 1930 there have been a few decisions in line with this ruling. That the newspaper was found liable for something it printed as a truthful news story is better described as one of the unexplainable decisions. Perhaps the outrageous nature of the story, its inherent bad taste, can be offered as an explanation for the ruling. While this kind of decision would be repeated occasionally in the future, it was rare and certainly does not deserve the status of a minority rule or doctrine.

PRIVACY AND THE CORPORATION

Two other privacy cases deserve mention before leaving this two-decade span. In 1912 Vassar College brought suit against the Loose-Wiles Biscuit Company in federal district court in Kansas City, Missouri, for marketing a confection called "Vassar Chocolates." While the college claimed that it was not suing for invasion of privacy, the complaint carried all the stock arguments usually found in an action based upon the right of privacy. Judge Arba S. Van Valkenburgh ruled that he could not invoke the right of privacy for two reasons. First, Vassar was a public institution. Citing *Corliss* v. *Walker* (see Chap. 4), Judge Van Valkenburgh wrote that when a person was a public character, the right of privacy disappeared. Even more fundamental, however, in its denial of a right of privacy was the court's argument that Vassar was a corporation and as such, it could not sustain an injury to feelings or undergo mental suffering, the basis for relief in a privacy suit.[20]

Of more interest to the press was a 1927 Maryland decision which indirectly involved the right of privacy.[21] Richard R. Whittemore was on trial for murder in Baltimore Criminal Court. As the defendant entered the lockup in the courthouse prior to his first day of trial, *Baltimore News* photographer William Klemm snapped a flash picture of him. The trial judge heard the noise and summoned Klemm to his office, where he ordered the photographer to surrender the photographic plate. Klemm gave the judge a blank plate instead, and kept the photograph. As court convened, Judge Eugene O'Dunne announced that he would not allow any pictures to be taken, either inside the courtroom or in the general vicinity of the trial. Despite the warning another *Baltimore News* photographer, William Sturm, on orders from his city editor, took seven pictures, all secretly, in court that day. The following day the *News* published two of Sturm's pictures and Klemm's photograph of Whittemore in the lockup. Judge O'Dunne instituted contempt proceedings against the management and photographers of the newspaper.

The newsmen appealed their convictions and argued that the trial judge exceeded his authority in issuing the contempt citations. Judge Hammond Urner, speaking for the Maryland Court of Appeals, disagreed with this contention. But the interesting aspect of the opinion was Urner's use of the right of privacy to justify the action by the trial court. "The liberty of the press," he wrote, "does not include the privilege of taking advantage of the incarceration of a person accused of a crime to photograph his face and figure against his will" (p. 120). Citing the *Pavesich* decision and other right-of-privacy cases, Urner argued that if Whittemore had not been in custody he could have defended himself from the invasion of the press. But since he was in custody of the state, the court was justified in intervening. This case did not constitute recognition of privacy in Maryland, which would not occur until 1962.[22]

While the *Sturm* case is of more historical interest than legal significance, it is, nevertheless, a good example of how ideas from one area of the law, in this case tort law, can influence and justify action in another. Obviously the court did not need a reason to justify the contempt citation: that the photographers were in some way interfering with the normal courtroom procedure was sufficient justification. But the use of invasion of privacy to sustain the contempt citation was novel and deserved notice.

As 1930 closed, the right of privacy still had not found a secure place in the American jurisprudence. However, with the beginning of the next decade the law would grow at a more rapid pace. And with this development there were attempts to minimize the range of freedom enjoyed by the mass media in reporting news and current events. The protections established in the first thirty years of the century received a severe test.

VI

Fifty Years of Privacy: 1931-40

The guarantee of a free press should continue to favor the newspapers, newsreels and radio commentators. Part of democracy's theory is that a free press is essential and it is in the public interest to endure small violences to privacy rather than to endanger the freedom of the press through too severe restrictions on its privilege.

RICHARD A. SNYDER [1]

During the fifth decade of its growth, the right of privacy began to spread more rapidly throughout the nation. By the end of 1940 five more states recognized the right, bringing to fifteen the number of state jurisdictions which protected the individual's right to be let alone. The idea received a hostile reception only in Wisconsin, where the supreme court declared that if such a right were to exist, legislative recognition would be needed.

The decade began with a California court's stating that there was no such thing as a common law right of privacy—but ruling that the plaintiff's constitutional right of privacy had been violated. It ended with a federal judge in New York arguing that Samuel Warren and Louis Brandeis had gone a bit too far in their original proposal.[2] In the ten years in between these two decisions, the boundaries of the law became mapped with greater precision, giving the press throughout the nation a more exact picture of what it could and could not do in reporting the day's events.

CALIFORNIA RECOGNIZES PRIVACY

In most cities in the civilized world there is a small group of women who make a living by plying what many call the oldest human trade—prostitution. Gabrielle Darley was one of these women. But in 1918, when she found herself on trial for murder, she began to have second thoughts about her life and where it had led her. After she was acquitted of the murder charge, she abandoned her trade and became rehabilitated. In 1919 Gabrielle married Bernard Melvin, became a housewife, and, in the words of Justice Emerson J. Marks of the California Court of Appeals, "thereafter at all times lived an exemplary, virtuous, honorable, and righteous life." [3] By changing the style of her life Gabrielle Darley Melvin also withdrew from the spotlight of publicity and enjoyed the solitude of private life—at least for a short time.

In 1925 the motion picture *The Red Kimono* began to appear in theaters in California and throughout the nation. The film was based on the true story of Gabrielle Darley Melvin's past life, and her maiden name was used in the film frequently. Advertising posters announced that the motion picture depicted the unsavory incidents in the life of Gabrielle Darley, the true name of the principal character. Mrs. Melvin brought suit for invasion of privacy, and this action prompted one of the strangest privacy opinions ever written.

Justice Marks began his opinion with a comprehensive discussion of the right of privacy—its history, its legal profile, and its status in the forty-eight states. He concluded that the use of the incidents in the plaintiff's life by the motion picture producers did not constitute an invasion of privacy. "When the incidents of a life are so public as to be spread upon a public record they come within the knowledge and into the possession of the public and cease to be private," he wrote (p. 290). Marks then considered whether the right of privacy existed in California and decided that "in the absence of any provision of law we would be loath to conclude that the right of privacy as the foundation for an action in tort, in the form known and recognized in other jurisdictions, exists in California" (p. 291).

But after declaring that no tort action for privacy was possible, Marks asserted that the California state constitution contained provisions which enabled the court to recognize the right to pursue and obtain safety and happiness without infringements by others. Section 1, Article I of the state charter, for example, guaranteed that all men "are by nature free . . . and have certain inalienable rights, among which are . . . pursuing and obtaining safety and happiness." And, according to Marks, these rights included the right to live free from the unwarranted attack of others upon one's reputation and social standing.

Applying this broad doctrine to the case at hand, Marks said, "The use of the appellant's true name in connection with the incidents of her former life in the advertisements was unnecessary and indelicate and a wilful and wanton disregard of that charity which should actuate us in our social intercourse and which should keep us from unnecessarily holding another up to the scorn and contempt of upright members of society" (p. 291). The justice said there were two basic elements in the case which created the producer's liability: the use of Mrs. Melvin's name in connection with the incidents in her life, and the use of her name "with no other excuse than the expectation of private gain by the publishers." Marks concluded that "whether we call this a right of privacy or give it any other name is immaterial because it is a right guaranteed by our Constitution that must not be ruthlessly and needlessly invaded by others" (p. 292). A petition for rehearing was denied by the court of appeals, and the supreme court of California refused to review the decision.

The Melvin decision, one of the most widely cited of all privacy cases, is strange for many reasons. For example, Marks emphasized that "the very fact that they [the incidents in Mrs. Melvin's life] were contained in a public record is sufficient to negative the idea that their publication was a violation of a right of privacy" (p. 290). It was the use of her name with these incidents which created the liability, he said. But, certainly, her name was part of the record as well: the transcript of the trial surely contained some reference to the defendant's identity.

Another point worth discussing is Marks's use of the state constitution as the source of his so-called right of privacy. In an article in the *California Law Review,* published eight months after the decision, Stanley G. Pearson pointed out that, in general, "provisions in declarations or bills of rights have been regarded as limitations upon the powers of government, rather than as sources of rights as between individuals." [4] To follow Marks's reasoning to its logical conclusion, there would really be no need for most of the tort law which has developed. Assault and battery, for example, could be dispensed with as a common-law doctrine because of the provision within the constitution guaranteeing "safety." Or trespass would not be needed in light of the guarantee of protected property.

To make any sense at all out of this decision, it is necessary to focus on the two elements in the case that tipped the scales in favor of the plaintiff. First, Marks said he was quite disturbed that the film was produced not as a documentary, but as entertainment for the purpose of making a profit. Also, Marks deplored the fact that after Mrs. Melvin rehabilitated herself (which he said was a goal of our society), this film was able to negate much of the hard work she had devoted to regaining her place in society. But even with these qualifications the *Melvin* case has provided us with a poor precedent. Unfortunately, it has gained great legal value, probably more because of its colorful nature than its legal logic.

Two more important cases followed the *Melvin* decision in California before the end of the decade. In 1939, in one of the first privacy cases involving a radio broadcast, a federal court refused to dismiss a privacy suit against Rio Grande Oil, Incorporated, the sponsor of a CBS program, "Calling All Cars." The plaintiff, Howard Mau, was a chauffeur who in 1937 had been shot while being robbed. The broadcast, a dramatization of the incident, had used Mau's name without his consent. The federal court refused the motion to dismiss, citing *Melvin* v. *Reid,* and stated that it was bound to follow the law where the tort was committed, in California. [5]

A year later, in Los Angeles, Jack Metter brought an action against the *Los Angeles Examiner,* which had published a photograph of his wife as she jumped to her death in a suicide leap from a downtown building. Metter asked the newspaper not to use either the story or the picture. Judge Thomas P. White of the district court of appeals sustained the trial court's directed verdict for the defendant newspaper. White used two arguments to support his decision: Mrs. Metter's right of privacy died with her, and her death was a public event. In explanation of the first argument, the justice said that the plaintiff could not assert a relational right of privacy. In addition, the complaint did not allege that anything was published which directly related to Mr. Metter.

As for the second basis, White said that by her conduct Mrs. Metter had waived her right of privacy. "She went to a public edifice in the heart of a large city and there ended her life by plunging from such high building. It would be difficult to imagine a more public method of self-destruction." The death resulted in an investigation by a public agency which became part of the public record, he said. "The incident described by respondent newspaper had to do with these circumstances, and therefore the publication . . . cannot be held to violate a right of privacy." [6]

The same year that the *Metter* case was decided in Los Angeles, the California legislature in Sacramento approved a second privacy statute for that state. (The first, it will be recalled, was repealed in 1915.) The measure was similar to the New York law, except that the legislature attempted to codify much of the judicial interpretation of the New York statute in addition to enacting the law itself. The California proposal, for example, expressly exempted the use of a name or picture "in any newsreel or in the news columns of any newspaper," or "as part of a group of persons in any photoplay or other motion picture, or in the exploitation thereof, provided such photoplay or motion picture is not in itself intended to advertise any other product." [7]

The California statute differed from the New York law in that it only provided a civil remedy. Also, intent to violate the law or invade an individual's privacy, which was not part of the New York law, was required by the California statute. The measure was approved by both houses of the state legislature, but was vetoed by Governor Culbert L. Olson, who said he wanted a "suitable privacy statute." [8] The fact that photoplays and motion pictures were exempted from the scope of the law suggests that the bill was a product of the motion picture lobby, attempting to protect itself from future decisions such as in *Melvin* v. *Reid*.

OTHER STATES RECOGNIZE THE RIGHT

Four other states—Ohio, North Carolina, Pennsylvania, and South Carolina—gave at least tacit recognition to a legal right of privacy before 1941. In 1938, actress Maxine Martin brought suit against the Roxy Theater in Cleveland for displaying her picture on an exhibit outside the theater. Miss Martin was a respected actress and objected to the display because it appeared that she was performing at the Roxy, a burlesque house. The court said that if she could prove special damages she possibly could collect for a libel, but that she could not collect damages for an invasion of privacy because she was a public character. Justice Merrick of the common pleas court of Cuyohaga County said: "Persons who expose themselves to public view for hire cannot expect to have the same privacy as the meek, plodding stay-at-home citizen. The glamour, genuine or artificial, of that business removes the participants from the realm of the average citizen." [9] Merrick never flatly stated that the right of privacy was recognized in Ohio, but in the final portion of his opinion he outlined the profile of the tort as it applied in Ohio—a tacit recognition, at least.

Two years later one of the most interesting and least publicized privacy decisions in American legal history was made by the same court. On 27 August 1940 the *Cleveland Press*, under the editorship of Louis B. Seltzer, began publishing the name of every citizen who signed a local Communist party nominating petition. With the list of names the *Press* published this notice.

Press Publishes Names Listed by Communists

If your name is published as a signer to the Communist election petition and you did not sign, you are asked to notify the *Press* at Cherry 0808 and your denial will be printed. In this way you will also assist the Board of Elections in its check for fraud in the petitions.[10]

Plaintiff Arnold Johnson argued that the publication of this information violated the signers' rights of privacy, and he asked for an injunction to stop further publication and for one hundred thousand dollars in damages. The defendant newspaper argued that freedom of the press prohibited prior censorship of the press, which was what an injunction would amount to, and that a court of equity did not have the power to restrain the press by injunction.

Justice Hurd, speaking for the court, agreed with the newspaper. "It is the general rule of law that a court of equity is without jurisdiction to impose censorship or control in advance of publication upon matter to appear in print" (pp. 377–78). Hurd said there were exceptions, such as obscenity, statements that tended to coerce, and lottery ads, but that the facts in this case did not constitute such an exception. The justice declared that nominating petitions were a part of the public record, open to public inspection at the secretary of state's office. "To suggest," he added "that the legislature intended to surround the procedure of nomination by petition with secrecy . . . is to do violence to elementary reasoning" (p. 380). Hurd argued that the nomination process is a function of great general or public interest. "To curtail the right of publication or to make the publisher liable to respond in damages would be a subversion of the constitutional guarantees of freedom of speech and of the press. . . . In other words, the rights of the public are paramount to the right of privacy of the individual, when the individual engages in conduct which vitally affects the public welfare and public concern" (p. 381). Hurd said Johnson's complaint failed to state a cause of action and he sustained the demurrer granted by the lower court.

INADVERTENT USE

North Carolina recognized the common law right of privacy in a case resulting from the inadvertent use of the wrong picture in a newspaper advertisement. It was common practice in the mid-1930s for traveling vaudeville shows to seek cooperation from local merchants to publicize their appearances in small towns. The Folies de Paree, in anticipation of its performance in Greensboro, North Carolina, bought an ad jointly with Melt's Bakery announcing the show. The ad included a picture of a woman clad in a bathing suit saying, "Keep that SYLPH-LIKE FIGURE by eating more of Melt's Rye and Whole Wheat Bread." The woman was identified as Mlle. Sally Payne, "exotic red-haired Venus" with the Folies de Paree; but through a mix-up at the *Greensboro Daily News* the woman pictured was really Nancy Flake, a popular singer.

The newspaper published a full explanation of the error and an apology. Nevertheless, Miss Flake brought suit for invasion of privacy. Justice M. V. Barnhill of the North Carolina Supreme Court said the publication of the plaintiff's picture in the ad without her consent gave rise to a cause of action. Noting his agreement with the *Pavesich* decision, Barnhill wrote: "If it be conceded that the name of a person is a valuable asset in connection with an advertising enterprise, then it must likewise be conceded that his face or features are likewise of value. Neither can be used for such a purpose without the consent of the owner without giving rise to a cause of action." [11] Justice Barnhill said the good faith shown by the newspaper in its apology could not be used to defeat the suit, but should be taken into consideration when damages were awarded.

The following year lower courts in Pennsylvania recognized the right of privacy in two decisions. In the first case, plaintiff Frances Carey Harlow objected to the use of her picture on advertising posters for a liquid hair preparation. The original owner of the pictures claimed that he had a written release from the plaintiff which authorized the publication of the photographs in advertisements. He had sold the pictures to a second party who had printed the placards and then sold the placards to a third party, who put the advertising message on them. Mrs. Harlow denied signing such a release and sued the third party, the Buno Company.

Philadelphia County Court Judge Eugene V. Alessandroni, before ruling on the merits of the case, announced, "In the absence of any decision on this subject by the appellate courts of this commonwealth, this court recognizes the existence of the right of privacy." Then Alessandroni ruled that he believed the plaintiff had given a release and there were no grounds for a suit. The judge said that it was impractical to require the purchaser of advertising from a publishing company to prove the authenticity of the release, for the purchaser would have to witness the execution of the release—which might have taken place months or years before he bought the material. "It is . . . apparent," Alessandroni said, "that the invasion of this right requires a direct trespass, the necessary element of which is intent." [12] The judge said he could find no evidence that the Buno Company intended to violate Mrs. Harlow's privacy.

The next year the same judge supported a plaintiff who sought to stop a physician from developing a picture he had taken of her disfigured face. The doctor, who was treating the plaintiff for coronary thrombosis, took the photograph without the patient's consent when she was semiconscious. Alessandroni said that the doctor had no right to take the photograph without the patient's consent, and that both husband and wife could maintain an action for invasion of privacy because "an act of this nature necessarily injures the other spouse." [13]

South Carolina was the last state to recognize a legal right of privacy during this ten-year period. The case, an unusual one, was decided in 1940. An agent for the defendant, the Life Insurance Company of Virginia, had attempted to persuade the plaintiff, Annie M. Holloman, to permit her son Roy to buy a life insurance policy. When she refused, the insurance agent lied to her son, told him that she had signed the insurance application, and wrote out a two-hundred-dollar policy. When the plaintiff discovered this bit of chicanery, she sued for invasion of privacy and claimed the insurance agent had used her name without permission. Acting Justice L. D. Lide wrote that while the court agreed that under certain circumstances the violation of the right of privacy did constitute a tort, in this case there had been no invasion of the plaintiff's rights.[14]

OTHER ATTEMPTS TO EXPAND RECOGNITION

Only one jurisdiction, Wisconsin, flatly refused to recognize a legal right of privacy in the 1930s. In an attempt to collect a debt from the plaintiff, the defendant had circulated flaming-orange handbills advertising the delinquent account. The plaintiff, Herbert W. Judevine, brought suit for invasion of privacy. Justice Chester A. Fowler of the Wisconsin Supreme Court, speaking for the judicial body, wrote: "We are of opinion, especially in view of the fact that truth is held no defense to the action where it has been recognized as it is to actions for injury to reputation through libel and slander, that if a right of action for violation of the right of privacy by such acts as are here involved is to be created, it is more fitting that it be created by the legislature by declaring such acts as it deems an unwarranted infringement of that right." [15] Other attempts were made in Wisconsin to establish a legal right of privacy, but all, including two legislative measures defeated in the early 1950s, have failed.

In Colorado two different attempts were made to establish a legal right of privacy before 1940. But on both occasions the courts found other grounds on which to base their rulings. In 1932 a widow brought suit against a mortuary association when they publicized, against her wishes, their delivery of her husband's casket by airplane from Walden to Denver, Colorado, during a bad snowstorm. The story and a photograph were published in an advertisement. The Colorado Supreme Court agreed that an injury had occurred, but ruled that the injury resulted from the violation of an implied contract, not from an invasion of privacy. Justice Haslett P. Burke said there was an implied agreement between the two parties that nothing would be done in the conduct of the services to outrage the plaintiff's feelings. Five years later another suit resulted when a Denver photographer used a picture of one of his customers in connection with a promotion for Millar's Universal Coffee. Again the Colorado Supreme Court chose to ground their decision on breach of contract instead of invasion of privacy.[16]

THE LADY AND THE CHAUFFEUR

The first attempt to gain recognition for a right of privacy in Massachusetts was mired in a divorce scandal in the city of Worcester. The *Worcester Evening Post* was sued when it published a picture of the plaintiff, June H. Thayer, and her chauffeur, Albert Desjardin. The picture was taken earlier at a Lowell, Massachusetts, airport at the request of the plaintiff's husband, Fred. The original photograph was a group shot of Fred Thayer, his wife, chauffeur Desjardin, an airplane pilot, and another man; but in publishing it the newspaper cropped out everyone but Mrs. Thayer and Desjardin and identified them with this cutline: "Albert Desjardin, chauffeur, who has been sued for $25,000 in alienation suit by Fred B. Thayer, wealthy and prominent resident of North Grafton . . . and Mrs. Jane Thayer, who is suing her husband for divorce, charging cruelty, abusive treatment and intoxication. The husband has entered a cross-suit and indications are that the action will be bitterly fought by both sides in Probate Court." [17]

The supreme judicial court of Massachusetts agreed that the plaintiff was libeled, but refused to accept her argument that her privacy was invaded. Chief Justice Arthur P. Rugg said that because Mrs. Thayer did not have a property right in the photograph, he could not support her contention that she had an absolute right to stop its publication without her consent. While dismissing this suit, Rugg made it clear that he did not deny the existence of a right of privacy in the commonwealth. The ruling dealt only with the facts at hand, he said; "it does not relate to violations of privacy which would involve acts in the nature of a nuisance, or which are appropriation of the photographic reproduction for the purposes of advertisement. Questions of that nature will be dealt with when they arise" (p. 164).

Seven years later, in 1940, Ullian Themo sued the *Boston American* when it published his picture on its front page. The facts in the case are sketchy, but it is known that Themo was pictured talking with a police captain in Cambridge, Massachusetts. Justice Henry T. Lummus ruled that the case did not force the court to consider if a right of privacy existed in Massachusetts since "if any exists, it does not protect one from having his name or his likeness appear in a newspaper when there is a legitimate public interest in his existence, his experiences, his words or his acts." Lummus said that if he accepted the defendant's argument, a newspaper would be prohibited from publishing a photograph of a parade or street scene without getting the permission of every individual in the picture. "We are not prepared to sustain the assertion of such a right," he added.[18]

In Montana in 1935 the supreme court of that state ruled that a photographer's unauthorized commercial use of a portrait he was hired to take was a violation of an implied contract, not an invasion of privacy. The plaintiff was a young girl from Butte who discovered that photographer Alfred Gusdorf had given a copy of her portrait to a third party for use in an advertising scheme. Justice Samuel Stewart said there was no need to rely on the proposition that a right of privacy existed in Montana since Gusdorf's action was a clear violation of an implied contract.[19]

An Illinois court in 1937 denied the request of a convicted murderer for an injunction to stop the broadcast of a radio program depicting his career in crime. While refusing to grant the injunction, the court did not deny the existence of a right of privacy.[20]

Finally, in Oklahoma a federal district judge inferred that the right of privacy was a part of the state's common law, despite the fact that the case at bar did not constitute a violation of that right. Paramount Pictures brought suit against the Leader Press, which sold advertising accessories to theaters for use with current motion pictures. Paramount and other film companies enjoyed almost a monopoly on this business, selling advertising posters and placards to theaters which leased their films. When Leader began selling a cheaper grade of advertisement, Paramount complained, arguing that use of the stars' names on the posters violated its right of privacy.

The court ruled against the film company on this count of the complaint, stating publicity—from any source—is a star's greatest asset. "Neither the stars nor the plaintiffs are in a position to claim the right of privacy for the stars, because their productions, faces and names are sold to the public," wrote Judge Edgar S. Vaught. Whether this case constituted recognition of the right in Oklahoma was not important, however, since in 1955 the state passed a privacy statute similar to the New York law.[21] To this date there have been no decisions in Oklahoma construing the law.

THE NEW YORK STATUTE

While other jurisdictions were approving or denying recognition of the law of privacy, most of the legal action remained in New York, where appellate courts worked to shape the boundaries of the privacy statute. Questions involving the incidental use of names, fictionalization, the protection of stage names, and the public interest were posed and answered before the end of the decade.

"TROPIC VENGEANCE"

True Detective Mysteries, published by the New Metropolitan Fiction Company, was representative of a large segment of the pulp magazine trade devoted to giving their readers "true" crime stories. In August 1928 the magazine published "Tropic Vengeance," a story of "the horrible fate of beautiful Blossom Martin," a young girl who had been ravished and killed by Eulogia Lozade. Several pictures accompanied the story, including one taken at Lozade's trial that showed Blossom's sister and mother seated in the courtroom next to an assistant prosecutor. The cutline described Mrs. Martin's reaction when Lozade walked into court: "The broken hearted mother cried out: 'I could kill that man with my own hands!' " [22]

Blossom's mother, Laura Martin, brought suit against the magazine for invasion of privacy, arguing that while the picture and cutline were accurate, they were used for purposes of trade without her consent. The lower court agreed, stating that the privilege of reporting newsworthy events did not include pictures of Mrs. Martin. Justice Ellis J. Staley wrote that in the reporting of a crime certain names and pictures cannot be excluded. The perpetrator of the crime places himself in the public domain, he said, as do the crime detectors and the victims. On occasion, when it is impossible to omit the part they played in a fair and intelligible chronicle of the events, the names and pictures of third parties are privileged. "In this case, however, I am unable to find any directly relevant justification for the inclusion of the plaintiff's picture in the article in question, even though the article is regarded as a legitimate historical chronicle of an actual happening" (p. 362). Staley added that he believed the addition of the picture and "lurid and passionate quote" was made to increase magazine sales.

A year later the appellate division of the supreme court reversed the decision, but did not write an opinion.[23] The memoranda decision merely cited *Binns* v. *Vitagraph Co.* (see Chap.

5), noting that the statute was not designed to prohibit incidental use of names and pictures in all commercial enterprises.

Three years later a New York attorney brought suit against the author of a book, *The Benson Murder Case*, for the use of his name without permission. Frank Swacker, a former United States special assistant attorney general, argued that Willard Wright had used his name in the story for its publicity value. The name Frank Swacker appeared in a list of characters in the front of the book, but in the text the surname Swacker was used alone.

Justice Meier Steinbrink said that there was no invasion of privacy since, aside from the name, there was no other parallel between the character in the book and the plaintiff. "The mere use of the plaintiff's surname and Christian name with his middle initial omitted without any other identifying feature cannot be held a sufficient basis for relief under the statute," Steinbrink wrote. He added that the statute was enacted to protect the privacy of persons, not to redress imagined wrongs or to subject authors to hazards against which "it is well-nigh impossible to guard." [24]

An outer limit on the use of names was put into effect in 1938 when the New York Supreme Court ruled that the use of a name 100 times in an article constituted a good cause of action. In that case prize fighter Solly Krieger brought suit against *Sports Novel Magazine* for publishing a story called "Deuces for the Duke" in which a prominent character, a prize fighter named Solly Krieger, was mentioned at least 100 times. Despite the defense argument that the story was fiction and use of the name coincidental, Justice Samuel Rosenman ruled that unless some proof could be offered that Krieger's claim was false, the article constituted an invasion of privacy.[25] There would be more cases dealing with incidental and coincidental use of names after 1940, but the rule established in the *Martin* and *Swacker* cases is still good law today.

WHAT IS IN A NAME?

Does the New York statute protect stage names from unauthorized commercial use? In answering this question, two federal courts came to opposite conclusions during the decade; but these opinions must be considered less than definitive because

New York state courts have not yet answered the question themselves.

In the first case, Claire H. Davis, who used the pseudonyms "Cassandra" and "Casandra," brought suit against RKO Radio Pictures for the use of her stage name in the movie *Bunker Bean.* The plaintiff was an actress, psychic, palmist, author, and lecturer. In the film, Cassandra was also a psychic, but was portrayed as a slovenly cheat and fake. District Judge Vincent L. Leibell refused to entertain the plaintiff's argument, ruling that the name Cassandra came from mythology and the producers of the movie had as much right to use it as did the plaintiff. Leibell said the New York law did not apply to stage or assumed names. The plaintiff's legal name, Claire H. Davis, was the only name protected.[26]

The following year a federal court of appeals stated in dicta a pseudonym was protected by the statute. Tess Gardella, an actress who used the name Aunt Jemima in advertisements for Log Cabin syrup and Aunt Jemima flour, brought suit against the Log Cabin Products Company when they hired another actress to do the commercials using the Aunt Jemima name. The defendant argued that the statute did not apply to stage names. Circuit Judge Martin T. Manton, noting that New York courts had not passed on the question, disagreed. "If the stage name has come to be closely and widely identified with the person who bears it, the need for protection against unauthorized advertising will be as urgent as in the case of a private name," he wrote. But the case was decided on different grounds. The trademark "Aunt Jemima" had belonged to the Quaker Oats Company, owner of Log Cabin Products, since 1890. Since Quaker Oats owned the name, no authorization to use it was needed.[27]

While no other cases have raised this question, it is generally accepted today that stage names are protected by the statute in most instances.

THE BREAK IN THE WALL: FICTIONALIZATION

In the early years of the decade, Picture Classics, Incorporated, prepared a pseudodocumentary travelogue film of New York City entitled *Sight-Seeing in New York with Nick and Tony.*

Four actors were used: two played the part of visiting school-teachers, two took the roles of guides. The film depicted the four persons as they toured the various tourist sights in the city, including Fifth Avenue, Washington Square, the Bowery, China-town, and the financial district. The four actors were used to add a continuity to the film, which was essentially a travelogue. Only the actors received stage direction; everything else in the film was "real life."

In one scene taken on Orchard Street on the city's lower East Side, a woman was shown selling bread from a sidewalk stand. Miriam Blumenthal, the peddler, was on the screen for six seconds as part of a group scene. No reference by sound or title was made to her; she stood as a silent reproduction of life and events in that part of the city. When she brought suit against the motion picture producers, she argued that her picture had been used without her consent for trade purposes. In a split decision the appellate division of the supreme court agreed and found the defendant guilty of an invasion of privacy. The court's very short opinion offered no clue as to how this case was distinguished from the similar suits, *Humiston* v. *Universal Film Manufacturing Co.* and *Merle* v. *Sociological Research* (see Chap. 5), in which the defendants were not found liable. The only plausible explanation was that the majority of the court considered the film a work of fiction, rather than a pure documentary, because of the use of actors.

In a sharp dissent Justices Edward R. Finch and James O'Malley criticized the majority opinion, arguing that the film was not a work of fiction, but an actual photograph of current events of public interest. "Such a production is not such trade as was contemplated by the legislature in the enactment of the statute," they wrote.[28] On appeal to the New York Court of Appeals, the majority opinion was sustained in a memoranda decision. In his monumental book, *Government and Mass Communications*, Zechariah Chafee, Jr., commented on the *Blumenthal* case and the New York privacy statute, which he said had not worked well. "Nothing could show better the dangers [to press freedom] which lurk in a broad statute." [29]

While the *Blumenthal* decision seems to be a strong blow against the documentary film makers, much of the punch of the majority opinion was removed four years later in *Sarat Lahiri* v. *Daily Mirror* when another New York court asserted: "It is hardly conceivable that the Blumenthal case was intended to stand for the proposition that the inclusion of passers-by in a current newsreel of a fire would give them a cause of action." [30] *Blumenthal* has rested, virtually unused, ever since. However, this was not the last time the New York courts would come face-to-face with the element of fictionalization.

PRIVACY AND THE ROPE TRICK

The Western world has long been fascinated by the mystics of India. The American Sunday newspapers, in their attempts to fill the gaudy supplements with eye-catching material, often looked to the East for feature stories on fakirs and their nail beds, snake charmers with their swaying cobras, and other exotic mysteries.

On 16 September 1934 the *New York Sunday Mirror* published a long photo feature, "I Saw the Famous Rope Trick (But It Really Didn't Happen)." Inspiration for the article came from a British society of mystics which offered to pay a large sum of money to anyone who could perform the famous Hindu rope trick. The author of the article revealed that Hindu mystics, using hypnotic powers, created an illusion which convinced observers that the rope actually rose into the air although it remained coiled on the ground.

Several photographs were used to illustrate the article, including one of a well-known Hindu musician playing a musical instrument as an accompaniment to a female dancer. The musician, Sarat Lahiri, brought suit for invasion of privacy, claiming that his picture was used for trade purposes without his consent. The action resulted in what has become one of the most widely cited privacy opinions in the history of the law.

New York Supreme Court Justice Bernard L. Shientag first ruled that the picture was not part of any advertisement, so that portion of the statute was not violated. But with respect to trade purposes, the situation was not as clear. Shientag wrote that, in general, recovery had been denied for the use of a photograph or name in a single issue when it was connected with the dissemination of current news and matters of information and general interest. "The public policy involved in leaving unhampered the channels for the circulation of news and information is considered of primary importance. . . . A free press is so intimately bound up with fundamental democratic institutions that, if the right of privacy is to be extended to cover news items and articles of general public interest, educational and informative in character, it should be the result of a clear expression of legislative policy" (p. 388).

Shientag suggested four rules or categories of material which might appear in a single publication of a newspaper. First, there could be recovery if the photograph was in an advertisement or was being used for advertising purposes. Next, if the picture accompanied an article of fiction in any part of the newspaper, recovery could be granted. Third, recovery was not possible if the photograph was related to current news or immediate public interest. The fourth category included the publication in the case at hand. Some articles were not fiction, but were not news either, Shientag said. (He defined news as "a response to an event of peculiarly immediate interest.") Articles of this type, he noted, included factual accounts of distant lands, tales of historic personages and events, reproductions of past news, and travel stories. "As a general rule," Shientag concluded, "such cases are not within the purview of the statute" (p. 389).

An important element in determining liability in cases falling in this last category was the relationship between the picture and the story. A tenuous connection, one in which the photograph was used primarily for promoting the sale of the publication, could destroy the privilege. With respect to the picture in the *Sunday Mirror*, Shientag wrote, "I think it has a relationship to the article. It is used to illustrate one of the points made by the author—the mystical quality of the East" (p. 389).

The greatest impact of Justice Shientag's decision was on future New York law. Time after time when New York judges were asked the same kind of question, they responded by citing the *Sarat Lahiri* decision. Shientag gave journalists and other laymen a kind of map to guide them through the legal maze of privacy when he codified the results of forty-seven years of litigation into four basic rules. His defense of the free press in a privacy action was one of the few made during the decade, as courts and judges turned away from the broad policy questions to the smaller problems involved in construction of the statute. These factors, plus the high quality of prose in the opinion, made the *Sarat Lahiri* case one of New York's leading privacy decisions.

The connection between a picture and a story was further explored the following year when a divorcée sued the *New York Evening Journal* for invasion of privacy. In a story in its magazine section on New York's "alimony racket," the newspaper had published a picture of Mrs. Henry Schley, the plaintiff, who "had her Blueblood Husband Jailed in A Dispute Over An Alimony Check." The court granted a judgment for Mrs. Schley on the grounds that the connection between the photograph and the article was too tenuous to come within the immunity granted.[31]

THE PUBLIC INTEREST—A KEY DEFENSE

The idea of public interest was the key to the *Sarat Lahiri* decision, and as the decade progressed, other courts found comfort in basing their opinions on the same grounds. Gertrude Sweenek sued Pathé News, Incorporated, for filming her as she exercised with other women in a gymnasium. Federal District Judge Grover M. Moscowitz found a public interest in the motion picture, and thereby protected Pathé News. The judge wrote that "while it may be difficult in some instances to find the point at which public interest ends, it seems reasonably clear that pictures of a group of corpulent women attempting to reduce with the aid of some rather novel and unique apparatus do not cross the border line, at least so long as a large portion of the female sex continues its present concern about any increase in poundage." [32]

The idea of public interest also played an important part in two cases resulting from the publication of a single book, *I Break Strikes* by Edward Levinson. Published by Robert R. McBride and Company, the volume was a history of the growth and development of that peculiarly American phenomenon, strikebreaking. Included were biographies and portraits of some of the

nationally infamous strikebreakers The book was not a particularly sympathetic account, as the strikebreakers were described
as hoodlums, gangsters, and other criminal types.

The first case began in 1936 as a criminal action against the
publisher. This was the first time in the thirty-three-year history
of the New York statute that the aggrieved party resorted solely
to the penal provision of the law. The complainant was William
Stern, also known as William Kid Steinie, whose exploits as a
strikebreaker were documented in the book in at least four different places. In addition, his picture was used on the frontis-
piece of the book. Stern charged that his privacy had been
invaded by the use of his name and picture and sought state
action against Robert R. McBride and Company.

Judge Louis B. Brodsky of the New York City Magistrates
Court was unsympathetic to the charge. He wrote that the use of
the statute was limited to stopping the unauthorized use of a
name or picture for advertising or trade purposes. "These provisions have no application to the use of such name or picture,
as part of, or in connection with, the text itself, or (in the case
of a picture) to illustrate the text (as contradistinguished from
mere advertising matter or trade use by word or picture) in a
newspaper or magazine article or in a book." Brodsky stated that
the subject of the book was one of great public interest. In addition,

under the heading "Freedom of Speech and Press," the constitution of the
state (article 1, section 8) provides that "every citizen may freely speak,
write and publish his sentiments on all subjects. . . ." The liberty of the
press consists in the right to publish, with impunity, truth, with good
motives, and for justifiable ends, whether it respects governments, magistrates or individuals. . . . To give to section 50 [the privacy statute] the
construction contended for by the complainant would necessarily impute
to the Legislature an intent in its enactment to restrain or abridge the
liberty of the press, in disregard of the express prohibition of . . . the
Constitution.[33]

In 1939 another "character" in the book brought suit, this time
a civil action, for the use of his name without consent. Justice
Salvatore Cotillo of the supreme court agreed with Judge Brodsky and ruled that no cause of action existed. The book concerned a topic of current interest, and the use of the plaintiff's
name was incidental to the main thrust of the account. Justice

Cotillo was not without an opinion on the evils of strikebreaking. "Despite its extensive dramatic color or sensationalism, the fact remains that here exists a social evil which this book sought to have the public recognize under its true colors" he wrote. "In the face of these social facts, the plaintiff's stand in this suit is ill taken." [34] Cotillo also based his decision on grounds of freedom of expression similar to those used by Judge Brodsky in the first case.

The concept that public interest in some way negates the individual right of privacy was just beginning to grow in the thirties. As more newspapers and magazines were brought to trial for alleged privacy violations, the defense of "published in the public interest" grew. Today, what an editor says is newsworthy, or what the public is interested in, is generally considered privileged publication, immune from a privacy suit. The battle begun in this decade, however, was not won for many years.

OTHER ASPECTS OF PRIVACY LAW

There was a series of other less important cases decided in New York before the decade ended. In 1937 "The Inquiring Photographer" column of the *New York Daily News* was placed within the bounds of protected material. An unemployed model sued the newspaper for using her name and picture without written consent. Justice Thomas C. Kaiden ruled that the column was not published for advertising or trade purposes.[35]

A year later the New York Supreme Court ruled that a minor could not give written consent for the publication of her picture. Marian Semler, a professional model, sued the publisher of *Silk Stocking Stories* for the use of her picture in its magazine. The defendant argued that the photographer had obtained the girl's consent when the picture was taken. Justice James P. Conroy ruled that the plaintiff was a minor and could not give consent.[36] Parent's consent must be obtained before the picture of a minor can be used.

The New York Supreme Court ruled in 1939 that nonresidents as well as residents could use the New York statute to institute an action in the state.[37] In the same year, a New York federal court ruled that if no cause of action is created in the jurisdiction in which the invasion takes place, then no recovery can be granted in other states. This confusing decision was the result of a suit by a patient against her doctors in Tulsa, Oklahoma. Three years earlier a six-inch steel surgical clamp had been discovered, by X-ray, in the plaintiff's abdomen. The two osteopaths gave a copy of the X-ray to a Tulsa newspaper reporter who sent the picture to King Features Syndicate. The *New York Journal* published the story and the picture in 1937, and the plaintiff, Ina Banks, sued for invasion of privacy in all states except Washington, Michigan, and Rhode Island—where existence of the right had been denied (she should have included Wisconsin in this category as well). The question the court had to face was, whose law is applied: the New York statute, the common law, or the law where the wrong was committed?

District Judge Edward A. Conger answered the question in this way: "In my opinion, the last event necessary to make an actor liable for invading this so-called right of privacy would be in that state where the seal of privacy was first broken. Where, in other words, did the plaintiff's name and X-ray picture first become public property?" [38] If this seal was broken in Oklahoma, then the law of that state would apply; if the name and picture became public property in New York, then the New York state statute would control. The court refused to answer the question of where the invasion took place until after the case was tried on the merits, but the principle established was important as more multistate problems occurred. [*]

FIFTY YEARS OF PRIVACY

"One snowy January evening in 1910 about a hundred professors and advanced students of mathematics from Harvard University gathered in a lecture hall in Cambridge, Massachusetts, to listen to a speaker by the name of William James Sidis." This is the way the famous "Where Are They Now" feature of the

---

[*] An important change in American legal procedure that should be noted at this point occurred in 1938. Since 1842, and the Supreme Court decision in Swift v. Tyson, 16 Pet 1 (1842), federal courts exercising jurisdiction on the ground of diversity of citizenship were not bound to apply the unwritten or common law of the state as declared by its highest court. They were free to exercise an independent judgment as to what the common law of the state was or should be. But in 1938 the United States Supreme Court struck down this procedure in Erie R. R. Co. v. Harry J. Tompkins, 304 U.S. 64. Justice Louis Brandeis wrote:

New Yorker began in the 14 August 1937 issue. Author Jared Manley was performing the weekly ritual of informing readers of the destiny of one of America's past heroes or heroines. His efforts would result in one of the nation's most famous privacy suits. The article continued: "He had never addressed an audience before, and he was abashed and a little awkward at the start. His listeners had to attend closely, for he spoke in a small voice that did not carry well, and he punctuated his talk with nervous, shrill laughter. A thatch of fair hair fell far over his forehead and keen blue eyes peered out from what one of those present later described as a 'pixie-like' face. The speaker wore black velvet knickers. He was eleven years old." [39]

This was one of the shining hours in the life of William James Sidis. His father, Boris, a scientist, named the lad after psychologist William James, whom he knew and admired. While William was still a baby, Boris began developing the child's mind with hypnosis. When the child was three, he could read and write English and French; when he was five, he prepared a scholarly treatise on anatomy. He completed his first seven years of schooling in six months, and at age ten was enrolled in Tufts College.

After Sidis' lecture at Harvard on four-dimensional bodies, Professor Daniel E. Comstock of the Massachusetts Institute of Technology predicted to reporters that the youth would grow up to be a world-famous mathematician. What happened to young Sidis? Did he fulfill his promise? This is the story Manley told in his *New Yorker* piece.

Sidis graduated from Harvard in 1914 with a bachelor of arts degree. At his graduation he told reporters who asked him his plans that he wanted to live the perfect life. "The only way to live the perfect life is to live it in seclusion," Sidis said.[40] But the perfect life was denied to the young scholar, at least for a little while. Upon graduation from Harvard Law School he took a post at a Texas university, only to be annoyed when placed at the center of interest.

"Except in matters governed by the Federal Constitution or by acts of Congress, the law to be applied in any case is the law of the state. And whether the law of the state shall be declared by its legislature in a statute or by its highest court in a decision is not a matter of federal concern. There is no federal common law." Ibid., p. 822. Consequently, after 1938 federal courts hearing privacy suits were obliged to apply state law regarding the right of privacy, and were not allowed to make decisions independently.

Then press reports on Sidis stopped until 1 May 1919, when he was arrested in Roxbury, Massachusetts, for leading a Communist demonstration. While free pending the appeal of his eighteen-month sentence for inciting a riot, Sidis jumped bail and went to New York, disappearing for five years. In 1924 an enterprising reporter found him working as a clerk in a Wall Street office for twenty-three dollars a week. Again he dropped out of sight for two years. In 1926 Dorrance Company of Philadelphia, a vanity press, published a scholarly work entitled *Notes on the Collection of Transfers*. The author was listed as Frank Folupa, but the press quickly discovered Folupa was really William Sidis.

Between 1926 and 1937 he popped in and out of sight throughout the eastern United States. It was in Boston's shabby south end that the *New Yorker* reporter found him, a heavy-set, middle-aged man with a prominent jaw, a thick neck, and a bushy reddish moustache. He was living in a dingy room, working as a clerk in a business house and collecting streetcar transfers. Twice each week he taught a small class in his room on the history of the American Indians. He told reporter Manley that the world just wouldn't let him alone. "The very sight of a mathematical formula makes me physically ill. All I want to do is run an adding machine, but they won't let me." The reporter asked about Professor Comstock's prediction of great fame for the young scholar. "It's strange," said Sidis with a grin, "but you know, I was born on April Fool's Day." [41]

THE CLASSIC CASE

Sidis brought suit against the *New Yorker* for invasion of privacy, claiming a cause of action under both the common law right of privacy and the New York statutory prohibitions. Judge Charles E. Clark of the prestigious Second United States Circuit wrote the final opinion in the case. Here was the classic encounter, classic in the sense that it was just this kind of snooping, prying, and harassment by the press that Samuel Warren and Louis Brandeis set out to halt in 1890. There was no question of advertising or implied contract. There was no important news event involved which dictated broad public dissemination of the matter for the public good. It was simply a case of a magazine's digging into the life of a private citizen who, for the past thirty years, had attempted to remain outside the glare of the public spotlight.

While sympathetic, Judge Clark took little stock in Sidis' arguments. Beginning with the cause of action brought under the common law, Clark reminded the plaintiff that none of the court rulings in states which recognize the right went so far as to prevent a newspaper or magazine from publishing the truth about a person, "however intimate, revealing or harmful the truth may be. . . . It must be conceded that under the strict standards suggested by those authors [Warren and Brandeis] plaintiff's right of privacy has been invaded. . . . But despite eminent opposition to the contrary we are not yet disposed to afford to all of the intimate details of private life an absolute immunity from the prying press." [42]

Clark said that at some point the public interest in obtaining information becomes dominant over the individual's desire for privacy. Warren and Brandeis, he said, were willing to lift the veil somewhat in the case of public officers. "We would go further, though we are not yet prepared to say how far. At least we would permit limited scrutiny of the 'private' life of any person who has achieved, or has had thrust upon him, the questionable and indefinable status of a public figure" (p. 809). William J. Sidis was once a public figure; while he attempted to cloak himself in obscurity, whether or not he fulfilled his early promise was still a matter of public concern. "We express no comment on whether or not the news worthiness of the matter printed will always constitute a complete defense. Revelations may be so intimate and so unwarranted in view of the victim's position as to outrage the community's notions of decency." But, the jurist wrote, "when focused upon public characters, truthful comments upon dress, speech, habits, and the ordinary aspects of personality will usually not transgress this line. Regrettably or not, the misfortunes and frailties of neighbors and 'public figures' are subjects of considerable interest and discussion to the rest of the population. And when such are the mores of the community, it would be unwise for a court to bar their expression in the newspapers, books, and magazines of the day" (p. 809).

Sidis charged that the article was malicious, so that the privilege normally given to accounts of this sort should not be granted. Clark denied this contention, saying that if the right of privacy was not invaded by the article, the existence of actual malice would not change that result. "Personal ill-will is not an ingredient of the offense," he wrote, quoting the Warren-Brandeis article (p. 810).

Clark then turned to the complaint brought under the New York statute, noting that only use for advertising and trade purposes was forbidden. "In this context, it is clear that 'for purposes of trade' does not contemplate the publication of a newspaper, magazine, or book which imparts truthful news or other factual information to the public" (p. 810). A publisher is immune from the interdict so long as he confines himself to the unembroidered dissemination of facts, Clark wrote. The *New Yorker* articles limited themselves to the unvarnished, unfictionalized truth, he added. In regard to Sidis' complaint that his name had been used in advertisements for the magazine article, Clark reiterated the long-standing rule: if the article itself is unobjectionable, the advertisement shares the privilege.

The decision in the *Sidis* case, leaving the former child prodigy with no recovery at all, is a good summation of the status of the law of privacy as of 1940. The case was discussed at length not only because it represents a leading precedent in the law of privacy, but because the clear, concise language of Judge Clark's opinion provides an excellent chart of the boundaries of the law as the first half-century ended.

The idea of a legal right of privacy grew from a law review proposal in 1890 to a recognized tort and statutory remedy by 1940. Perhaps it did not grow as fast or as much as its proponents hoped and expected. Undoubtedly it expanded more rapidly than its detractors desired. But while it grew, the freedom of the press to provide a truthful and accurate chronicle of the day's news remained unfettered. In the first fifty years plaintiffs enjoyed little success in stopping the news media from carrying out their basic function of informing the public. In this sense the proposal by Warren and Brandeis failed. But the other aspect of the right of privacy, the right of an individual to be free from the commercial exploitation of his name or picture, took a firm foothold in American jurisprudence. Advertisers and other businessmen were stopped time after time from milking profits from the property of others. In the gray area between these two extremes —the so-called entertainment function of the media—there was less certainty in 1940. Problems regarding dramatization and fictionalization had surfaced in the preceding fifty years, but rules or guidelines were yet to be constructed.

As the privacy law's second half century began, American courts would note an increase in the number of privacy actions as more and more citizens became aware of their legal rights. New media, such as television, would create additional knotty problems for the judicial branch to unravel. And while the law would grow, and more rules would be enunciated, the basic principles developed in the first fifty years of the law of privacy would change little in the next twenty-five years.

VII

The Second Half Century Begins: 1941-50

In any single privacy case two opposing forces press in upon the judge. . . . On the one hand, he is urged to uphold the right of free speech, the right of a society to know the truth, the right to make full use of the wonders of modern civilization which spread intelligence instantaneously to the farthest ends of the earth. On the other hand, he is urged to protect the sensibilities of the individual from the brash and vulgar attentions of the mob, to fence off a small corner of human existence against the predatory advances of selfish commercial interests.

LOUIS NIZER [1]

If the growth of the law of privacy was unspectacular in the first fifty years of its existence, as the second half century opened things began to pick up. The law of privacy received recognition in six additional jurisdictions during the forties, despite the fact that the nation was at war for more than three years. Twenty states, plus Alaska and the District of Columbia, were protecting the right of privacy by 1950.

While the number of reported decisions decreased somewhat during the forties in comparison with the previous decade, courts throughout the nation explored new as well as old problems. In New York, courts began to clarify the gray area of the law between hard news and pure advertising. For example, the question of what constituted fictionalization received attention in several lawsuits. In other jurisdictions, courts attempted to add meaning to the concepts of "public interest" and "public figure."

With each court decision more boundaries appeared on the map which charted the law for newsmen and lawyers alike.

CIVIL SERVANTS AND POLITICS

The first new jurisdiction to recognize the law of privacy during the decade was Oregon. The case involved not the mass media but the unauthorized use of an individual's name on a telegram sent to the state's chief executive. The plaintiff, George Hinish, was a federal civil service employee, prohibited by law from engaging in political activity. The defendant, Meier and Frank Company, operated an optical department in their general merchandise store. The manager of the department was Kenneth Braymen, also a defendant in the suit. In 1939 the Oregon state legislature approved Bill 70, a measure to tighten the restrictions on the sale and fitting of eyeglasses, and the proposal was on the governor's desk for signature. Since the measure would have forced the closing of their optical department, the Meier and Frank Company worked strenuously to prevent its approval. As a part of this campaign Braymen signed the plaintiff's name to the following telegram sent to Governor Charles A. Sprague: "There is no demand for optical bill seventy except by those who are financially interested in its passing. It is not a bill set out by the people. I urge you to veto it."

Hinish brought suit for invasion of privacy, and for the first time the state supreme court was faced with the question of whether the right was protected in Oregon. Justice Hall S. Lusk wrote:

We are called upon, as Mr. Justice Holmes says somewhere, "to exercise the sovereign prerogative of choice" between the view that the courts for want of a precedent are impotent to grant redress for injury resulting from conduct which universal opinion in a state of civilized society would unhesitatingly condemn as indecent and outrageous, and the view that the common law, with its capacity for growth and expansion and its adaptability to the needs and requirements of changing conditions, contains within itself the resources of principle upon which relief in such a case can be founded.[2]

Justice Lusk concluded that the common law contained the resources needed to grant relief and announced that the right of privacy was protected under Oregon law. In addition, he said Hinish's complaint clearly stated a cause of action for a breach of the right.

Three years later Florida announced protection for the right of privacy in a suit involving the novel *Cross Creek* by Marjorie Kinnan Rawlings, who in 1938 won a Pulitzer Prize for her novel, *The Yearling*. The plaintiff, Zelma Cason, argued that the book contained an unfavorable biographical sketch which referred to her as an "ageless spinster resembling an angry and efficient canary." Like California, Florida based its recognition of the right of privacy on a constitutional provision—in this case, Section 4 of the Florida Declaration of Rights. The provision stated: "All courts in this State shall be open so that every person for any injury done him in his lands, goods, person or reputation shall give remedy, by due course of law, and right and justice shall be administered without sale, denial or delay." [3] An invasion of the right of privacy was an injury to the person, Justice Armstead Brown wrote, and therefore the right was protected by the Florida courts.

The objectionable character sketch was a small part of the entire novel, which had received wide circulation and praise as a Book of the Month Club selection. The character in the novel was called Zelma—no surname—and lived in the same county as the plaintiff. Both Zelmas managed orange groves and both were active in village and county government. On the whole, the sketch presented Zelma in a favorable light, as "one who was worthy of . . . friendship—a fine, strong, rugged character—a highly intelligent and efficient person, with a kind and sympathetic heart, and a keen sense of humor." [4]

After the appellate court recognition of the right of privacy, the case was sent back to the lower courts for trial. A jury brought in a verdict for the defendant, and the plaintiff appealed again. This time the court ruled that because the book was fictional it did not have the requisite qualities of newsworthiness to protect it from a suit, and the plaintiff was entitled to some kind of recovery. However, since the plaintiff did not show that she had sustained any actual or compensatory damage, Justice C. E. Chillingsworth ordered a new trial with directions that Miss Cason recover only nominal damages.[5]

The next jurisdiction to recognize the right of privacy was Arizona in 1945. Because the Arizona Supreme Court's opinion was terse, it is difficult to establish all the facts in the case. The plaintiff, Charles Reed, complained that his photograph was published in a magazine in connection with a crime and that because the account was not newsworthy, his right of privacy had been violated. After reviewing many of the leading decisions, Justice Joseph H. Morgan ruled that the doctrine of a right of privacy was recognized as a part of Arizona common law and that the plaintiff's complaint stated a good cause of action.[6]

"TUSCALOOSA TOWN TALKS"

One day in 1905 John Lindgren, town blacksmith in Tuscaloosa, Alabama, told his wife and two children that he was going to nearby Birmingham to buy stock for his shop. He hitched up two mules to his surrey, withdrew his seven-hundred-dollar bank account, and began his journey. The next day Lindgren's surrey was found near a bridge over a river between Tuscaloosa and Northport. Residents testified that they had heard a shot the night before. Both the buggy and Lindgren's coat, found in the surrey, had bullet holes in them. Later that day the blacksmith's empty wallet was found. On the theory that Lindgren was murdered for the seven hundred dollars he was carrying, police arrested John Sobrey, the man who had found the mules and returned them to town.

After many months Sobrey was released for lack of evidence, but the public still held doubts about his claimed innocence. One obstacle that blocked prosecution was the lack of a corpse: Lindgren's body was not recovered. Then in 1930 Lindgren's body was returned to Tuscaloosa from California, where he had died of cancer. He had not been murdered, or mugged and robbed: he had skipped town with the family bank account and had established himself in California. His body was returned to Alabama because of a provision in his will.

This strange tale was related to radio listeners in Tuscaloosa in 1946 during a popular radio program, "Tuscaloosa Town Talks," on station WJRD, owned by James Doss. Lindgren's two married daughters, Roberta and Katrina, brought suit against the station for invasion of privacy. After announcing that Alabama protected the right, Justice Davis F. Stakely went on to consider the merits of the complaint before the court.

Stakely admitted that he sympathized with the feelings of the two girls, but reminded them that the freedoms of speech and press were guaranteed to preserve "a vital source of public information." [7] "In other words, the right of privacy does not prohibit the broadcast of matter which is of legitimate public or general interest" (p. 253). The question was, did the story of John Lindgren fall into the category of privileged material? Justice Stakely wrote: "By his own acts John Lindgren made himself a public character. The passage of time could not give privacy to his acts because the story of John Lindgren is a part of the community. It is embedded in the public record through the imprisonment of John Sobrey on a charge of murder and his fight in the courthouse to prove his innocence. . . . The will of John Lindgren is a public record. The broadcast was based on fact" (p. 253). Stakely said that under some circumstances unwarranted and offensive publicity about Lindgren might violate his daughters' right of privacy, but in this case there was no cause of action.

A few months later Michigan, which in 1899 had denied the existence of a common law right of privacy in *Atkinson* v. *Doherty* (see Chap. 4), announced that the right to be let alone was protected there. The plaintiff was Bernice Pallas, an actress employed by theatrical producer Earl Carroll. The defendant, Crowley-Milner Company, a Detroit department store, used a publicity picture of Miss Pallas to illustrate a one-quarter-page cosmetic ad in a Detroit newspaper. In light of the *Atkinson* decision, the plaintiff did not plead invasion of privacy, but argued that there was a right to be free from unauthorized and offensive publicity.

Justice Emerson Boyles, without deciding whether the use of the picture constituted an invasion of privacy, said that there could be circumstances in which the unauthorized use of a photograph would give rise to an action for damages. To this extent, he said, the state protected the right of privacy. "We recognize a fundamental difference between the use of a person's photographic likeness in connection with or as part of a legitimate news item in a newspaper, and its commercial use in an advertisement for the pecuniary gain of the user." Whether or not this particular use was a violation of the right of privacy was to be answered at a trial, Boyles said. At the trial the jury said the action by the department store did not constitute an invasion of privacy. Four years later the Michigan Supreme Court affirmed the jury verdict that Miss Pallas waived her right of privacy by embracing the role of a show girl or model.[8]

UNFAVORABLE LIGHT

Curtis Publishing Company was sued in 1948 by an irate taxi driver after the *Saturday Evening Post* published a satirical article by cabby James J. Brennan entitled, "Never Give a Passenger a Break." The case marked the official recognition of the right of privacy by the District of Columbia. In 1927, it will be recalled, the right received a semiofficial recognition in *Peed* v. *Washington Times Co.* (see Chap. 5). The suit against the *Post* was filed in federal district court by Muriel Peay, a cab driver who was photographed talking to the author, Brennan. Miss Peay's name was never mentioned in the story or in the cutline under the photograph.

The satire was described by Judge Alexander Holtzoff as "a caustic, merciless, diatribe depicting taxicab drivers in the Nation's Capital as ill-mannered, brazen, and contemptuous of their patrons."[9] This excerpt from the article includes the *Post* description of the zone fare system. "Only the natives who make a life study of the zone system know exactly how much is legal. It's easy to tell whether you've got one of those or some poor trusting visitor. For instance, when they point to the Capitol and ask if it's the White House, that automatically doubles the fare. Any guy unpatriotic enough not to know his Capitol should be penalized."[10]

The cause of action for privacy was based on the use of the plaintiff's picture as merely an illustration of "one" Capital cabby. Judge Holtzoff said that while the *Peed* decision was was not binding, it was persuasive. "Modern life with its accompanying increase in public media of communication, such as newspapers, monthly and weekly magazines, moving pictures, radio and television, has created novel situations, that in turn gave rise to the problem of protecting the individual who desires seclusion and freedom from intrusion into his private life as well as from undue and undesirable publicity . . ." (p. 309). Because of this development Holtzoff said that the District of Columbia recognized the right of privacy and that the use of an individual's picture without consent constituted an invasion of this right. Since Muriel Peay was not a public figure, her privacy was invaded.

The decision in this case is hard to reconcile with many of the cases previously discussed. *Sarat Lahiri* v. *Daily Mirror*, for example, appears to offer a similar fact situation—an unrelated photograph used to illustrate an article on a general topic (see Chap. 6). Of course *Sarat Lahiri* was a case brought under the narrow New York statute, while Muriel Peay's suit was brought under common law. Nevertheless, it seems strange at this point in the development of the law to find that what was apparently a news picture used with a feature or news story provided the basis for a privacy suit. The *Peay* case represents, subtly no doubt, a new direction of judicial reasoning for a narrow class of mass media privacy cases.

While it would become clearer in future cases,[11] it was here that a favorable light–unfavorable light test was first used. Stated simply, the test provides that when an individual's picture is used with an unrelated news or feature article, the court is more likely to sustain the action if the article places the individual in an unfavorable light than if it presents him in a complimentary role. In *Peay*, the article made poor Muriel appear to be one of the capital's unethical cab drivers, even though she wasn't specifically named.

From a purely moral or ethical position, this test makes sense. If nasty things are implied in print about an individual, someone should probably pay the penalty. But looking at this test from the standpoint of history and the development of privacy law, it makes no sense whatsoever. A privacy suit compensates an individual for the suffering he experiences when his name or picture or life is exposed to the public needlessly. Why should the nature of the publicity—be it good or bad—have anything to do with it?

William Prosser categorized this kind of case as "putting an individual into a false light." He suggested that this conduct was one of four broad categories of action which constituted an illegal invasion of privacy.[12] But Prosser overstated his case somewhat. If a general rule can be outlined, it must be narrower than merely false light. When all the cases that fall into this category are considered, it becomes clear that usually the plaintiff was successful in his lawsuit only if he was placed in an unfavorable false light. There were several instances during the forties and the fifties when a false light privacy suit failed because the plaintiff was pictured in a complimentary manner, not in a derogatory fashion.[13]

What is important, however, is not false light, but the fact that there have been several instances when the unauthorized use of an individual's photograph with an unrelated news article constituted an invasion of privacy, even though the use of the same picture without the article probably would not have been actionable. Editors must be wary when selecting legitimate news photographs to illustrate unrelated articles. This is a lesson it took the *Saturday Evening Post* staff many years to learn.

THE LENS GRINDER

Indiana recognized the right of privacy in 1908,[14] but the first important mass media case was not litigated until 1949. Clifford Reed, an optical lens grinder, brought a suit against the Continental Optical Company for the unauthorized use of his photograph in an advertisement. The picture was taken by the United States Army when Reed was on duty with a mobile optical unit near the front lines during the Second World War. The photograph was sent out as a news item and used in several newspapers throughout the nation. Continental used the picture in an advertisement, hinting that Reed endorsed its brand of lens-grinding equipment.

The interesting aspect of the case was the argument used by Continental in its attempt to defeat the suit. The optical firm argued that while Reed was in the service he was a public figure who waived his right of privacy and that the use of the photograph by the nation's press was proof of this waiver. Justice

Harry L. Crumpacker agreed that the plaintiff, while in the service, lost his right of privacy in connection with the army's legitimate use of his photograph. But "that situation cannot be stretched into a license to private business to use the same for advertising its wares for individual profit," Crumpacker said.[15] The court ruled that Continental's action constituted an invasion of privacy.

Right of privacy suits were brought for the first time in two additional states, Nevada and Minnesota, during the forties, but neither resulted in a recognition of the tort. In Las Vegas a waitress challenged a city ordinance requiring employees of the city's casinos and clubs to register with city police and to be photographed and fingerprinted. The photographs were disseminated to various area police departments for identification purposes. The plaintiff, Barbara Jeane Norman, argued that the ordinance violated the privileges and immunities clause of Article 4, Section 2, of the United States Constitution; the Nevada constitutional guarantees of life, liberty, and pursuit of happiness; and her fundamental right of privacy.[16]

District Judge Milton B. Badt skirted the privacy issue by ruling that the ordinance did not violate anyone's right of privacy and that its provisions constituted a legitimate governmental function undertaken in the public interest. This case is frequently cited as constituting recognition of the right of privacy in Nevada.[17] But intricate legal gymnastics would be needed to make the *Norman* case stand for that proposition. Privacy must be regarded as an open question in Nevada.

In Minnesota the existence of a legally protected right of privacy also remained an open question after the first lawsuit in 1948. But Federal District Judge Gunnar H. Nordbye's opinion in the case was well reasoned and well written and is worth quoting. The case began when *The Times* (Minneapolis), "The Picture Newspaper," published a photograph of Carl A. Berg in the late 1940s in connection with its story on his protracted divorce proceedings. The picture, a close-up, had been taken in court, but when it was published, it was impossible to discern where Berg had been photographed. The news story accurately related the proceedings of the divorce and child custody hearings, and

Berg's only complaint was that his picture was used without authorization.

After relating the long history of the growth of the law of privacy, and the fact that Minnesota had no state decision regarding the doctrine, Nordbye said that it was unnecessary to decide whether or not the right was protected. "For even assuming that the courts of this State would embrace as a part of its common law the doctrine of the right of privacy, the showing herein under the admitted facts will not sustain a right of recovery." [18] The Berg story was of public interest, Nordbye added. He admitted that there existed a wide and marked diversity of opinion about what constituted legitimate news, but he said he was certain that news of these proceedings could be included in that category.

That the American public is interested in news concerning court proceedings and court trials is evident. Traditionally, since pioneer days people have flocked to trials when courts were in session out of curiosity or perhaps in order to see drama which their daily lives did not provide and that this same curiosity and interest is evident today is to be observed in any courtroom when there is a proceeding involving a criminal case of interest or the sensational details of some divorce suit or matrimonial triangle, and to those who cannot attend, the newspapers assume to furnish a daily account of the proceedings. [P. 960]

Nordbye wrote that a court should be cautious before attempting to interfere with the traditional rights of the press. People were concerned with what was happening in the world because in many ways it affected their lives. Matters such as divorce proceedings and controversies between parents over the custody of children touched the lives of many persons and for that reason were of great interest. Then, in referring to the Warren-Brandeis law review article, he noted that the authors complained that the press was overstepping in every direction the obvious bounds of propriety and decency.

The authors made that observation in the staid days of the Nineties, when the standards of our theatres, newspapers, magazines and current literature were considered to be higher than they are today; but over half a century has passed since that writing and no legislation has been called to the court's attention which has in any way assumed to limit such improprieties. That we have gone much further in that time in attaching importance in the news to trivial things and sheer gossip regarding the intimate details of the lives of important and near-important people is undoubtedly true, but in proceedings of this kind the courts should not attempt to determine whether the Press is to blame or whether it is merely catering to the present mores of the people. [P. 962]

BARBER v. TIME

It is difficult to undertake a discussion of the development of the law of privacy in the forties without mentioning Dorothy Barber, *Time* magazine's famous "starving glutton." The *Barber* case and *Melvin* v. *Reid* (see Chap. 6) represent two of the most famous, and yet poorest, precedents in the short history of the right of privacy. Like *Melvin*, the *Barber* case makes little sense when considered as part of the great quantity of privacy law accumulated by 1942. Yet it happened, and is frequently cited ahead of some of the more representative cases as a leading precedent in the law. It was a bad decision and can only be explained by the outrageous circumstances upon which the case was based.

In March 1939 Mrs. Dorothy Barber checked into Kansas City (Missouri) General Hospital and complained to doctors that she was constantly hungry. "I can finish a normal meal and be back in the kitchen in ten minutes eating again," *Time* quoted her as saying.[19] The doctors quickly put her to bed, after ordering her a big meal from the kitchen, and prepared to make some routine laboratory tests on their new patient. While Mrs. Barber ate her hospital dinner she told the physicians that despite her unusual eating habits, she had lost twenty-five pounds during the past year.

The press soon heard of the Barber case, and before long representatives of local newspapers and wire services were at the hospital attempting to get a story and pictures. One International News Service photographer took a picture of the patient despite her protests, and local media featured the story for a few days. The *Time* magazine article appeared in the 13 March 1939 edition in the "Medicine" section under the headline, "Starving Glutton." In a tightly written, 150-word narrative the magazine told readers the unembellished story of the medical curiosity, gleaned from a United Press dispatch from Kansas City. *Time* also used the INS photograph, which was a close-up of the patient showing only her face, head, and arms, with the bedclothes drawn up over her chest. Under the picture was the cutline, "Insatiable-Eater Barber, She Eats for Ten."

Mrs. Barber filed suit against the magazine for invasion of privacy. *Time* countered with the argument that the article was a newsworthy account of an occurrence of great public interest. *Time* lost. Commissioner Laurence M. Hyde of the Missouri Supreme Court ruled that "if there is any right of privacy at all, it should include the right to obtain medical treatment at home or in a hospital for an individual personal condition (at least if it is not contagious or dangerous to others) without personal publicity (p. 1207). Hyde argued that while the ailment was possibly a matter of some public interest because of its unusual nature, the magazine did not have the right to use the plaintiff's name and picture as well. "It was not necessary to state plaintiff's name in order to give medical information to the public as to the symptoms, nature, causes or results of her ailment" (p. 1207). Also, he thought the title of the piece was objectionable. Hyde affirmed the jury verdict and the three-thousand-dollar judgment against the magazine.

Hyde's argument would contain a good deal of logic if the discussion only concerned what was normally or ethically right or wrong. But the right of privacy did not develop along that line. The law, generally speaking, prescribed that when an individual became part of an event or situation of great public interest, whether that individual was a former child prodigy, the wife of a murder victim, or a participant in a divorce scandal, the right of privacy was lost. By almost all standards set both before and after her case, Dorothy Barber temporarily lost her legal right of privacy.

Another curious factor was Commissioner Hyde's suggestion that use of the facts without the name would have precluded a successful suit. Obviously, without identification, no suit could be maintained. But if there was any part of the story that definitely was public, it was Dorothy Barber's name, which was a part of the admission records of Kansas City General Hospital, a public institution.

Barber v. *Time* is one of a small number of privacy decisions in which courts have limited the coverage of news by the press because of extreme circumstances. The facts in the case seem to have overtaken the law. Decisions in such cases are not consistent: the personal judgment of the court or the jury is the most important element, and people are unpredictable.

Even so, the *Barber* case is not a good precedent. Courts rarely make such rulings. The press is usually given a free hand to publish stories about people and events in which the public is interested. Because of its colorful nature, *Barber* has become a widely cited privacy decision. While this would not be the last time a court would make such a decision, the case of *Barber* v. *Time* remains unrepresentative.

NEW YORK CASES

While other states recognized and developed the common law of privacy, New York was still the jurisdiction with the greatest amount of privacy litigation. Most problems stemmed from publications in the gray area between news and advertising, and it remained to be determined exactly what was and was not privileged material. The 1946 case of *Molony* v. *Boy Comics Publishers* shed light on some of these problems.

A COMIC BOOK PORTRAYAL

On 28 July 1945, while on a training flight over New York, a United States Army B-25 bomber crashed into the seventy-ninth floor of the Empire State Building. The force of the impact, followed by several explosions, killed fourteen persons and severely burned and maimed many others. The elevator in the 102-story structure stopped, and panic seized many persons inside the building. One of the day's many heroes was Donald P. Molony, age seventeen, a pharmacist's mate in the United States Coast Guard. Molony remained calm and displayed great presence of mind in quickly procuring medical equipment, evacuating a large number of building occupants, and administering first aid to many victims. For his heroism he received many awards and wide publicity.

Six months after the incident, *Boy Comics* carried a five-page cartoon story of Molony's feat entitled, "Real Hero: The True Story of the Empire State Building." The text was taken from the news account in the New York *Journal-American;* the illustrations were cartoon sketches. Molony brought suit against the magazine for invasion of privacy and won. The New York Supreme Court ruled that a comic book, distributed for profit, must be differentiated from a newspaper or magazine, even though the cartoons related to current events. The appellate division of the supreme court, however, reversed the lower court ruling in a three-to-two decision and held that the magazine was not liable for damages.[20]

Molony's chief argument was that the account was fictional: it made him appear to be a kind of superhero who rushed from the damaged building with a woman under each arm. Justice John Van Voorhis of the appellate division was not moved by this plea, writing that nothing which was described in the magazine reflected badly on the plaintiff (the favorable false light mentioned earlier) and that the errors were really only minor inaccuracies. He said that the article could not be classed as fiction merely because it was presented pictorially or because it was carried in a magazine that carried other fictional pieces. "It is the article itself rather than its location that is the determining factor."[21]

FICTIONALIZATION IN NEW YORK

During the same year in which the appellate division denied Donald Molony protection, another plaintiff had more success with essentially the same argument of fictionalization. This story began before the Second World War, in Norfolk, Virginia, where the plaintiff, Mildred F. Sutton, and a man named Valentine Lawless were co-workers and friends. When fighting broke out, Valentine joined the Army Air Corps and was assigned as a gunner in a B-17. Mildred married an engineer and began a family in Norfolk, forgetting Val as one would forget any co-worker after leaving a job.

Val died when his bomber was shot down during a raid over Linz, Austria, but before he perished he sent his brother Edward a letter requesting the establishment of a small trust fund. The fund of thirty-six hundred dollars was to be used to provide a "perfect rose" each week for Mildred Sutton. But Mildred refused to accept the flowers. The story of the trust fund was made public during a court contest over Val's will and received wide publicity. Nevertheless, it was not until the New York *Daily Mirror* published a dramatic version of the events in its Sunday supplement that Mrs. Sutton lost her patience and brought suit for invasion of privacy. "Here, told for the first time in all its poignant and dramatic detail, is one of the great true love stories of our time. . . . A Flower A Week Forever for A Girl He Could Not Have, . . ." the *Daily Mirror* proclaimed. The story began with a description of the Norfolk courthouse where "there were on file the legal papers in a litigation which would make the name of Mildred Sutton one with those of Eurydice and Beatrice and Heloise and Roxanne and all the other heroines of fact and fable who have been loved, sometimes unknowingly, and lost." [22]

The article, presented in a narrative style with illustrations, was basically true. The author did imply there was a romantic link between Mildred and Val before he left to join the army, which was not true, and there were a few other embellishments, but nothing seriously inaccurate or misleading. However, the story was obviously a romanticization and Mrs. Sutton objected to this. She also objected to one of the illustrations, which depicted a woman holding a rose, arguing that it was designed to lead people to believe she had accepted the roses and regarded Val with romantic sentiment. But the article stated clearly that she had refused the flowers.

The supreme court ruled that the *Daily Mirror* account was a sensationalized version of facts embellished with matters drawn from the author's imagination, and awarded a judgment to the plaintiff. On appeal the defendant argued that there was no basis for a suit because the account was a newsworthy presentation of an event of great public interest. The appellate division ruled that it could not dismiss the complaint, that a good cause of action had been stated, and affirmed the lower court's ruling. [23]

Two supreme court justices, David Peck and Bernard L. Shientag, dissented, arguing that the article was more truth than fiction and should be protected. Peck's dissent was long and, in spots, eloquent. He attacked the majority argument that because the article was at least partly fictional, it therefore was designed to entertain rather than to inform and consequently did not enjoy the privilege normally reserved for news reports. Peck's dissent represented a minority point of view expressed frequently in cases involving fictionalization. As such it deserves to be quoted as a sample of this philosophy.

> That the article is dramatic, romantic or sensational is not of consequence if the content is truthful. Fictional or fanciful is quite different in connoting untruth, exploitation of plaintiff rather than exposition of news. Embroidered or embellished may be an innocent dressing up. They raise the question of whether sane literary license is allowable in newswriting where news reporting is permissible. . . . [P. 239]

> Nor can we see that any issue is created by the allegation of the complaint that the article was designed for entertainment value and is hence "trade." The privilege and latitude of the press in disseminating news cannot be made to depend upon or legally be tested by classifying news as informative, educational, amusing or entertaining, with educational and informative given immunity and amusing or entertaining classed as "trade." . . . A newspaper is a composite of the educational, informative, amusing and entertaining, some of which would defy classification and much of which is combinative. [P. 242]

PRIVACY AND ANIMALS

Two other New York court decisions made during the forties deserve noting. In 1945, H. Ruth Lawrence brought suit against a photographer who sold a picture of her dog to an advertising agency for use in a campaign for the National Biscuit Company. The defendant, Jane Ylla, a renowned animal photographer, was hired by the plaintiff to take the dog's picture, but was not authorized to sell it. The court said that the plaintiff's suit could not be based on the right of privacy because "that statutory right of privacy concededly does not cover the case of a dog or a photograph of a dog." [24] In other words, people have a legally protected right of privacy, animals do not. The plaintiff did have recourse, however, based upon her contractual relationship with the photographer.

Two years later, world-famous Boston Symphony Orchestra conductor Serge Koussevitzky brought suit against Allen, Towne and Heath, Incorporated, to stop the publication of his biography.[25] Koussevitzky argued that the publisher used a copy of his picture without permission and that the book contained false and objectionable matter. Justice Bernard L. Shientag, who was one of the dissenters in the *Sutton* case, ruled that there was no invasion of privacy because Koussevitzky was "well within the orbit of public interest and scrutiny." [26] That the account may contain untrue statements did not make it fiction, Shientag wrote, and the right of privacy law did not apply to an unauthorized biography unless it was fiction. Shientag added that a literal interpretation of the phrases "trade and advertising purposes" would have resulted in hampering freedom of speech and press. "It is clear, therefore, that the right of privacy statute applies to the unauthorized use of name or picture to sell a collateral commodity. That was the precise situation presented in the Roberson case, and was what the statute was primarily intended to cover" (p. 783).

Shientag's comment was the narrowest interpretation of the law yet presented in a ruling opinion. It was obviously too narrow—the New York statute had previously and would continue to include instances in which there was no collateral commodity involved. This argument represented the extreme freedom of expression position, a point of view which was adopted during the fifties in construction of the Utah privacy statute. But in New York it was not good law.

But while this point of view was not good law, it accurately represented the ideas of Bernard Shientag, a true friend of the press and one of the New York Supreme Court's privacy specialists. Shientag, a respected author and member of the New York Supreme Court since 1930, wrote some of the best and most famous privacy opinions handed down in the state. His long, authoritative opinion in the *Sarat Lahiri* case (see Chap. 6) remains today as a model for construction of many sections of the New York privacy law. It is, with the *Roberson* decision (see Chap. 4), and perhaps the *Binns* opinion (see Chap. 5), one of the most widely cited New York rulings. In most cases Justice Shientag, who held a firm belief in the importance of an unfettered, uninhibited press, found himself voting against the plaintiff's claim of invasion of privacy. His death in 1952 at age sixty-five deprived the New York bench of a great scholar and true libertarian.

WHAT IS IDENTIFICATION?

It must be obvious by now that for a plaintiff to prosecute successfully an invasion of privacy complaint he must show, among other things, that he was publicly identified, that his complaint concerns publicity about him. Usually this requirement presents no problem. Use of a name and picture with events surrounding an individual's life provides sufficient identification. But a name is not the exclusive property of an individual. There are many men in the United States, for example, who call themselves John Smith. Without the use of some other identification, such as an address (John Smith of 123 Elm) or occupation (John Smith, the bartender) or event (John Smith, the man who shot the robber), the use of a common name alone usually does not create a liability. Frank Swacker did not collect because the name Frank Swacker was used in a novel (see Chap. 6). In 1941 Mr. and Mrs. Rudy Nebb of Georgia brought suit in a New York federal court against the Bell Syndicate because a comic strip called "The Nebbs" was being nationally syndicated. Even the first names of the members of the two Nebb families matched. But Judge Henry W. Goddard ruled that "the words 'his name' in the statute apply to the use of a name coupled with circumstances tending to refer to the plaintiff and not merely a similarity of names." There must be an intent to capitalize on another's name and identity.[27]

It is a general rule, then, that similarity of names is not enough to show that an identity has been appropriated. But as with most of the rules in the law of privacy, there is a glaring exception, a case which cannot be explained. This time a California court handed down the decision. In the late 1930s actress-singer Marion Kerby resided in Los Angeles, attempting to make a living as a performer while pursuing her hobby of studying American folklore. About the same time Hal Roach Studios distributed a film in the "Topper" series, a comedy about a man, his wife, and St. Bernard dog who were killed in an auto accident, but who returned to earth in the form of spirits or ghosts. The female character in the film was named Marion Kerby.

To advertise the movie the studio sent out one thousand letters on pink stationery to men in the area. The handwritten message was:

Dearest:
Don't breathe it to a soul, but I'm back in Los Angeles and more curious than ever to see you. Remember how I cut up a year ago? Well, I'm raring to go again, and believe me I'm in the mood for fun.

Let's renew our aquaintanceship [*sic*] and I promise you an evening you won't forget. Meet me in front of Warner's Downtown Theatre at 7th and Hill on Thursday. Just look for a girl with a gleam in her eye, a smile on her lips and mischief on her mind.

> Fondly,
> Your Ectoplasmic Playmate,
> Marion Kerby

When the letters were delivered, Marion Kerby, the actress-singer, was the only Marion Kerby in the Los Angeles phone book. Needless to say, she received many unwanted phone calls and personal visits following the studio mailing. She brought suit for invasion of privacy—and won. Judge Shaw, speaking for the California District Court of Appeals, ruled the defendant's conduct constituted a serious invasion of privacy. "Here the plaintiff was, without her consent, plucked from her regular routine of life and thrust before the world, or at least 1,000 of its persons, as the author of a letter not written by her and of a nature to at least cast doubt on her moral character and this was done in a manner to call down on her a train of highly undesirable consequences." [28] To the studio's plea that they didn't even know the plaintiff existed, that there was no attempt to represent her as the Marion Kerby who signed the letter, the judge ruled that some steps should have been taken to find out if there was a real Marion Kerby.

This was a harsh ruling, one which would probably not have been made in New York, where, of course, there is a statute, a specific mandate. The common law, under which the California decision was made, is more nebulous, more flexible, and much more unpredictable. The *Kerby* case stands as the only reported common law decision based upon this kind of a fact situation. Other cases arose in New York in the fifties, but they followed the established precedent that a person's identity, not just his name, must be appropriated to establish a cause of action. How other common law jurisdictions will decide similar cases in the future remains unanswered.

USE OF AN IDENTITY

The rulings above explain what happens when a name and not an identity is used. But what about the reverse situation—appropriation of an identity but not the name? Three cases decided in the mid-forties shed light on this problem.

The first suit was instituted against RKO Radio Pictures in a Massachusetts federal district court. The plaintiffs were Minna Wright, her son Joel, and daughter Vera Burdette. The family complained that characters in a movie, *Primrose Path,* actually represented their lives, and that this was an invasion of privacy. The movie was based on a novel, *February Hill,* by Victoria Lincoln, who grew up as one of Vera's playmates. But the setting had been moved from Massachusetts to California, the names were not similar, and other differences were apparent as well.[29]

In the second case the plaintiff was Ethel Levey, the first wife of George M. Cohan, famed theatrical performer of the early 1900s. The plaintiff and Cohan were divorced in 1907 after eight years of marriage. The suit was filed in New York federal court against Warner Brothers Pictures, producers of a semi-fictional film biography of Cohan called *Yankee Doodle Dandy,* starring James Cagney. While her name was not mentioned in the film— in fact, no mention was made that Cohan was ever divorced—the plaintiff nevertheless insisted that the film constituted an invasion of privacy. Mrs. Levey argued that a character in the movie called Mary re-enacted events that were a part of her life with Cohan.[30]

A third suit was brought against author John Hersey by Frank E. Toscani in a New York state court. The publication in question was Hersey's best-selling novel, *A Bell for Adano,* the story of a United States Army civil affairs detachment; its commander, Major Victor Joppolo; and the occupation of a fictitious Sicilian town, Adano, during the Second World War. Toscani asserted that the story of Joppolo was really a portrayal of his own war experiences when he was the senior civil affairs officer in Licata, Sicily, and that his life and personality were therefore being exploited.[31]

In all three cases the plaintiffs' arguments failed to convince the courts. The *Wright* case was decided in Massachusetts, a state which had always avoided recognition of the legal right of privacy. Federal District Judge George Sweeney said that in his opinion Massachusetts' state courts prohibited recovery in privacy actions unless the publication "discredits the plaintiffs in the minds of any considerable and respectable class in the community"; however, the facts in this case did not fit this definition.[32]

Mrs. Levey's complaint was dismissed because, according to District Judge William Bondy, "similarities, if any, between the events of the plaintiff's life and the episodes shown in the picture [*Yankee Doodle Dandy*] are too insignificant to characterize the plaintiff, and are merely incidental to the theme of the film."[33] Bondy said the New York statute required a representation of a person at least approaching likeness, and such a representation was not found in the film.

Finally, in the *Toscani* case the court refused to accept the plaintiff's argument that a word portrait, such as the one used by Hersey in *A Bell for Adano*, was included within the definition of "portrait" in the Civil Rights statute. "Giving the language [of the statute] . . . its ordinary meaning," wrote Justice Joseph M. Callahan, "we find that it was not intended to give a living person a cause of action for damages based on the mere portrayal of acts and events concerning a person designated fictitiously in a novel or play merely because the actual experiences of the living person had been similar to the acts so narrated."[34]

What these decisions mean, then, is that an author or playwright has a fair amount of leeway in using events from real life in a novel or drama, provided he avoids identification. The burden appears to be on the plaintiff to demonstrate that he is the person characterized in the book or play; and in the forties, courts demanded a fairly high level of evidence, more than just a series of parallel events in the lives of both the fictional character and the plaintiff. The outer limit of this rule is not clear. In *Cason* v. *Baskin,* the Florida case discussed earlier in this chapter, the author patterned a fictional character after a local citizen and was found liable. But not only were the personalities and appearances of the real and fictional characters nearly alike, but the locale was the same and the author used the plaintiff's Christian name for her fictional counterpart. The outer limit probably rests somewhere between the *Toscani* and *Cason* decisions.

Also, plaintiffs in the cases just discussed were private citizens, as opposed to public figures. In the next chapter it will become apparent that courts grant authors and dramatists a good deal more freedom in using the lives of public figures, such as criminals, as the basis for plays and books, again as long as there is no identification.

WHAT CONSTITUTES AN ENDORSEMENT?

Endorsements, or the use of an individual's name to promote the sale of a product, is a common practice in American advertising. As a rule, endorsements cannot be used without authorization from the individual whose name or picture is being publicized. But is the use of an individual's name or picture in an advertisement always considered an endorsement? Two courts were asked this question during the forties, and their answers added another page to the growing volume of privacy law.

During the late 1930s and early 1940s Davey O'Brien was one of America's most famous football stars. The tough little quarterback from Texas Christian University played with the Philadelphia Eagles of the National Football League after being named an All-American in 1938. In 1939 O'Brien's picture was used on the annual Pabst Blue Ribbon football calendar with other members of the 1938 All-American team. On the calendar, in addition to the pictures and all the major college and professional football schedules, were a picture of a bottle of Pabst and a glass and some advertising copy. O'Brien brought suit in a Texas federal court for invasion of privacy, despite the fact that the state had never recognized the tort. Not only were his name and picture being used to promote the sale of beer, the plaintiff argued, but he was a member of a group which frowned on the use of alcohol and the calendar thus damaged his reputation.

Pabst had obtained the picture from the Texas Christian University sports publicity office for the price of one dollar, and the photograph was used on the calendar with the consent of the university athletic department. Because the use of the picture was "legal," the real question was, did the use of the picture constitute an endorsement? Circuit Judge Joseph C. Hutcheson said it did not. He ruled that O'Brien was a public figure who had sought publicity, and this calendar was just more publicity. There were no statements or representations made on the calendar which constituted an endorsement; and in any case, O'Brien wasn't suing for endorsement value, but for invasion of privacy. And no invasion had occurred. The court avoided deciding whether a right of privacy action could be instituted in a Texas court.[35]

Six years later Milton H. Wallach filed suit in New York for invasion of privacy when his name was used in a newspaper advertisement. The facts in the case were not reported completely, but it is known that the advertiser used a news story in his paid advertising space to attract attention to his ad. The two items were not related in any way except that both occupied paid advertising space. Wallach argued that his name, which appeared in the news report, was used to promote the advertiser's product—hence a trade purpose. Justice Benjamin F. Schreiber disagreed. He noted that every incidental mention of a name does not constitute an invasion of privacy. "It cannot be said that it was the intention of the legislature to prohibit the mention, otherwise lawful, of a person's name in a commentary or news report, unrelated to the advertising of any product or business, merely because such news or commentary appears in paid advertising space and in physical juxtaposition to advertising matter." [36]

The matter of endorsements was not settled by these two cases, and more problems arose in the fifties and the sixties. But the proposition was established that mere placement of a name or picture in an advertisement or on advertising matter, such as a calendar, did not automatically constitute an unauthorized endorsement.

SUMMARY

The law of privacy expanded greatly during the forties, the sixth decade of the life of the tort. While courts still placed high value on freedom of the press, it was clear that in cases of outrageous circumstances even the right of the press would be forced to give way to an individual's right to seclusion. The First Amendment defenses were not used as frequently by jurists during this decade to protect the mass media. The major boundaries of the law were established, and judges devoted more of their time to the technical tasks of trimming and pruning the tort law and privacy statutes. In this process there seemed to be a marked divergence in some respects between the interpretation of the law in New York and in the common law states.

Newer media, such as motion pictures and radio, were brought under the existing rules of privacy. In the next decade television would also encounter restrictions based on privacy law. But whatever happened in the forties was only a preview of the fifties, the decade in which privacy law came of age.

VIII

Privacy Comes of Age: 1951-60

---

*Those who would forbid publication entirely without consent
overlook the proper function of the newspaper and other media
of communication and expression in modern democratic society.
Whether we like it or not we have no more privacy than the
proverbial goldfish. If we participate in any manner in the life
of a community, we live in public. What is news is a matter of
place and circumstance. . . .*

LEON R. YANKWICH [1]

In the few, short years since the end of the 1950s, television producers, magazine writers, and other popular historians who attempt to package and sell the recent past for mass consump-
tion have described the decade with many adjectives. The
"Fantastic Fifties," the "Phenomenal Fifties," the "Fabulous
Fifties"—phrases such as these have been used in one place or
another to characterize this ten-year period. Whether the decade
deserves such a description remains an open question. There is
little doubt, however, that these adjectives accurately reflect the
growth of privacy law during the era. By 1960 the right of privacy had come of age.

During the fifties, seven new jurisdictions recognized a legally
protected right of privacy, six through the common law and one
by statute. For the first time, the law was recognized by a majority of jurisdictions in the nation.* The number of cases reported

* The seven new state jurisdictions were Connecticut, Illinois, Iowa, Mississippi,

146

between 1951 and 1960 easily doubled the number in any previous decade. In addition, law journals and other legal periodicals came alive with views and reviews on the decade's most exciting legal "discovery," the law of privacy. The fact that Texas and Nebraska firmly refused to recognize the right had little effect in dampening the zeal of the privacy proponents.

The two most discernible trends during the decade were the smaller number of suits against newspapers and other news media, and the increasing number of actions against television and the popular detective magazines. At least six important decisions were reported involving each of the last two media. But growth was the key word during the decade, and things began to happen first in Mississippi.

THE SHERIFF AND THE PHOTOGRAPHER

Does a public officer have a right to assault a newspaper photographer who took his picture without consent? The need for an answer to this question resulted in Mississippi's recognition of the right of privacy in 1951. A citizens' protest was under way at the Prentiss County courthouse against the construction of a building which, according to the protesters, was going to be used for the illegal sale of beer. The citizens wanted the county sheriff, Sale Martin, to stop construction of the structure, but he told them that he did not have the authority to take such an action. A local newspaper photographer, Harold Dorton, after shooting a picture of the protesters, took a picture of the sheriff as he was leaving his office to go to lunch. Martin attacked the photographer, hitting and kicking him. The photographer sued for assault and battery and won, despite the sheriff's argument that the picture-taking was a violation of his right of privacy. Martin appealed, but the Mississippi Supreme Court, while announcing recognition of the right of privacy, affirmed the lower-court decision. Justice Harvey McGehee, speaking for the

Montana, West Virginia, and Oklahoma. With twenty states already recognizing some form of legally protected right of privacy, these states brought the total to twenty-seven. Alaska, which recognized the right as a federal territory in 1926, and Hawaii, in which there have been no recorded privacy cases, attained statehood in 1959. At the end of the decade, then, twenty-eight of the fifty states, and the District of Columbia, protected the right of privacy.

court, ruled that "one who engages in public affairs and public life to an extent which draws the public interest upon him may be deemed to have consented to the publication of his name and photograph in connection with a legitimate news story. . . ." [2]

Illinois and Montana each announced legal protection for the right of privacy in the following year. In Illinois, Virginia Eick complained that the Perk Dog Food Company had used her picture in an ad promoting dog food without securing her consent. The plaintiff was blind, and her photograph was used as part of a contest both to promote the sale of dog food and to provide seeing-eye dogs for the visually handicapped. The advertising copy announced: "Dog owners, your purchases of Perk Dog Food can give this blind girl a Master Eye Dog."

The plaintiff complained that in addition to using her picture without permission, the advertisement falsely depicted her in need of a seeing-eye dog, when in fact she already owned one. After noting that this was the first Illinois case on the question, Justice Ulysses S. Schwartz of the appellate court ruled that the state would protect the right of privacy. As for Miss Eick's suit, "the complaint states a good cause of action for violation of plaintiff's right of privacy by defendant's unauthorized use of her picture for advertising purposes." [3]

In Montana things were not quite so simple as what was probably the most unusual privacy suit on record unfolded in the late forties and early fifties. The antagonists were John P. Welsh, tenant, and Griff Pritchard, landlord. Welsh and his wife Katherine rented a house from Pritchard from July 1948 to April 1949 for sixty-five dollars a month. On 15 April Pritchard announced he wanted possession of the house by the first of May, but Welsh refused to comply, putting the rent for May and June in his landlord's bank account.

On 25 June the seventy-two-year-old Pritchard and his paralytic wife Dora moved into the front room of the Welsh house, bringing with them, piece by piece, a straight-backed chair, a rocker, a radio, newspapers, magazines, and finally a bed. The couple stayed there for two days without any trouble; but when Welsh attempted to move Mrs. Pritchard outside, the landlord came at his tenant with his cane yelling, "Don't you touch that woman, old man." Welsh hit Pritchard, who went down and landed on a small throw rug. As he lay outstretched upon the floor, Welsh skidded the rug out the front door and onto the porch, where the rug halted. Pritchard, however, did not stop, and rolled down the steps onto the lawn. Suffering pain in his right shoulder and the right side of his chest, Pritchard staggered back into the living room, again to face his foe. In that living room he and his wife stayed for the next seventeen days and nights, unwanted guests of unwanted tenants.

After Welsh finally got Pritchard out of the house he filed numerous damage suits against his landlord, including an action for invasion of privacy. No similar suit was ever tried in Montana, but Justice Harry J. Freebourn readily agreed that the right was legally protected in the state. "That Pritchard invaded the privacy and the right of privacy of the Welshs is beyond question," he added.[4]

SENSATIONALISM OR NEWS?

One day in late August 1954, eight-year-old Jimmie Bremmer disappeared from his Sioux City, Iowa, home. He was missing for one month until his mutilated and decomposed body was found in a nearby field on 29 September. That evening the Sioux City *Journal-Tribune* published a front-page picture of the site where the body was discovered. At the bottom-center of the photograph the small boy's exposed body was visible. The parents sued for invasion of privacy.

The Iowa Supreme Court first had to decide whether the right of privacy was protected in the state. The answer was affirmative: Justice Ralph A. Oliver noted that the state must bow to the great weight of authority favoring recognition. But the next question, whether the *Journal-Tribune* picture constituted an invasion of that right, was tougher. The newspaper argued that discovery of the body was a top-ranking news story of great public interest. The plaintiff agreed that the public was concerned that the missing boy was found dead, but insisted that there could be no legitimate public interest in the condition of the youth's body.

Justice Oliver, who wrote the court's opinion in the five-three decision, agreed with the Journal-Tribune Publishing Company. "From a news standpoint the public is interested in the appearance of the body of such a local victim. Such appearance may be pictured by words or by photographs or both." To the plaintiff's argument that the picture was simply a sensational device to increase the sale of newspapers Oliver replied: "The courts are not concerned with canons of good taste, and pictures which startle, shock, and even horrify may be freely published, provided they are not libelous or indecent, if the subject of the picture consents or if the occasion is such that his right of privacy does not protect him from the publication." [5]

THE BUGGED APARTMENT

Two years later West Virginia recognized the right of privacy when a tenant brought suit because her landlord had planted a listening device in her apartment. The plaintiff, Adeline Roach, asserted that the landlord had overheard her confidential and private conversations. Judge Leslie F. Given of the supreme court of appeals ruled that because of the "decided preponderance of authority favoring the view that there is a legal right of privacy" the plaintiff was entitled to maintain such a suit in West Virginia. [6]

Connecticut was the final state to give clear recognition to a common law right of privacy during the decade. Twelve years earlier another plaintiff had asserted her right of privacy in a Connecticut court and lost. [7] In that suit a mother argued that an erroneous news report that her daughter had been killed in an auto accident constituted an invasion of privacy. Justice John M. Comley of Hartford County Superior Court ruled that, assuming the state protected the right of privacy, the facts in the case did not constitute an invasion of that right.

In 1959, however, the facts were different, and the defendant New Haven *Register* was not as lucky. The plaintiff, Pamela Korn, complained that her picture was published in the newspaper for advertising purposes without her consent or knowledge. The defendant's only argument was that there was no right of privacy in Connecticut. Justice Howard W. Alcorn neatly disposed of this argument by ruling that "the recognition of the right as a basis for a tort action in jurisdictions faced with the question unaided by statute, and the practical unanimity of recent opinion, place the right within the purview of the common law." [8]

The common law right of privacy was asserted in Tennessee in a suit that resulted from the publication of a baby picture by the Vanderbilt University student newspaper, *The Hustler.* Another student publication, *The Chase,* originally had published the picture of two-year-old Pamela Langford with a humorous caption. The child's father, a minister in the community, brought suit against *The Chase* for libel. A copy of the picture from the publication was included with the plaintiff's pleadings in the libel suit.

Before any judicial action was taken, however, *The Hustler* published a news story about the libel suit and included a reproduction of the allegedly libelous picture. Langford then brought suit against *The Hustler* for libel and invasion of privacy. The Tennessee Supreme Court ruled that the pleadings in the libel suit—including the picture—were privileged information and *The Hustler* was not liable for defamation unless its report was inaccurate or malicious.

Justice Pride Tomlinson was equally unsympathetic to the Langfords' action for invasion of privacy. He said that, assuming Tennessee did protect the right of privacy, there was no basis for the Langford suit because *The Hustler* story merely related facts which were a matter of public record in the Davidson County Circuit Court. "From a practical standpoint, aside from any precedent, it is, this court thinks, unrealistic and illogical to hold that there has been an invasion of this common law right of privacy of an individual by publishing a matter which that individual has already made a matter of public record, available to the eyes, ears, and curiosity of all who care to look, listen or read." [9]

Some authorities have asserted that this decision constituted recognition of the right of privacy by Tennessee. It is difficult, however, to stretch Tomlinson's language to that point. Despite a recent ruling by a federal district court judge in Tennessee that recognition was implicit in this case, Tennessee still should be considered as one of the many states in which recognition of the right of privacy remains an open question.[10]

TWO STATUTES

The Oklahoma legislature in 1955 adopted a privacy statute which, in most respects, was identical to the New York law.[11] While there were two nonmedia federal court decisions prior to the enactment of the legislation,[12] there were no state-court decisions considering recognition of the right. Since the passage of the statute, there have been no reported cases based upon the law.

But there are two unusual features about the law that are worth noting. First, it made the use of a name or portrait for advertising or trade purposes a felony, not a misdemeanor, as in New York. Maximum punishment was a fine of one thousand dollars and five years in prison. In 1965 the law was repealed and replaced by an almost identical statute which classified the offense as a misdemeanor.[13] Also, the Oklahoma statute, like the 1909 Utah law, provides a cause of action for close relatives if the offended party is dead. Relatives may sue up to fifty years after the death of the individual whose privacy was invaded.

COLLATERAL COMMODITIES

While there were no cases construing the Oklahoma privacy law, an important decision was made during the fifties which was based on the 1909 Utah privacy statute. The action, the first reported suit based on the statute, wound its way in and out of both federal and state courts for several years, and resulted in an interesting construction of this forty-five-year-old law.

The plaintiffs were Alice M. Donahue and her daughters, the widow and children of theatrical performer Jack Donahue. Warner Brothers Pictures filmed the life story of theater star Marilyn Miller, including her rise to fame in vaudeville and musical comedy. Her co-star in two famous Broadway shows, *Sunny* and *Rosalie,* had been Jack Donahue, and the film depicted not only his roles in these shows but part of his life as well. The plaintiffs complained that the film contained many factual errors and depicted Donahue, who died in 1930, as unctuous, forward, and brash. Mrs. Donahue and her daughters lived in California, and Warner Brothers' corporate home was New York; but the suit was brought in Utah because, while the Utah statute is almost identical to the New York law, it does extend the right of recovery to heirs.

The action began in Salt Lake County District Court, but was quickly moved to federal district court upon a diversity of citizenship petition by the defendant.* The federal district court granted a summary judgment for the defendant, but this ruling was reversed in a three-two decision by the court of appeals. Circuit Judge Sam G. Bratton ruled that the film was based primarily on fiction and imagination, designed to entertain and amuse, and that this removed it from the protection usually granted to the publication of information and educational matters or the dissemination of news.[14] Bratton refused to accept the argument that Donahue's accomplishments as a performer made him a public figure. The guarantee of freedom of the press could not protect the film either. "The constitutional guaranty of free speech and free press in its full sweep does not undertake to create an inviolate asylum for unbridled appropriation or exploitation of the name, picture, or personality of a deceased public figure for purely commercial purposes . . ." (p. 13).

In a strong dissent Judge Orie L. Phillips took exception to Bratton's broad construction of the statute, arguing that under the New York law the film would be protected. Untrue statements alone did not constitute fictionalization, he wrote, and he asserted that only fictionalization was prohibited under the Utah statute.

Because several factual matters were not completely clear in the record, the case was remanded to district court with the understanding that unless a jury found that the film was informative or educational, and without error, it constituted an invasion of privacy. At the district court the plaintiffs, who were having their own way to this point, requested that the case be moved

* A federal court may assume jurisdiction in a case under Article 3, Section 2, United States Constitution, when all the parties on one side of a lawsuit are from different states than the parties on the other side of the suit. This jurisdiction is said to be based on diversity of citizenship.

back to the state court for a more authoritative construction of the statute. The defendant, with little to lose, agreed. At the trial in the state district court the jury, using the standards laid down by the federal court of appeals, found that there was no invasion of privacy. The plaintiff then appealed this decision to the Utah Supreme Court for a final ruling in the case.

Justice Allan Crockett, speaking for the Utah court, said that to construe the statute properly, it was necessary to look at its historical background. Crockett pointed out that when the New York law, upon which the Utah statute was modeled, was first tested, the New York Court of Appeals said: "It [the statute] is a recognition by the lawmaking power of the very general sentiment which prevailed throughout the community against permitting advertisers to promote the sale of their wares by this method. . . ." [15] Crockett noted that this was the narrow meaning of the New York law when the Utah statute was enacted in 1909. He continued: "It is well settled that when the legislature of a state has used a statute of another state or country as a guide for the preparation and enactment of a statute, the courts of the adopting state will usually adopt the construction placed on the statute in the jurisdiction of its inception" (p. 261).

Crockett ruled that the narrow construction of the New York statute represented the intent of the Utah legislature in 1909. What of the later case law which broadened the construction of the New York law? Crockett complained that it was not satisfactory, that too much uncertainty had developed.

> A publisher would be required to ask these questions: Is the matter essentially educational or informational or fictional? Is it legitimate news? Is the subject a public or private character? Has he waived his right of privacy or not? If so, is that particular matter included in the area of waiver or not? The twilight areas of uncertainty between the alternatives are such that a publisher would have to be constantly negotiating a hazardous course between educational and non-educational, fact and fiction, public and private character, from one quandary to another so that the situation would be both impracticable and intolerable. . . . [P. 263]

Crockett said he rejected the idea that the statute was designed to distinguish between educational or informational matter and fictional material. "A natural and sensible interpretation of the statute . . . leads to the conclusion that the legislature was thinking of the use of names, etc., for advertising purposes, or for the sale of some collateral commodity and they had no thought of extending it to other classes of publication hereinbefore referred" (p. 265).

The Donahues, who won a substantial victory in the federal courts but insisted on obtaining a state construction of the statute, lost. There was no invasion of privacy under the narrow reading of the Utah law provided by the state's supreme court. This interpretation remains as the law in Utah today.

A short time after the *Donahue* decision, Richard L. Dewsnup, writing in the *Utah Law Review*, lamented: "In light of this decision it appears that films, books, newspapers and like publications cannot, in themselves, invade one's statutory right of privacy." [16] Dewsnup's appraisal of the Utah statute is probably correct; but it is not cause for despair. By using Justice Crockett's interpretation, the privacy statute becomes a model of certainty and clarity —goals which the law strives for but rarely reaches, especially in the area of privacy. For example, clarity is not one of the hallmarks of the New York statute.

Under the supreme court's guidelines, then, in order to invade an individual's privacy in Utah, it is necessary to use his name or picture in the promotion of a product, be it spaghetti or mouthwash or used cars. The construction is very clear, very neat, and leaves little for lawyers to argue about. It is tempting to suggest that the law of privacy would be much better off if all jurisdictions followed the Utah rule—there would certainly be less threat to newsmen and other writers and photographers. However, such a suggestion precludes the possibility that there are any worthy invasion of privacy claims outside those involving collateral sale. But, in light of the extreme lapses in good taste exhibited by some members of the press in the past eighty years, this possibility is difficult to discount. Still, the Utah idea has a lot to offer.

THE RIGHT REJECTED

Despite the fact that privacy finally gained a foothold in a majority of jurisdictions during the fifties, two states, Nebraska and Texas, brusquely rejected attempts to make the right a part of the common law.

In Texas, some close relatives of Ben Milner brought suit against the *Sherman Daily Democrat* when on 1 July 1949 it published a news story describing Milner's death in an auto accident. The story, which reported the funeral arrangements and listed Milner's close relatives, included this reference to the deceased: "Milner was one of a group of Grayson County men who were indicted last year in Collin County grain theft cases. He was the second of the group to die in a traffic accident." The plaintiffs complained that the story invaded their privacy. The newspaper argued that the story was a normal obituary and that the reference to the indictment was merely used as a means of identifying Milner to readers.

Justice William M. Cramer of the civil court of appeals at Dallas noted that Texas courts were limited to the enforcement of rights under the common law as it existed on 20 January 1840, the first day of statehood. "The right of privacy as such not being recognized under the common law, as it existed when we adopted it, and our Legislature not having given such rights by statute, no recovery can be had in Texas under the facts in this record." [17]

Three years later, in 1955, Nebraska rejected the right in a humorous case which involved, among other events, a staged armored-car robbery in downtown Omaha. The owners of Ranks Army Store, as an advertising gimmick, hired stuntman-actor Jim Brunson to stage a re-enactment of the famous Massachusetts Brinks armored car robbery. Brunson insisted that police permission be obtained before the phony robbery took place, and the Omaha store owners assured him they would get the needed consent. But they did not and Brunson and his gang of bogus bad men were arrested by the police and taken to jail. All participants were later released, but the story received wide publicity.

Three days after the fiasco, Ranks published two ads in the *Omaha World Herald* which referred to the fake holdup. In one, Ranks noted that Brunson had "put on such a sensational stunt that the whole crew were thrown in the clink." The other advertisement proclaimed: Ranks Gang Captured. The public can sigh in relief now because the Ranks gang, led by Omaha's leading desperado, Jim Brunson, was captured Saturday. . . ." [18]

Brunson sued Ranks for invasion of privacy, arguing that he had not consented to the use of his name in the advertisements. Justice Frederick Messmore ruled that Brunson could not maintain such an action in Nebraska because a legally protected right of privacy was not a part of the common law and was not guaranteed by statute. "We submit that if such a right is deemed necessary or desirable, such right should be provided for by action of our legislature and not by judicial legislation on the part of our courts" (p. 525).

THE CANDID CAMERA

Wisconsin first rejected recognition of the right of privacy in 1936, in *Judevine* v. *Benzies–Montanye Fuel & Warehouse Co.* (see Chap. 6). But in 1956 another attempt was made to gain legal protection for the right in one of the fabled privacy cases. While its impact on the development of the law in Wisconsin and elsewhere was negligible, the case of *Yoeckel* v. *Samonig* is worth discussing, if only as a good story.

Sam Samonig was the owner and proprietor of Sad Sam's Tavern in Delafield, Wisconsin. In addition to his bartending chores, Sam was a demon with a flash camera and did not hesitate to demonstrate his prowess as an amateur lensman. On the evening of 30 June 1954, Sam surprised one of his customers, Norma Yoeckel, while she was in the lady's rest room and photographed her before she realized what had happened. When Norma returned to the barroom, she observed Sam showing his patrons pictures he had taken of other women in similar circumstances. She said she could not be certain that her picture was among the handful being passed around, but in any case, she sued Sam for invasion of privacy.

The Wisconsin Supreme Court was less than sympathetic, ruling that the decision in the 1936 *Judevine* case must stand as a refusal to recognize the right. Perhaps even more persuasive than the *Judevine* precedent, however, was the fact that the Wisconsin legislature had refused both in 1951 and again in 1953 to enact privacy statutes which had been introduced. Justice Edward J. Gehl wrote that "particularly because of the refusal of the legislature at two sessions to recognize even a limited right to protection against invasion of the right of privacy, we are compelled to hold again that the right does not exist in this state." [19]

Wisconsin thus emphatically reaffirmed its decision to deny recognition. This was the last major ruling against recognition of the right of privacy and today, as in 1956, there are but four states—Rhode Island, Wisconsin, Texas, and Nebraska—which have explicitly denied the existence of a law of privacy.

LOVE AND THE LAW

It should be fairly clear by now that there are some aspects of the law of privacy that make little sense. Even in this general description of the growth of privacy as a legally protected right there are times when the strange ways of the law play havoc with all good intentions to make the subject understandable. Perhaps if the development of both the common law and the New York statute stopped in the 1930s or 1940s, before rulings on fictionalization and unfavorable false light became accepted as doctrine, or if all jurisdictions followed the Utah rule of collateral sale, things would be a good deal simpler. But the development did not stop, and the Utah rule applies in but one jurisdiction—and today there are some rather knotty problems in the ball of twine called the law of privacy. Two California cases decided during the fifties, *Gill* v. *Curtis Pub. Co.* and *Gill* v. *Hearst Corp.*, do little to unravel these knots.[20]

John and Sheila Gill owned and operated a confectionery and ice cream concession in Los Angeles' Farmer's Market. One day in the mid-1940s, famed photographer Henri Cartier-Bresson took a picture of the couple as they sat side-by-side at their public ice cream counter. The photograph was taken from the side and showed the two young people seated at the counter, the man with his arm around the girl. Other persons were also visible in the photograph. This picture, which was used in two different magazines, became the basis for both lawsuits.

The actions began in 1951. The suit against Hearst Publishing Company was based on the use of the photograph in an October 1947 issue of *Harper's Bazaar*. The picture illustrated an article entitled "And So the World Goes Round," a short piece on love in which the pictured couples (including the Gills) were said to be "immortalized in a moment of tenderness."

The action against Curtis Publishing Company, which bought the Cartier-Bresson photograph from Hearst Publications, was based on the use of the picture in the *Ladies Home Journal* in May 1949 to illustrate another article about love—this time on the many varieties of love between men and women. The picture of the Gills was captioned: "Publicized as glamorous, desirable, love at first sight is a bad risk." After linking the photograph to "love at first sight," the author of the article described that kind of love as "instantaneous powerful sex attraction—the wrong kind of love."

In the *Curtis* case,* District Court of Appeals Judge Minor Moore ruled that by linking the photograph to "love at first sight—the wrong kind of love," the *Ladies Home Journal* invaded the Gills' right of privacy. "One need not be hypersensitive to be offended or humiliated at being denominated in such a manner." [21] While he conceded that the picture of the couple could have been used in connection with a legitimate news story, use of the photograph with the love article violated their privacy.

Curtis appealed the decision, but lost again in the supreme court. Justice Jesse W. Carter, in response to the defendant's argument that the publication was protected by the freedom of the press, wrote:

> Freedom of speech and freedom of the press have been urged as a ground for denying the existence of the right of privacy. The right of privacy does undoubtedly infringe upon absolute freedom of speech and of the press, and it also clashes with the interest of the public in having a free dissemination of news and information. These paramount public interests must be taken into account in placing the necessary limitations upon the right of privacy. But if this right of the individual is not without qualifications, neither is freedom of speech and of the press unlimited. [22]

Carter asserted that the article could have been published without the picture, which was not absolutely necessary to the presentation, and that he could see no public interest in the plain-

---

* These actions are easiest to understand if the *Curtis* case is considered before the *Hearst* decision, despite the fact that the rulings were made in the opposite order.

tiffs' likenesses. The caption and the article, he said, depicted the Gills as dissolute and immoral persons, and robbed them of public esteem.

The Gills' success against Curtis, however, was not duplicated against Hearst. In the first place, the statute of limitations had expired for any right of privacy action involving the October 1947 publication in *Harper's Bazaar*. Therefore, the only action that could be maintained against Hearst was a suit for an invasion of privacy based on the sale of the photograph to Curtis. After sparring in the lower courts, the case reached the supreme court and Justice Jesse W. Carter, the jurist who wrote the *Curtis* opinion. The Hearst Company argued that while it had sold the picture to Curtis, it did not consent to the use of the photograph with the article on "Love"—and especially not to its connection with "the wrong kind of love." The publishing company asserted that in order to sustain the plaintiff's contention that there was a cause of action, the court must rule that the photograph, standing by itself, was an invasion of privacy. Justice Carter and a majority of the supreme court obliged the defendant and did exactly that. Carter wrote: "Members of the opposite sexes engaging in amorous demonstrations should be protected from the broadcast of that most intimate relation . . . even though the display is in a public place." [23] The justice said he failed to see any substantial public interest in the bare publication of a couple in an amorous pose.

But Carter did not have the last word on the subject. A year later the supreme court reversed itself and ruled that mere publication of the photograph standing alone did not constitute an actionable invasion of privacy. Justice Homer R. Spence wrote: "The right to be let alone and to be protected from undesired publicity is not absolute but must be balanced against the public interest in the dissemination of news and information consistent with the democratic process under the constitutional guarantees of freedom of speech and of the press." Spence agreed that the photograph had no particular news value, but was designed to serve the function of entertainment. "However, the constitutional guarantees of freedom of expression apply with equal force to the publication whether it be a news report or an entertainment feature." The court ruled that the Gills waived their right of privacy by assuming their pose in a public place. "In short, the photograph did not disclose anything which until then had been private, but rather only extended knowledge of the particular incident to a somewhat larger public than had actually witnessed it at the time." [24]

The pair of *Gill* actions offers a good indication of the departure of the law of privacy in some jurisdictions from its original premise, that is, the protection against the exposure of one's private life to public view. Publication of the picture alone was not actionable; but tied to an uncomplimentary article, the photograph stood as the basis for a cause of action. This was another instance of the "unfavorable false light" idea discussed in Chapter 7.

William Prosser in 1960 expressed the fear that the branch of the tort which he described as "false light" was capable of swallowing up the entire tort of libel.[25] If this should happen, it will be only because courts and judges have lost sight of the theoretical basis of the law of privacy. Leon R. Yankwich, who in 1954 was the chief judge of the United States district court in Southern California, wrote shortly after the final disposition of the *Gill* cases: "If the invasion of the right of privacy is made dependent upon whether the resulting publication is or is not complimentary we are out of the domain of privacy altogether and are in the domain of defamation. For in privacy, the invasion exists if there is no right to publish, regardless of whether the publication offends in the eyes of others." [26] There have been no decisions since the *Gill* cases to indicate that the courts are moving away from this standard. Indeed, there are decisions reinforcing this doctrine. Until jurists take a strong stand in differentiation of the two torts, confusion will reign in the law of privacy.

THE DEFENSE OF NEWSWORTHINESS

Throughout the growth of the law of privacy the concept of newsworthiness has proved to be the most effective and durable weapon in the press's arsenal of defenses. This concept has often been referred to in the preceding seven chapters, but a series of decisions in the fifties provides an opportunity to discuss the idea at greater and, it is hoped, more profitable length.

Almost without exception, American courts have excluded the newsworthy story or picture or name from the purview of actionable invasions of privacy. Warren and Brandeis suggested in their 1890 article that such items be protected from suit. American jurists, long imbued with the notion that an informed populace was one cornerstone of a strong democracy, have generally agreed that the rights of the individual must give way to the general societal good when the newsworthy is involved.

When attempting to define "newsworthy," one finds that a broad range of ideas and subjects has been considered at one time or another newsworthy items. However, the concept of newsworthiness can be broken down into three basic parts: public interest, public figure, and public record. Broadly speaking, when the topic under discussion is of legitimate public interest, or when the subject is a voluntary or involuntary public figure, or when the facts of the story have been taken from the public record, there can be no successful action for invasion of privacy.

Certainly there are many nuances and shades of difference within this broad statement—these account for the exceptions to the rule, such as the *Barber* v. *Time* case (see Chap. 7). But over time, newsworthiness has stood as the first line of defense in privacy actions and has usually carried the day. The following cases will help illuminate the concept and the ideas behind it.

NO REMEDY FOR EVERY ANNOYANCE

On 25 August 1948 the Boston *Post* published a photograph of a serious auto accident in which a fifteen-year-old school girl was killed. The girl's body was visible in the picture and she was identified as the daughter of Mr. and Mrs. James J. Kelley. The parents brought suit for invasion of privacy because of the publication of the picture and also because they were mentioned in the account. Massachusetts, it will be recalled, had never recognized the right of privacy, always finding another means of disposing of the suit. The results in this case were the same, as the supreme court ruled that even if the right of privacy was protected, there was no violation of that right in this case.

Justice John V. Spalding asserted that if the court followed the plaintiff's wishes, the press would be tied in knots by lawsuits. "A newspaper could not safely publish the picture of a train wreck or of an airplane crash if any of the bodies of the victims were recognizable. The law does not provide a remedy for every annoyance that occurs in everyday life. Many things which are distressing or may be lacking in propriety or good taste are not actionable." [27] Justice Spalding agreed that the publication of the picture was indelicate and perhaps lacked good taste. But it was not actionable. He also ruled that the single reference to the parents in the story could hardly be considered an invasion of privacy.

In a similar case four years later in Fayette County, Alabama, a mother attempted to collect damages for invasion of privacy when a local newspaper published a picture of the body of her son who had been shot in the head and killed. The picture was taken at the funeral home by a photographer for *The Northwest Alabamian and The Fayette Banner* and showed a metal object protruding from the youth's head. The story, which accompanied the picture, reported that the youth was killed in Winfield, Alabama, and that a women had been arrested in connection with the shooting. The victim was on parole at the time of his death after serving a sentence in the Alabama state penitentiary. Justice Robert T. Simpson ruled that even if a relational right of privacy existed in Alabama—and it did not—there was no cause of action. "Her [the plaintiff's] son had become such a public character that, had he not died, the photographs and publication of the circumstances of his death were matters of legitimate public interest in the proper dissemination of news through the newspapers and he had thus forfeited his claim to privacy. . . ." [28]

NEWS IN THE MAKING

Probably the last thing John Jacova expected when he walked into the cigar shop of the Casablanca Hotel in Miami Beach one day in the early fifties was that he would be on television that night. But sure enough, Jacova was one of those unfortunate souls who happened to be in the wrong place at the wrong time. While he was reading the newspaper he had just purchased, two Miami Beach police officers shoved him up against a wall, claimed he was a gangster called Tony, and charged that he was operating a gambling room in the hotel. All the while television newsmen were filming the scene for the evening news.

After showing the police his identification, Jacova was released; but that night on the evening television news, after watching films of a police gambling raid on a restaurant, he saw himself on the screen, being questioned by two police officers in the cigar shop. During the twelve to fifteen seconds Jacova was pictured, an announcer reported that the cousin of Tony Tronolone, the restaurant operator who was arrested in the restaurant raid, was picked up at his apartment for questioning.

Jacova filed suit for invasion of privacy, arguing that the film made it appear he was being arrested and that he was Tony Tronolone's cousin. Justice B. K. Roberts disagreed, saying that the narration did not match the picture and that no reasonable man would infer that Jacova was Carmen Tronolone. "So far as the telecast showed, he was just an unidentified person, standing against the wall and apparently being interrogated by the officers." [29]

Undaunted, Jacova argued that even if he was not mistaken for a gambler, the television station had no right to include him, an innocent bystander not involved in the raid, in their news film. Roberts reviewed many cases involving newspapers, magazines, and newsreels, and finally ruled that Jacova still did not have a cause of action. The fact remained, he wrote, that Jacova was in a public place and present at a scene where news was in the making. Roberts agreed that a television film editor, like a newspaper editor, has a responsibility to protect individual rights. The scene in which Jacova appeared could have been edited from the film when it was discovered that he was only a bystander. But, Roberts added,

it should also be remembered that a television newscaster must, like a newspaper reporter, attempt to get before the public "today's news, today." . . . The public has an interest in the free dissemination of news. . . . In the free dissemination of news, then, and fair comment thereon, hundreds and thousands of news items and articles are published daily and weekly in our newspapers and periodicals. This court judicially knows that it frequently takes a legal tribunal months of diligent searching to determine the facts of a controversial situation. When it is recalled that a reporter is expected to determine such facts, in a matter of hours or minutes, it is only reasonable to expect that occasional errors will be made. Yet, since the preservation of our American democracy depends upon the public's receiving information speedily—particularly upon getting news of pending matters while there still is time for public opinion to form and be felt—it is vital that no reasonable restraints be placed upon the working news reporter or the editorial writer. [P. 40]

Roberts ruled there was no unreasonable invasion of privacy.

PRIVACY'S CHILD

The Columbia, South Carolina, *State* carried this item in its news columns on 13 March 1956: "A chubby, blonde 12-year-old mother of a day-old healthy baby boy greeted visitors cheerfully yesterday, but declined to have her picture taken or talk generally with reporters." The story continued, giving the names of the mother and father, Troyce and Lewis Meetze, their ages, the baby's weight, the name of the grandparents, and assorted other details one might find in any birth announcement. The Associated Press picked up the story and, despite the Meetzes' wishes to the contrary, the birth of the baby was given great publicity. The couple filed suit against the AP for invasion of privacy.

Justice G. Dewey Oxner of the South Carolina Supreme Court said he had sympathy for the couple, but admitted there was little the court could do. "The right of privacy is not an absolute right. Some limitations are essential for the protection of the right of freedom of speech and of the press. . . ." [30] Oxner said that it was rather unusual for a twelve-year-old girl to give birth to a child. "It is a biological occurrence which would naturally excite great public interest. Moreover, it was an event which the law required to be entered as a public record" (p. 610). Oxner said the reporter had been a bit obnoxious, but his action did not constitute an invasion of privacy. "We regret that we cannot give legal recognition to Mrs. Meetze's desire to avoid publicity but the courts do not sit as censors of the manners of the Press" (p. 610).

The Associated Press was sued again, three years later, in the same state, this time by four men accused of conspiracy and assault and battery. Two days after Christmas in 1956, Guy Hutchins, a high school band director, was waylaid, seized, and beaten by a band of hooded night riders. A week later at a press conference officials of the South Carolina Law Enforcement Division announced that six men had been arrested for the crime. Official police mug shots were given to the press for use in newspapers and on television. The Associated Press made a composite of the six photographs and transmitted it across the nation as a wirephoto. Four of the six men arrested sued the AP for invasion of privacy.

Federal District Judge Charles C. Wyche ruled that there was great public interest in the case and the public had a right to know the facts, a right that was paramount to that of the plaintiffs. "In deciding a right of privacy issue a court is, in essence, deciding whether the news organ in question has abused the privileges of a free press. While it may not be determinative in and of itself, the fact that the Associated Press received its information here from the chief executive of the state and the highest law enforcement officers in the state at a news conference called by the Governor for this purpose is of relevance and significance in deciding the question." [31] The fact that the plaintiffs had placards and numbers on their chests was not important in a privacy suit, Wyche said. When the plaintiffs became associated with an event of great public interest, they necessarily sacrificed their right to privacy.

TIME LAPSE AND PRIVACY

The infamous career of John Dillinger, America's number one outlaw during the 1930s, touched the lives of many persons, and any attempt to recount the exploits of the killer was bound to involve other individuals as well. Indeed, one of these individuals figured in a series of six stories by Elgar Brown on the life of Dillinger published in the spring of 1949 by the Chicago *Herald-American.*

The first installment of the series was illustrated by three photographs, one of which was a picture taken in 1934 of Dillinger and the Lake County, Indiana, prosecuting attorney, Robert Estill. The photograph, which showed Dillinger standing next to Estill, with a hand on his shoulder, carried this caption: "Victim of the Dillinger curse was Robert Estill, Lake County, Ind.

prosecuting attorney, who foolishly struck a friendly pose with the noted outlaw. The killer's subsequent toy-gun escape from a Hoosier jail spelled the end of Estill's career. He was virtually laughed out of office and public life." [32] The story added that Dillinger was captured in Arizona and was brought back and lodged in the Crown Point Jail—from which he escaped. The story also noted that Estill died after leaving public office.

The writer was wrong on at least one fact: Estill was still alive. Estill demonstrated this by filing suit against the newspaper for invasion of privacy. But Circuit Court of Appeals Judge Otto Kerner refused to accept Estill's argument. "Regardless of the circumstances under which the picture was taken, and whether or not the pose was wholly inadvertent, as plaintiff alleges in his complaint, he was at that time a public official and, as such, whether inadvertently or not, he became one of the figures in a story of considerable public interest at that time. That being the case, we think it cannot be said that the republication of that story constitutes any invasion of his private rights" (p. 1022).

As in the *Sidis* case (see Chap. 6), then, time lapse did not remove the label of public figure from Estill. Another federal judge made a similar ruling three years later in California. The plaintiff in this case had attempted in 1952 to dissuade a woman from jumping off the Golden Gate Bridge in San Francisco. A photographer took his picture and it appeared in the San Francisco *Call-Bulletin* on 22 April. Almost two years later the picture was published again, this time in the *Saturday Evening Post*, to illustrate an article on suicides. The caption named the woman —who eventually jumped—and the plaintiff. Nothing in the accompanying article referred to the picture, which was used to depict one kind of suicide.

A privacy action was started in federal court against Curtis Publishing Company on the ground that use of the picture after two years violated the plaintiff's right of privacy. The court disagreed, ruling that "the mere passage of time generally does not destroy this privilege [of newsworthiness], at least when the time elapsed is only two years." Judge Oliver D. Hamlin, Jr., also pointed out that there was nothing derogatory about the picture. "Indeed, it was most laudatory." [33] This stress on the fact that the picture was complimentary places this case in the favorable light category, the rule of thumb being: if you are going to use someone's picture out of context, try to make it a complimentary use, not a derogatory one.

NEWSWORTHINESS

It is difficult to overemphasize the importance of the defense of newsworthiness. Without it, the press would find it almost impossible to present a fair account of the day's news without opening itself up to numerous privacy suits. Equally important, however, is the question of whether right of privacy suits could withstand the constitutional challenge brought on First Amendment grounds without the broad exceptions granted to the publication of news and information.

For the newsman, the study of the law of privacy revolves around a definition of the concept of newsworthiness. An understanding of what has been considered newsworthy in the past provides important guidelines for the future. The important point which must be remembered is that in a lawsuit, a judge will be the editor who decides what is or what is not newsworthy. Theoretically, there is the grave possibility of censorship of the press by the courts; in reality, however, this has not occurred. Courts in nearly all cases have deferred this decision to both editors and readers by including a broad range of topics and material within the definition of "newsworthy." While there is no guarantee that this practice will continue indefinitely, the journalist has little to fear if he concentrates on presenting the "news" in a responsible fashion.

IX

New Interpretations of Old Laws:
1951-60

It is characteristic of every era, no less than of our contemporary world, that events which have caught the popular imagination or incidents which have aroused the public interest, have been frequently revived long after their occurrence in the literature, journalism, or other media of communication of another day. The events, being embedded in the communal history, are proper material for such recounting.

JUSTICE W. T. FOX [1]

While the law of privacy was expanding in other parts of America, case law in New York kept pace during the fifties. New problems arose, and old ones needed fresh appraisals. Courts in Pennsylvania were busy resolving privacy questions also, as for the first time a state other than New York or California reported more than two or three privacy decisions during a decade.

But the law of privacy expanded into new media as well as new jurisdictions. And for the first time it was possible to isolate a series of cases involving two distinct outlets—television and magazines featuring stories about crime and criminals. Decisions made during the decade with regard to both areas stand as law today.

MORE FICTIONALIZATION PROBLEMS

Ever since the 1920s New York courts had been wrestling with the problem of semifactual and sensationally written magazine and newspaper articles. The few guidelines that did exist shifted frequently, like ripples in a sand dune, and added little certainty to the law. Often the particular justices or court hearing the appeal had as much or more influence on the decision than the facts in the case. With an appellate bench as large as that in New York, this personal factor can be very complex. The few apparent rules are flexible. Fictionalization, for example, will destroy the privilege usually granted to newsworthy items. But what is fictionalization? The mere presence of inaccuracies in an article does not necessarily make it a fictional piece. How much inaccuracy is needed? There is no trustworthy answer.

The appellate division of the New York Supreme Court faced this kind of problem in 1953 when prize fighter Lee Oma brought suit against *Pageant Magazine* for the publication of his picture with an article entitled, "Let's Abolish Boxing." While primarily factual, the article was written in a racy, sensational style and stressed the corruption and degradation in boxing. Oma's photograph was published on the back cover of the magazine with the caption, "Lee Oma, Tycoon—this man can make $25,000 on a single deal, but it might cost him his life. Why? See page 24." Oma was not mentioned in the article, but the reference in the caption to the health hazards of boxing was explored. Justice Charles D. Breitel ruled that the article, despite its sensational nature, was about a matter of the highest public interest. "The lines may not be drawn so tight as to imperil more than we protect," he wrote.[2]

A similar case arose five years later, this time involving the infamous *Confidential Magazine*. The facts of the case were poorly reported by the appellate division, but it is known that in January 1956 *Confidential* printed what the court called "a sordid article" about a man named Robert Goelet. Goelet sued *Confidential* because, he said, the use of his name was not for the legitimate purpose of disseminating news or actual events, but to increase magazine sales. Justice Francis L. Valente did not accept this argument. He admitted that *Confidential* was a poor-quality magazine and that the article was spicy and lurid. But he wrote,

. . . we are not unmindful of the daily content of our current newspapers and periodicals. In addition to the vast growth of the gossip columns, we find therein detailed reports of the piquant facts in matrimonial litigation, and the colorful escapades and didoes of well-known persons which are not unlike those in the article about which plaintiff complains. Even a cursory examination of the contents of some of our daily newspapers makes evident that such stories are part and parcel of the reading habits of the American public. We cannot undertake to pass judgment on those reading tastes. The increased circulation of magazines such as "Confidential" is mute testimony that the public is interested in the kind of news those magazines purvey.[3]

Valente said the court could only grant a remedy when there was a use of a name or picture for the purpose of advertising or trade through commercialization.

But the question of fictionalization was not settled—and it still is not, despite a United States Supreme Court ruling on the subject in 1967.[4] A writer walks on unsettled ground when he begins to fictionalize or sensationalize his otherwise factual article.

MORE IDENTIFICATION PROBLEMS

In Chapter 7 the problem of identification was discussed with the aid of several leading cases. During the fifties the New York courts again dealt with the problem, but this time handed down what is probably the definitive opinion on the subject. The case resulted from a criminal complaint brought against publisher Charles Scribner's Sons on behalf of Joseph A. Maggio of New York City. The defendant had published James Jones's *From Here to Eternity,* a highly regarded novel about events in Hawaii during the hectic months surrounding the Japanese attack on Pearl Harbor. Author Jones was a member of Company F, 27th Infantry Regiment, stationed in Hawaii during the period. The complainant was a member of the same company.

One of the main characters in *From Here to Eternity* was a soldier named Angelo Maggio. However, the fictional Maggio was not in the 27th Regiment, nor did he in any way portray acts performed by the real Maggio. Complainant Maggio based his entire case on the similarity of last names, but the court refused to accept the argument. City Magistrate Dunaif ruled that "to violate the statute, the name must be used in such a context as to unequivocally point to and identify the complainant. . . . Where a name is used, it, like a portrait or picture, must upon meeting the eye or ear, be unequivocally identified as that of the complainant. In the case of a name having no public recognition, this can be established only by a clear showing that the details surrounding the fictional character portrayed are such as to identify the complainant as the person of that name in that particular setting." [5]

ENDORSEMENTS REVISITED

Does the use of a name in a news story, which is in turn reprinted as a part of an advertisement, constitute an invasion of privacy under the New York statute? The courts in New York had faced this problem before, it will be recalled, but the issue was not settled. In the mid-1950s, when Joseph C. Flores brought suit against the Mosler Safe Company for the use of his name in one of their advertisements, this question became a key issue in the case.

The news story was a report of a warehouse fire. Flores, an upstate New York motel keeper, was conducting business in the building when the fire was accidently started, and his name was mentioned three times in the story. The Mosler advertising circular carried a picture of the burning building plus the news story. The advertising message urged readers to buy a Mosler safe to protect their valuable business records in case of fire. But there was no suggestion that Flores endorsed Mosler safes.

The plaintiff argued that this was clearly the use of a name for advertising purposes. The defendant asserted that the use of the name was incidental to the advertisement and totally unrelated to the advertiser's product. Attorneys for the safe company pointed to the *Wallach* v. *Bacharach* decision (see Chap. 7) in which a New York court ruled that the use of a name in an independent and unrelated news item published in paid advertising space to attract attention to the ad was not a trade or advertising purpose. But Judge Albert Conway, and a majority of the court of appeals, was not persuaded. Because Mosler chose to reprint the entire original news story, including the portion that mentioned the plaintiff's name, in a circular designed to solicit customers, the court ruled that there was an invasion of privacy. [6]

Conway also based his opinion on what some courts during the fifties began calling the "right of publicity." This concept was discussed at length first in 1953 by Federal Circuit Judge Jerome N. Frank in *Haelan Labs Inc.* v. *Topps Chewing Gum,* a case which involved baseball stars' pictures in bubble gum packages. In his opinion Frank attempted to define the right: "We think that in addition to an independent right of privacy . . . a man has a right in the publicity value of his photograph, i.e. the right to grant the exclusive privilege of publishing his picture. . . . This right might be called a 'right of publicity.'" [7]

The idea that a man has property value in his features and should be able to capitalize on this property was not really new. In a sense, it was the motivation for many earlier privacy lawsuits. While some persons were undoubtedly sincerely chagrined to see their pictures or names in advertisements, others regretted not the publicity, but the loss of the profits from the campaign. In this respect the right of publicity was a companion to the right to privacy for many years. But personalities, those who have dedicated their lives to the public by appearing in films, performing on television, or participating in professional sports, have at times found it difficult to restrict the use of their names and pictures by unscrupulous advertisers. It was this situation that undoubtedly prompted Judge Frank to argue that a separate doctrine was needed. The so-called right of publicity does not compensate the individual for mental suffering resulting from unwarranted publicity. Instead, it provides the individual with remuneration for the use of his features, personality, or name to sell a collateral item. As such, it has nothing at all to do with the news gathering side of the mass media.

But Judge Conway's attempt to base his decision in the *Flores* case on this newly enunciated right of publicity was weak, for it is doubtful that the use of Joseph Flores' name stirred many New Yorkers to rush out and buy a new Mosler safe. In other words, the property value in a name should be proportional to the fame of the personality. There would be little value to an advertiser to announce that Joseph Flores, upstate New York motel operator, endorsed Mosler safes. Consequently, it is difficult to see why Flores should be remunerated for a value that barely existed. His best argument, which was the one he used, was that he was distressed because his name was associated with the Mosler safe. This was the traditional right of privacy argument.

THE DEFENSE OF CONSENT

Newsworthiness has been discussed as one of the two primary defenses in a privacy suit. Consent is the other one. From Samuel Warren's and Louis Brandeis' plea for privacy in 1890 to contemporary court decisions, the rule that the individual's consent to the publicity destroys his right of privacy has remained constant. But the defense of consent can be more complicated than it appears. In 1959, for example, New York courts were asked whether consent to publicity for one use can be expanded to include a second use as well. The vehicle for the legal query was one of the state's most interesting privacy cases.

Mary Jane Russell was one of New York City's highest-paid and best-known high fashion models. In the vernacular of the trade, she was "class," and her picture frequently graced the covers of the nation's leading women's magazines. In addition to her work as a model, she was a housewife and mother and a respected member of her community. In 1954 she posed for celebrated fashion photographer Richard Avedon, who was taking a series of pictures for Marboro Book Stores. The print used by the book firm features Mary Jane in one bed, a male model in an adjoining bed, each reading an educational book. The caption for the picture, which was used in full-page newspaper ads and on a poster, was, "For People Who Take Their Reading Seriously." Miss Russell agreed to the use and signed this release: "The undersigned hereby irrevocably consents to the unrestricted use by Richard Avedon, advertisers, customers, successors, and assigns, of my name, portrait, or picture for advertising purposes or purposes of trade and I waive the right to inspect or approve such completed portraits, pictures, or advertising matter used in connection therewith." [8]

Five months after the picture was taken, Marboro told Avedon that a negative was needed to make more posters. The negative, however, was sold by Marboro for two hundred dollars to the Springs Cotton Mills, a bed-sheet manufacturer. Springs Mills had a reputation for publishing bawdy advertisements and consequently had difficulty getting good models to pose for them. The Russell negative was a real catch and was put to use as soon as it could be retouched. The Springs Mills version of the photograph placed Miss Russell in the company of an elderly man who was reading a copy of *Clothes Make the Man,* a rather well-known "dirty" book. The picture, which was used in Springs Mills ads in many national magazines, was described by New York Supreme Court Justice Matthew M. Levy as that of a "willing call girl waiting to be used by a stranger, whetting his sexual appetite" (p. 17).

The photograph was also used by the bed-sheet company in a contest. Readers were asked to caption the picture, and prizes were to be awarded to the most creative writers. The advertising copy promoting the contest announced: "We bought this picture to advertise Springmaid Sheets, but we can't write the caption. Elliott Springs tried, but all he came up with was 'Lost Weekend,' 'Knight Errant,' 'Lost Between the Covers,' and 'You Can't Go Wrong With A Springmaid Sheet'" (p. 17).

Mary Jane Russell sued Marboro, Springs Mills, and numerous and sundry other individuals for invasion of privacy. After preliminary legal skirmishing, the question in the case was reduced to: Did the plaintiff completely abandon her right of privacy when she signed the model release statement? The New York Supreme Court ruled that the model did relinquish her right of privacy with respect to the original picture. Justice Matthew M. Levy said that "without question, the consent clearly entitled an assignee [such as Springs Mills] to use the same picture that was used by the original advertiser" (p. 27). However, because Springs Mills did not use the same picture, but had retouched it substantially, the case had to be considered in a different light. Levy concluded: "If the picture were altered sufficiently in situation, emphasis, background or context, I should think that it would no longer be the same portrait, but a different one. And as to the changed picture, I would hold that the original written consent would not apply and that liability would arrive where the content of the picture has been so changed that it is substantially unlike the original" (p. 27).

Note that Justice Levy was referring to the content of the picture itself and not the purpose for which it was used. Presumably, if Springs Mills had used the original picture, without alterations, there would have been no invasion of privacy, even when the photograph became part of the caption-writing contest.* The lesson of the *Russell* case is that written consent—the kind signed by Mary Russell—must be interpreted as a very broad approval of use. At least in New York, it is only when the original photograph is substantially altered, or connected to defamatory words, that the model has a legal recourse.

PRIVACY IN PENNSYLVANIA

If any jurisdiction rivaled New York during the fifties as a hotbed of privacy litigation, it was Pennsylvania. A series of important cases was decided during the decade that provided some interesting instructional points, including a contrast between the favorable and unfavorable aspects of false light.

THE QUESTION OF TIME LAPSE

In 1951 a suit was initiated by a Birmingham, Alabama, girl, Eleanor Sue Leverton, against Curtis Publishing Company for the publication of her picture without consent in the *Saturday Evening Post*. When Eleanor was ten years old, she was hit by a speeding automobile as she crossed an intersection. A photographer at the scene photographed the child as she lay in the street, unhurt but terrified. The motorist was fined for running a red light, and the next day the story and picture appeared in a Birmingham newspaper. Twenty months later the *Post* published an article on pedestrian carelessness by David G. Wittels entitled, "They Ask to Be Killed." Wittels reported, "Safety education in schools has reduced child accidents measurably, but unpredictable darting still takes a sobering toll." Eleanor's photograph was used to illustrate the article, and it was implied that the accident had resulted from her own carelessness.

After a federal district court jury awarded the twelve-year-old a sizable judgment,[9] Curtis appealed to the Third United States

---

* While a privacy suit probably would have failed, an action for libel most likely would have succeeded—depending, of course, on the content of the caption.

Circuit Court, complaining that the photograph was newsworthy
and hence privileged. In his opinion Circuit Judge Herbert F.
Goodrich said there were two relevant questions to be answered.
First, did the twenty-month time lapse destroy the newsworthiness privilege enjoyed by the picture immediately after the accident? Second, was the newsworthiness privilege destroyed by
using the photograph in connection with the article on pedestrian
carelessness?

Judge Goodrich ruled that the time lapse did not affect the
privilege. The Birmingham newspaper originally publishing the
photograph, for example, could have used it months later in a
roundup of traffic accidents. However, use of the picture out of
context could not be tolerated. For, while the plaintiff was newsworthy with regard to her accident—even for an indefinite period
of time afterward—use of the picture with the *Post* article, which
implied that she had been careless, destroyed the privilege.
Goodrich concluded: "The sum total of all this is that this
particular plaintiff, the legitimate subject for publicity for one
particular accident, now becomes a pictorial, frightful example
of pedestrian carelessness. This, we think, exceeds the bounds of
privilege." [10]

Five years later another suit was filed against Curtis Publishing
Company, again for using a news photograph to illustrate an
unrelated article. The suit represents another instance of placing
the plaintiff in a kind of false light. The plaintiffs were three
Philadelphia policemen who were photographed in 1945 after
apprehending a robbery suspect. One of the pictures, which was
published by the Philadelphia *Inquirer*, showed the three officers
lunging after the suspect, who did not want his picture taken.
In January 1948, twenty-six months later, the *Saturday Evening
Post* published the photograph to illustrate an unrelated feature
article entitled, "Crime Was My Business," an autobiographical
account by a former California police chief. The caption under
the picture read: "One of the compensations in a policeman's life
is the thrill he gets out of walking into a potentially dangerous
situation and knowing that it is his presence there that brings
order. 'If I had it to do all over again,' says Mr. Powers, 'I'd still
be a cop.' " [11] The plaintiffs' names were not used, and no mention
was made of the circumstances under which the picture was

taken. In the *Post*, the photograph appeared to depict three uniformed officers restraining a suspect or a prisoner.

The lawsuit was not filed until the mid-fifties and consequently a Pennsylvania two-year statute of limitation precluded any recovery by the plaintiffs. However, Superior Court Justice Robert E. Woodside did discuss the merits of the case in the hope of clarifying the state's common law of privacy. Woodside noted that this suit differed from the *Leverton* case in two important respects. In *Leverton,* the *Post* story implied imprudent conduct on the part of the plaintiff, thus placing her in an unfavorable light. However, in this case the reader was left with a good impression that an officer's presence brings order, thus placing the plaintiffs in a favorable light. Also, Eleanor Leverton was a private citizen, whereas these plaintiffs were public officers. "When there is no defamation, we have grave doubts whether a tort is committed by the publishing of a picture of governmental officials or employees engaged in the performance of an official duty . . . " (p. 100). The Pennsylvania justice then added this comment on freedom of the press: "Furthermore, it must not be forgotten that the right of privacy infringes upon freedom of speech and press and clashes with the interest of the public in the free dissemination of news and information, and that these paramount public interests must be considered when placing the necessary limitations upon the right of privacy" (p. 101).

The *Leverton* case played a part in another Pennsylvania decision during the decade, this one involving a news story about a gambling investigation. On 25 January 1952 the *Quakertown Free Press,* a Bucks County weekly newspaper, published a front-page story on a slot machine investigation in an adjacent county. According to the story, state police had reported no evidence of any unlawful activity in Bucks County since the raid on a floating dice game six months earlier. The *Free Press* report continued: "It has been an even longer time since slot machines have been uncovered in the county. It was August 10 of last year to be exact that State Police seized seven slot machines after a raid on the estate of Carl Schnabel in West Rockhill." [12] The story was true, but the newspaper neglected to report that Schnabel had been acquitted of the gambling charges. Schnabel sued, arguing that the lapse of time since the raid destroyed the newsworthiness of the item.

Justice Charles A. Jones of the Pennsylvania Superior Court did not agree. Publication at the time of the raid was not an invasion of privacy, and the lapse of time did not change that. "By his possession of the slot machines, the appellant relinquished his asserted right to be let alone; and the passage of the six-month interval did not wipe away the notoriety occasioned by his possession of the machines" (p. 615). Jones said that in publishing a fact already known to the public which had obvious relevance to the printed story at hand, the defendant publisher did not exceed the privilege granted to newsworthy items. The *Leverton* rule regarding time lapse would stand.

BEYOND THE FACTS

The final important Pennsylvania case during the decade concerned fictionalization and demonstrated how jurisdictions outside New York have been even less tolerant with those who tamper with the facts. The story began in Philadelphia in the late summer of 1949. Theresa Allizzo Aquino and John N. Masciocchi, a forlorn "pair of star-cross'd lovers," were wed secretly before a justice of the peace. In addition to promising to love, honor, and obey Theresa, John also promised someday to provide a home for her and to renew their wedding vows in a church. Then the teen-agers returned to their parents' homes and the marriage was never consummated. When Theresa's parents learned of the marriage the following day they were not happy, but were willing to give their blessing if John would keep his promises to their daughter. John refused, stating that he had married Theresa only to spite her parents, who had been opposed to the courtship. A divorce action began immediately and, since John did not contest the matter, was completed in relative secrecy. The Philadelphia newspapers, according to regular policy, reported the filing of the divorce action and the granting of the decree. Also, an opinion by the court on a legal point was published in the legal reports. Nevertheless, none of Theresa's friends or relatives was aware of what had occurred—until 30 December 1950, when

The Sunday Bulletin (Philadelphia) published a long feature story on the marriage and divorce.

The facts in the *Bulletin* story were basically true. Most of them had been reported previously in the brief accounts of the divorce proceeding. But the style of the piece was narrative and the writer embellished the article with such details as "imaginary" conversations between the two teen-agers. Entitled "Marriage for Spite," the story was published in a prominent position and gained wide readership. A suit was filed by Theresa and her parents for invasion of privacy.

Justice Robert E. Woodside, who wrote the opinion for the superior court, first outlined the general problem courts faced in deciding most privacy actions. "Without well defined limitations the right of privacy might dangerously encroach upon freedom of speech and freedom of the press. Legal actions for invasions of the right of privacy must not be a vehicle for the establishment of a judicial censorship of the press. The courts are not concerned with establishing canons of good taste for the press or the public." [13] The facts in the article were a part of the public record, Woodside said, and to prevent the press from reporting these items would constitute an unwarranted interference with the right of the press to disseminate news. Therefore, if the story reported just the facts, there could be no legal action.

But the *Bulletin* reporter went beyond the bare facts. "Only by reading the article," Woodside said, "can one appreciate how the author permitted his imagination to roam through the facts, and how newsworthy events were presented in a style used almost exclusively by writers of fiction" (p. 537). The article was about a newsworthy event, which ordinarily would fall within the scope of proper immunity pertaining to the publication of current events, but the fictionalization or embellishment pushed it outside this scope.

TELEVISION AND TRADE PURPOSES

As the 1950s opened, strange new gadgets began to appear on the rooftops of homes throughout the nation. Television, the latest electronic entertainment medium, found its way into more and more living rooms. As the medium expanded, questions arose regarding the law of privacy, and courts were faced with both new and old problems.

The New York courts were the first to meet these new problems in an early 1950 case involving monkeys, the Washington Redskins professional football team, and Chesterfield cigarettes. Arsene Gautier was a well-known animal trainer-showman whose act featured ponies, dogs, and monkeys. On 5 December 1948 he was hired to perform at Griffith Stadium in Washington, D.C., between halves of the Washington Redskins-New York Giants football game. When Gautier discovered that the contest would be televised, he protested, arguing that he was neither prepared nor being paid for a television performance. But the show went on, and so did the television cameras. During the half-time activities, which were televised as well, announcers advertised Chesterfield cigarettes. Gautier brought suit in a New York court on grounds that his name and picture were used for advertising and trade purposes. The New York Supreme Court ruled that Gautier was due compensation because his name and picture were used without consent, in violation of the statute. A five-hundred-dollar judgment was awarded the animal trainer.[14]

The appellate division reversed the supreme court decision, and in one of his most important privacy opinions, Justice Bernard Shientag noted that commercial messages had never enjoyed the protection given to news and information. "The compelling public interest in the free flow of ideas in the market place does not extend to advertising matter." Certainly, commercials were presented during Gautier's act. But, Shientag pointed out, advertising on television and radio was different from newspapers, where ads were clearly separated from news columns. "The unique necessities of radio and television . . . require that in large part programs appear under the sponsorship of commercial advertisers. To hold that the mere fact of sponsorship makes the unauthorized use of an individual's name or picture on radio or television a use 'for advertising purposes' would materially weaken the informative and educational potentials of these still developing media."[15] Shientag ruled that in the absence of exploitation of a name or picture in the commercial announcement or in direct connection with the product itself, there was no use "for advertising purposes."

What about trade purposes, the broader category which in the past has included entertainment features? Shientag again disagreed with Gautier's argument and ruled that television was free to report or disseminate information of public interest. There was no legal foundation in the contention that television coverage of the animal act exceeded the legitimate bounds of public interest. No fictionalization, no humorous narration had been added; the act was presented in an unembroidered, unembellished fashion without variation. Also, Shientag noted, "the extent of the infringement on the plaintiff's privacy would in this case seem to be minimal. There was no substantial invasion of the plaintiff's 'right to be let alone' in telecasting an act voluntarily performed by plaintiff for pay before 35,000 spectators" (p. 436).

The New York Court of Appeals, the state's high court, affirmed the appellate division opinion, citing most of Shientag's arguments. Justice Charles W. Froessel wrote that "unless the plaintiff's name or picture were in some way connected with the 'commercial,' the mere fact of sponsorship of the telecast would not suffice to violate the statute in this respect." [16]

It is difficult to overemphasize the importance of this decision, especially with respect to the concept of "advertising use." What Justice Shientag did was to give the electronic media the same protection offered the print media, putting column rules between the commercials and programs, so to speak. If this had not been done, it probably would have been difficult to bring the mantle of protection around even sponsored *news* programs. The *Gautier* case, while not dealing specifically with the news media, had an impact on all aspects of television production.

"THE BIG STORY"

Soon after the *Gautier* decision the television networks were faced with a problem that plagued the print media for some time: what is the status of the dramatized re-enactment of actual events? The first important suit began in Washington, D.C., Federal District Court and was filed by Charles S. Bernstein, surely one of history's more unfortunate souls.

In 1919 Bernstein was convicted of bank robbery in Minnesota and served nine years of a forty-year sentence before his innocence was determined and he was pardoned. In 1933 he was arrested in Washington, D.C., on a first-degree murder charge. He was convicted, but his death sentence was commuted to life imprisonment. Then, through the work of many persons, including Washington *Daily News* reporter Martha Stroyer, he was pardoned again when it was shown he was probably innocent.

On 18 January 1952 the National Broadcasting Company's "Big Story" presented a dramatization of the work reporter Stroyer did to free Bernstein. The only true names used in the program were those of reporter Stroyer and the president of the United States. But Bernstein nevertheless sued for invasion of privacy, arguing that his friends recognized the portrayal as his story and that the actor who portrayed the convict resembled him. The story was based on facts, but was dramatized and fictionalized for the television production.

In a long, well-reasoned opinion, District Judge Richard B. Keech ruled that the facts presented no actionable invasion of privacy. The first point Keech made was directed at the plaintiff's contention that he was no longer a public figure and hence should be left alone. Keech agreed that society should not sanction the unwarranted revival of a rehabilitated criminal's past mistakes in a manner that identifies him in his present private setting with the old crime. Yet he noted such persons were not protected from the redisclosure of embarrassing facts in an old newspaper or in court records. The protection "which time may bring to a formerly public figure is not against repetition of the facts which are already public property, but against unreasonable public identification of him in his present setting with the earlier incident." [17]

Even more basic than this argument, however, was that Bernstein's affairs were already known to the public because of the considerable publicity given the murder case before, during, and after the many trials. Also, Keech noted there was no identification in the television drama, nothing to link the fictional David Crouch with Charles Bernstein. "This court holds as a matter of law that a criminal proceeding widely publicized for a period of at least eight years and containing elements of decided popular appeal does not lose its general public interest in a period of four years or even 12 years" (p. 835). Keech asserted that the producers of the program made a careful and honest attempt to conceal the identity of all persons except the reporter. And he saw a distinct social value in the program as well. "The 'Big Story' program was of current public value in demonstrating how an alert reporter, who has an interest in seeing right prevail, may help an innocent man escape the unhappy consequences of a wrongful conviction, and perhaps might inspire some other reporter to greater efforts or some young person to embrace a newspaper career" (p. 835).

The *Bernstein* decision set the standard for several other similar cases. In California a federal court ruled in 1956 that a National Broadcasting Company radio production of "Dragnet" which re-enacted the events surrounding the escape of a black panther from a carnival was not an invasion of the animal owner's privacy. Again, the plaintiff's name was not used, and the material, while based on fact, was fictionalized.[18] The following year a federal district judge in Delaware used the decision in the *Bernstein* case to deny recovery in another action based on NBC's "Big Story." Judge Caleb M. Wright ruled that all the facts were in the public domain. "In matters of this nature courts must balance the right of the individual to be free from unwarranted exposure with the right of the public to have the uncensored dissemination of ideas whether they are purely newsworthy or form the basis of an entertainment medium." [19]

While courts were unanimous in refusing recovery for fictionalization where no identification was made, the use of the plaintiff's true name in a dramatization presented a different problem. In 1956, Kenneth D. Strickler, a United States Navy commander, was en route from Honolulu to San Francisco on a commercial airliner when the plane developed engine trouble and was forced to make an emergency landing in the Pacific. During the evacuation of the plane and prior to the Coast Guard rescue, Strickler played a heroic role in keeping passengers calm and organizing the survival efforts.

These acts were dramatized some months later on an NBC telecast. The story was embellished and fictionalized to some extent, but Strickler's real name was used. He brought suit in a California federal court, where District Judge Harry C. Westover ruled that the complaint stated a cause of action for invasion of privacy and the case should go to trial.[20] Note that the only difference between this case and the three discussed above is that the plaintiff's name was used. The implications of this point will be discussed shortly after another kind of fictionalization problem is noted.

FICTIONALIZATION AND THE DETECTIVE MAGAZINE

The detective magazine, if not peculiar to American society, is certainly typical of certain parts of it. Evolving as it did from the dime novels of the last century and through the *Police Gazette* of the early twentieth century, the detective magazine today is a slick, cheap disseminator of sensation and morbidity. While there are certainly gradations within the field, most are poorly produced and represent the worst in American journalism. Heading an army of police reporter and photographer stringers scattered across the nation, the editors of these publications give readers the sick and gruesome details of the nation's most sensational crimes. But to do a smooth job they sometimes have to compromise the truth. During the fifties the privacy law began to catch up with some of these compromises.

In 1945, Ralph H. Garner and Grace M. Smith went on trial in Virginia for the murder of Grace's husband, Frank, and were convicted. Before their appeal was heard, Triangle Publications presented to a national audience the sensational "facts" of the trial. In its publications, *Timely Detective Cases, Uncensored Detective,* and *Official Detective,* Triangle published stories entitled "Mystery of the Hanging Corpse," "Rope's End," and "Wayward Wives Make Merry Widows." In all three accounts Ralph and Grace were portrayed as the principal participants in the murder and also were depicted as adulterers. The couple, after their murder convictions were reversed by the Virginia Court of Appeals, sued Triangle for invasion of privacy.

The publisher claimed Mr. Garner and Mrs. Smith were public figures and as such, subjects of legitimate comment in the news. But Federal District Judge Irving Kauffman refused to grant the defendant's motion for a summary judgment. He ruled that the right to invade a person's privacy in order to disseminate public information did not extend to a fictional or novelized representation of a person, no matter how public a figure he or she might be.[21]

The *Garner* decision served as a precedent in two other similar suits during the decade. In both cases the story was fictionalized and the plaintiff's name was used in connection with a sensational crime. In one decision the judge ruled that the "story was in essence not a vehicle of information but rather a device to facilitate commercial exploitation." In the other the court ruled that "there is no difficulty in ascertaining that what plaintiff complains of is not news reporting, but the use of her photograph in connection with a 'story' with strong appeal to the idle and prurient." [22]

In two other contemporary cases, *Rohzon* v. *Triangle Publications* and *Jenkins* v. *Dell Pub. Co.*, courts refused to sustain actions based on similar fact situations.[23] The only difference was that in these two instances the stories involved were reportedly more accurate, so there was little fictionalization. In the *Jenkins* case Circuit Court of Appeals Judge William H. Hastie refused to accept the argument that the magazine was entertainment and consequently did not deserve protection from liability. Hastie wrote that in the modern mass media entertainment and news were mixed.

Few newspapers or news magazines would long survive if they did not publish a substantial amount of news on the basis of entertainment value of one kind or another. This may be a disturbing commentary on our civilization, but it is nonetheless a realistic picture of society which courts shaping new juristic concepts must take into account. In brief, once the character of an item as news is established, it is neither feasible nor desirable for a court to make a distinction between news for information and news for entertainment in determining the extent to which publication is privileged.[24]

If these five cases seem to lead to a contradictory and confusing standard, it is undoubtedly because fictionalization is the grayest of all the gray areas in the law of privacy. New York courts struggled with the concept of fictionalization for decades and, as will be seen in Chapter 11, have not yet resolved it. There is no firm legal definition of fictionalization. Do just a few inaccuracies constitute fictionalization? If not, how much inaccuracy is needed? Or is purposeful inaccuracy required? The list of questions could be virtually endless. Then, when a fair definition of fictionalization is arrived at, does this fictionalization automatically remove the material from the protected area? Or, as Judge Hastie said, must we expect entertainment and fictionalization in our news columns? There are obviously more questions than answers.

But despite the confusion, these cases do present at least one important guideline which reporters and editors should tuck away for later use. If a writer wants to fictionalize or dramatize a story, the safest course to take is to change the names of the participants. There have been no recorded decisions in which a publisher was held liable when there was no link made between the character in the drama or story and the plaintiff. Identification is a requirement of any successful suit; without it the plaintiff will lose. Therefore, if you fictionalize, do not identify. The question will thereby be kept from the hands of the most unpredictable participants in any lawsuit—the jury. If there is no cause of action, there is no jury trial. And if there is no identification, there is no cause of action.

X
Privacy Today:
From 1961 to the Present

Time works changes, brings into existence new conditions and purposes. Therefore, a principle to be vital must be capable of wider application than the mischief which gave it birth.

LOUIS BRANDEIS [1]

The development of the privacy law in the sixties reflected seventy years of growth both of the law and of a nation. The problems encountered were in some ways the same ones encountered in the preceding seven years. In other ways the questions raised during the sixties were unique.

For the first time the United States Supreme Court decided a suit involving privacy and the press. The high court's decision in *Time, Inc.* v. *Hill,* [2] handed down in January 1967, charted many new boundaries for the law, but left most scholars and jurists bewildered. Numerous old questions remained unanswered, and several new issues were raised in Justice William Brennan's sometimes confusing opinion. Many scholars hoped for a second Supreme Court ruling to illuminate the mysteries in *Time, Inc.* v. *Hill.* [3]

Elsewhere, privacy won recognition in five more states—Arkansas, Maryland, Delaware, South Dakota, and New Hampshire—bringing to thirty-four the number of American jurisdictions recognizing a legal right of privacy (thirty-three states and the District of Columbia). Courts in New York and in other jurisdictions re-evaluated problems involving consent, public records, and public interest. And privacy suits in at least three jurisdictions were affected by collateral but unrelated state statutes, such as retraction laws and open records provisions.

ARKANSAS AND MARYLAND RECOGNIZE PRIVACY

The story of the decade begins in the South, where Arkansas and Maryland both recognized the right of privacy in 1962 in two nonmedia cases. In Arkansas, a housewife brought suit against a photographer when one hundred and fifty thousand postcards bearing her picture were sent throughout the state. Mrs. Mary Dodd had hired the photographer to make her portrait in 1960, but did not consent to its use on the postcard, an advertisement for the photography studio.

The defendant admitted that Mrs. Dodd's photograph was used, but by mistake, for normally he obtained consent first. Supreme Court Justice Ed F. McFaddin affirmed the trial jury verdict in favor of Mrs. Dodd, ruling that "in an action like this one—for violation of the right of privacy—there may be such a recovery, just as in cases of willful and wanton wrong." [4]

The question of whether Maryland recognized the right of privacy was first raised in 1932 in *Graham* v. *Baltimore Post Co.*, an unreported Baltimore Superior Court ruling. [5] Knowledge of the facts in the case is incomplete, but it is known that Helen Graham's portrait was used in advertisements which appeared in the *Baltimore Post*, on many Baltimore theaters, and on advertising placards on taxicabs. When Mrs. Graham brought suit for invasion of privacy, the *Post* argued that its action was protected by freedom of the press. *Post* attorneys also asserted that because the advertising message was truthful, there could be no recovery. Justice Eugene O'Dunne dismissed both arguments in ruling for the plaintiff. "Truth of the matter published is . . . not a defense to the abuse of the right of freedom of the press which invades the right of personal privacy to which the plaintiff . . . is undoubtedly entitled." [6]

While this case constituted a recognition of sorts, official recognition by an appellate court did not come until 1962, in the case of *Carr* v. *Watkins*. Elmer Carr brought suit against three defendants—two police officers and a security officer at a government laboratory—because they had told his employer that Carr had been charged with child molesting in 1954. They had failed to add, however, that Carr had been cleared of the charges. On the basis of this incomplete report Carr had lost his job.

Justice Hall Hammond said he could find no record of recognition of the right of privacy in Maryland, but could see no reason why it should not be recognized in a proper case. Looking to precedent outside his state, Hammond noted that recovery was not usually allowed for an oral invasion of privacy, publication of some kind was normally needed. However, he said there was a small line of cases in which oral harassment of a debtor by a creditor constituted grounds for an action. He constituted: "We follow the cases last cited as to the sufficiency of an oral communication to support an action for invasion of privacy which has the other requisites." [7] Hammond ordered a trial to determine the pertinent details in the case.

RECOGNITION OF PRIVACY IN DELAWARE

The right of privacy was first asserted in Maryland's sister state of Delaware in 1960, but it was not recognized at that time. Judge Francis A. Reardon sued the Wilmington *News Journal* after it published remarks by local officials who were critical of the judge's policies. Reardon said his name was used without his consent. Justice Howard W. Bramhall ruled that even assuming Delaware recognized the right of privacy, Reardon did not state a cause of action. The article in this case, Bramhall said, was a legitimate report of a public hearing on a subject of great public interest—revival of the whipping post as a punishment for some crimes in the state. "The general purpose of protecting the right of privacy relates to one's private life, not when that life has become a matter of legitimate public interest." [8]

The whipping-post law was the center of controversy again in 1963 when John P. Barbieri brought suit against the same newspaper for reporting that he was the last person to feel the lash under Delaware's whipping-post law. The comment was made in a report of a state senate debate on whether whipping should be a mandatory punishment for certain crimes. Barbieri complained that the report that he was whipped in 1952 at the New Castle Correctional Institute was an invasion of privacy. He agreed that in 1952 he was a public figure because of his trial for breaking and entering and his subsequent punishment, and had at that time lost his right of privacy. But during the nine-year interim, Barbieri said, he reformed and was no longer in the public eye.

After announcing that Delaware did recognize the right of privacy, Supreme Court Justice Clarence A. Southerland wrote that he disagreed that the lapse of time in itself recreated or reinstated a plaintiff's right of privacy: "The right of the press to republish the unpleasant facts still exists if those facts are 'newsworthy,' i.e. if they still are of legitimate public concern." [9] The published statements concerning the plaintiff in this case were not actionable, he noted, "because the subject matter dealt with— the use of corporal punishment to deter crime—was one of acute public interest in this State during the year 1961. . . . It was a legitimate subject of public interest, and the plaintiff's connection with it—the last man to have suffered the penalty—had a real bearing on the matter" (p. 776).

Barbieri relied heavily on the 1931 California decision in *Melvin* v. *Reid* (see Chap. 6), arguing that the newspaper could have told his story without mentioning his name. But in a rare backhanded slap at a sister jurisdiction, Justice Southerland wrote that he was not at all impressed with the outcome of the thirty-two-year-old California case. "With deference to the California Court of Appeals, we must express a serious doubt whether the basis of the decision—the unnecessary and indelicate use of plaintiff's name—is a sound one on which to sustain an action for invasion of privacy. Such a rule would in reality subject the public press to a standard of good taste—a standard too elusive to serve as a workable rule of law" (p. 776).

A PUBLIC EMPLOYEE'S PRIVACY

South Dakota recognized the right of privacy in 1963 when Guy Truxes, a postal employee in Sioux Falls, brought suit against the Sioux Falls *Argus Leader* for using his picture on 23 October 1960 to illustrate a story on the state's elderly citizens and the financial problems posed by retirement. Below the picture of the plaintiff, who was shown sorting mail, was this caption: "GOVERNMENT SETS PACE—The Federal government, unlike most industries, maintains a retirement age of 70 instead of the usual 65. 'Many men are in their prime at 65,' says a government official. Sioux Falls postal employee Guy Truxes, 69, will retire Jan. 1 when reaching retirement age." The photograph was made with the knowledge and consent of the plaintiff, but Truxes argued that it falsely portrayed him as one of the state's elderly citizens plagued with financial hardship.

After announcing recognition of the right of privacy in South Dakota, Judge E. D. Roberts noted that in privacy suits courts were required to balance the interests of the public in the free dissemination of news and information with the rights of the individual to be protected from brash and unwarranted publicity. In this case, Roberts said, it was significant that the photograph was taken with consent after arrangements were made with the postmaster. "The taking of the photograph under these circumstances of a public employee while engaged in the discharge of his duties was not an infringement of his right of privacy." [10]

NEW HAMPSHIRE RECOGNIZES PRIVACY

New Hampshire was the last state to recognize the right of privacy during the decade. The plaintiff, Carl H. Hamberger, and his wife rented a house from the defendant, Clifford C. Eastman. A short time after moving into their home, the Hambergers discovered a microphone in their bedroom. The couple filed suit for invasion of privacy against Eastman when they found the wires from the device led to the landlord's home. New Hampshire Supreme Court Justice Frank R. Kenison ruled that "what married people do in the privacy of their bedroom is their own business," and added, "If the Peeping Tom, the big ear and the electronic eavesdropper (whether ingenious or ingenuous) have a place in the hierarchy of social values, it ought not to be at the expense of a married couple minding their own business in the seclusion of their bedroom. . . ." [11]

The various new kinds of listening and spying devices partially changed the face of privacy law during the decade. This change is underlined by the fact that two states, Maryland and New Hampshire, recognized the right in cases which did not involve publication. What happened was that the law of privacy, which until the fifties was linked primarily to the mass media, was beginning to undertake new forms to meet the social needs of the community. This trend had little or no effect on the law as it applied to the media. But there can be little doubt that in the future the law will expand even more to protect the individual from the many devious and reprehensible methods used for spying and information gathering.

PRIVACY ASSERTED IN IDAHO AND NEW MEXICO

Attempts were made in two other states to gain recognition of the right of privacy during the sixties. In Idaho, in another non-media suit, Curtis Peterson brought an action against the Idaho First National Bank for disclosing to his employer facts regarding his personal bank account. Justices C. J. Taylor and Joseph McFadden refused to recognize the privacy claim, ruling that "plaintiff's complaint fails to state a claim upon which relief can be granted," because an invasion of privacy required some kind of public dissemination of the matter.[12] The information had to go at least beyond Peterson's employer, the court said. However, the court did find that the bank could be held liable for breach of the implied contract to keep a depositor's account records confidential.

A more important case, because it involved the news media, was decided in New Mexico in 1962. On 15 July 1960 the *Albuquerque Journal* published this news item: "Richard Hubbard, 16, son of Mrs. Ann Hubbard, 532 Ponderosa NW, was charged with running away from home, also prior to date, several times endangered the physical and moral health of himself and others by sexually assaulting his younger sister. Court ordered a suspended sentence to the New Mexico Boy's Home on the condition he serve 60 days in the Juvenile Detention Home." [13] The news report was a verbatim copy of the official juvenile court record filed in the office of the district court. But Richard Hubbard had only one sister, Dolores, and she sued for invasion of privacy. She argued that the privilege of newsworthiness, which the newspaper claimed shielded the story, applied only to Richard, who was a public figure by virtue of his problems with the law. Justice James C. Compton disagreed, ruling that the newspaper account was accurate, newsworthy, and written "in a reasonable manner for a proper purpose" (p. 475). Justice Compton said it was unfortunate, but the plaintiff had become an involuntary public figure "caught up in the web of news and public interest" (p. 475).

WHAT CONSTITUTES CONSENT?

In previous chapters certain problems surrounding the defense of consent were discussed. But in the sixties several cases were litigated which point out the many shades of meaning of this deceivingly complex concept.

The first suit was filed in New York by Sam and Sally Schneiderman against the *New York Post* and the owners of the Berkshire Country Club. The management of the club had published an advertisement at least two times which reported the Schneiderman marriage and noted that the couple had met at the Berkshire Country Club. The defendants argued that although no written consent had been obtained, the plaintiffs had agreed to the use of their names as guests at the club. That kind of advertisement was a common practice, they claimed. Justice Louis L. Friedman of the New York Supreme Court ruled that the defendants were liable nevertheless. A single publication of the notice might have been considered an incidental use, but its reprint "exemplifies an effort towards soliciting and inducing readers to patronize the named country club." [14]

The same year the former personal manager of Jackie Gleason brought suit against the Columbia Broadcasting System in an attempt to stop the broadcast of a television show, "The Million

Dollar Incident," because he was named and portrayed in the program. The story, which depicted a fictional kidnaping of Gleason, did have a character representing the plaintiff, George "Bullets" Durgom. But CBS argued that Durgom had known about the broadcast for many months and had even helped the network in preparing its presentation. Certainly his actions must constitute consent, the network said.

Justice William C. Hecht, Jr., disagreed and ruled that the "right to enjoin a proposed use of a person's name for trade, without his *written* consent is absolute, regardless of the detriment resulting to the defendant. . . ." [15] He added that the network knew or should have known that they were including Durgom as a character at their own risk since the statute required his written consent.

In Louisiana in 1961 another consent question arose, but in this case the defendant had previously obtained the plaintiff's consent to use his picture in an advertisement. (Remember, only in the four states with privacy statutes is *written* consent *required*.) However, the consent had been given nine years earlier. Cole McAndrews had enrolled at the defendant's health studio in Baton Rouge in 1950 and after a few months of workouts had given proprietor Alvin Roy permission to use his "before" and "after" pictures in an advertisement. But Roy did not use the photographs until 1959. When the lawsuit was initiated, the health-studio owner argued that it was McAndrews' responsibility to revoke his consent if he no longer wanted the pictures used.

The Louisiana Court of Appeals disagreed with the defendant and ruled that a consent given in 1950 would not remain in effect indefinitely. Roy should have renewed the consent before he used the photographs. Judge Robert D. Jones wrote: "We are of the opinion that it would be placing an unreasonable burden on the plaintiff to hold he was under the duty to revoke a gratuitous authorization given many years before. As defendant was the only person to profit from the use of the pictures, then, under all the circumstances, it seems reasonable that he should have sought renewal of the permission to use the old pictures." [16]

The final case in this quartet was decided two years later in a Pennsylvania federal court and involved Boston Celtics basketball star Bill Sharman. Sharman, recipient of the National Basketball Association's most valuable player award in 1955, solicited modeling agencies to use his photograph in advertisements. His picture, not his name, was selected by the Ted Bates advertising agency for use in a Schmidt's Beer campaign. Sharman posed in a bowling alley, wearing a bright red bowling shirt and holding a bowling ball. After the photography session he signed a model release or consent form.

The Bates agency took the picture, retouched it by adding a bottle of Schmidt's Beer and a glass, and affixed the advertising copy. But the ad was not a testimonial and Sharman's name was never used. Shortly after the advertisement was published, Sharman filed suit, claiming that he did not know his photograph would be used in a beer campaign. He said that as a professional athlete the association with the beverage hurt his reputation. Also, citing the famous *Marboro* case (see Chap. 9), in which the New York Supreme Court ruled that even though a written consent was obtained from the plaintiff, substantial alteration of the photograph constituted a violation of the privacy law, he argued that his release was not valid because the picture had been altered by the addition of the beer bottle and glass. Judge Harold K. Wood was not sympathetic to the complaint, and ruled that there was no invasion of privacy. He said that consent was always a complete defense, adding: "In the case at bar, by execution of the release Sharman conclusively consented to the use of his picture." [17]

Consent is primarily a problem for the advertising man, not the newsman. But as a key defense in privacy suits, both its possibilities and its exceptions should be understood. In New York, Virginia, Oklahoma, and Utah, only written consent will stand up in court. In other jurisdictions, written consent, while not always required, is the safest kind to have. Consent does not last forever and, after many years, it may be necessary to renew consent before a photograph or picture may be used safely, especially if the consent was originally given gratuitously. Also, as underlined by the *Durgom* case, gratuitous consent may be revoked at any time —even the day before a broadcast. Finally, consent is not a license to use a picture or name in all possible ways. It is generally applicable only to the specific purpose for which it was given. If a broad consent is arranged, even this will not permit such changes as a major alteration of a photograph or portrait. As Justice Hecht ruled in the *Durgom* case, a court will assume that the defendant had knowledge of the requirement of the law before he acted. The plea, "We didn't know," is never sufficient.

NO FALSE-LIGHT SUITS IN CALIFORNIA?

The suggestion that the publication of a nondefamatory falsehood about an individual constitutes an invasion of privacy received a sharp setback in California in 1961. The case developed from a report published in the *Los Angeles Times* that Erwin P. Werner, city attorney during the 1930s, was to be married for the third time. Werner had served in city government during a turbulent political era. His first wife, Helen, during the twenties had won the sobriquet of "Queen Helen" because of her domination of Los Angeles politics. In the late thirties both Werner and "Queen Helen" were indicted during a liquor scandal in the city. He was acquitted, but Helen served ten months in jail for grand theft. Werner was ultimately disbarred, but was reinstated in 1954 by the California Supreme Court.

The *Times* marriage announcement recounted all of the above and more. Many old skeletons were dragged out of Werner's closets, and the account contained some inaccuracies. When he brought suit for invasion of privacy, the substantive legal problem involved Werner's status as a former public figure. Justice John J. Ford of the district court of appeals stated the question as "whether a person who has theretofore acquired the status of a public personage may claim an invasion of his right of privacy when a newspaper publishes an article about him, the subject matter of which is within the general scope of what is understood to be within the public domain, if such article contains false and misleading statements. . . ." [18]

But Ford never answered this question, for the court decided the case on a collateral issue. California, the justice noted, has what is called a retraction statute which governs court action when libelous matter is involved. Under the statute, if an individual believes he was libeled, he must ask that a correction be made by the offending publication before he files his lawsuit. If he fails to make this request, or if the correction is published, the plaintiff may not claim any recovery other than special damages or reimbursement for actual monetary loss.

Ford noted that Werner failed to request a correction of the *Times*'s story, and because he was unable to prove special damages, his libel suit against the newspaper failed. In addition, however, Ford asserted that the privacy suit was also governed by the provisions of the retraction statute. "In enacting section 48a of the Civil Code [the retraction statute], the Legislature declared the public policy of the state. . . . To extend the tort of invasion of privacy to the extent necessary to reach a determination that the appellant's [Werner's] amended complaint states a cause of action would be to ignore such declaration of public policy and dilute the effect of such legislation" (p. 123).

In other words, when the legislature approved the retraction statute, it declared that it was the state's policy to protect a publication from the costly damages of a libel suit by giving it an opportunity to correct the error which led to the suit. The ultimate publication of the truth was more important than giving the defendant a substantial monetary compensation for the largely unmeasurable damage to his reputation. Werner refused to give the *Times* the opportunity to correct its errors. By granting him recovery for the false publication under a different tort, that of privacy, the court would be sanctioning the evasion of the state's retraction statute.

The broad ruling by Justice Ford seems to preclude any recovery in California under the false light privacy category unless a retraction is at least requested. Whether a privacy action would stand if the request was denied, or if the correction was printed, is not clear from the opinion. However, it is clear that California has taken a first step to protect the press from the pitfalls of a false light privacy suit by extending the protection afforded to defamatory words to nondefamatory falsehoods as well.

The public figure defense was cited in litigation in California during the decade. John K. Carlisle, the first husband of Janet Helen Morrison, better known as movie actress Janet Leigh, brought suit against the magazine *Motion Picture* when it published the facts of the couple's teen-age marriage. Under the title, "Janet Leigh's Own Story—I Was a Child Bride at 14," the magazine told the story of their wedding in Reno, one-night honeymoon, and the subsequent annulment. There were some errors in the piece.

Carlisle attacked the publication with three arguments. First, he said he should not be put in the public spotlight, because he was not a public figure. Judge Philip Conley disagreed, stating that a corollary to the rule that public figures lose their right of privacy is that "people closely related to such public figures . . . to some extent lose their right to the privacy that one unconnected with the famous or notorious would have."[19] Conceding that he may have been a public figure when related to Janet Leigh, Carlisle argued that eighteen years had passed and surely he had moved from the spotlight in that time. Again Conley disagreed. "If the necessary elements which would permit the publication of factual matters are present, mere lapse of time does not prohibit publication" (p. 746).

Finally, Carlisle argued that even if he still was a public figure, the inaccuracies within the article destroyed the privilege of newsworthiness. Conley refused to accept this argument as well. "The mere fact that there are errors in the account does not constitute an invasion of privacy. . . . We do not believe that the imagination of the writer of the article as exercised here creates a tort that would not otherwise exist . . ." (pp. 747, 748). There would be no recovery for Carlisle, Conley said. The law of privacy must be restricted to protection of those with ordinary sensibilities, not the supersensitive. He also pointed out that the marriage and annulment were hardly private matters, as they were a part of the public record.

THE PUBLIC RECORD

It is virtually a maxim in the law of privacy that any report taken from the public record is privileged under the heading of newsworthiness. Yet circumstances can prevail that undermine the maxim, and dire consequences can result for the news media. A Florida case provides a clear example.

On 14 June 1958 the Tampa *Tribune* published, as usual, the circuit court docket entries under the heading of "News of Record." One portion of the docket, which is a public record, noted judicial commitment of persons for treatment as narcotic addicts. The following entry was included:

Suits Filed
State of Florida vs. Virginia Patterson,
Commitment of narcotic; James M. McEwen, Attorney

Orders and Decrees
The State of Florida vs. Virginia Patterson
Order of Commitment [20]

Miss Patterson had become addicted to demerol, a narcotic drug, during a physical illness. She sought voluntary commitment for treatment, and the court entered an appropriate commitment order. When she was rehabilitated from her addiction, she sued the *Tribune* for invasion of privacy; and the ensuing case, a nightmare of legal jargon, is a frightening example of how a well-meaning newspaper can run afoul of the law.

Section 28.21 of the Florida Statutes requires the clerk of courts to keep a progress docket, which is open to public inspection in absence of some specific prohibition. It was this docket the *Tribune* item quoted. However, another state statute, Section 398.18(1), restricts the inspection of the records of narcotic commitment proceedings. This law was enacted to permit addicts to come forward for treatment without the fear of publicity. The plaintiff argued that by publishing the docket record, the *Tribune* had publicly proclaimed that she was committed as an addict. The court agreed. Judge Jack F. White wrote: "The docket entries unquestionably disclosed the fact of commitment and the identity of the plaintiff as the one who was committed. In this situation we are constrained to the view that the entries became and were, in effect, part of the 'records' of the commitment proceedings within the spirit and intendment of the statute" (p. 625).

Judge White said publication of just the order of commitment was worse than if the entire record had been published, since that would have revealed the voluntary nature of the plaintiff's commitment. To the lay reader, he added, publication of the order alone might even suggest criminal dealings in narcotics.

The *Tribune* argued that since the order was included in the docket, it was assumed it was a public record. If there was a villain, the newspaper added, it was the clerk who failed to restrict inspection of the commitment orders as the statute commands. Unfortunately, the argument carried little weight. "The fact that information which is not in the public domain has been obtained innocently does not license a publisher, charged with the knowledge of the proscribed character of the information, to publish it further and thus compound the wrong" (p. 627).

It can be argued that the public-record maxim still holds true, because in this case the commitment order was not a part of the public record. Merely believing that an item is part of the public record, as the *Tribune* reporter did, is not sufficient to sustain a defense in a privacy suit. The old tort-law aphorism—it is not what you aim at, but what you hit—is a healthy reminder.

MORE EXTREME CIRCUMSTANCES

Mrs. Flora Bell Graham, the wife of a Cullman County, Alabama, chicken farmer, visited the county fair with her two children in October 1961. After being coaxed by her children, Mrs. Graham agreed to a walk through the fun house. Upon leaving the building air jets in a platform on which she was walking blew her dress up over her head. With the exception of her underclothing, her body was exposed from the waist down. As chance would have it, a photographer snapped a picture of the scene and it was published four days later on the front page of the local newspaper as a promotional news item for the fair. Needless to say, Mrs. Graham was displeased and she sued for invasion of privacy.

Several factors seemed to preclude recovery. In the first place, it was a news picture. Also, the photograph showed only the plaintiff's back. Her sons were in the picture, but only friends recognized the boys and made the connection. Finally, there was nothing private about the incident. It was witnessed by scores of persons at the fair and was certainly a public occurrence. But the Alabama Supreme Court was not disposed to decide the case in this fashion. "We can see nothing of legitimate news value in the photograph," Justice Robert B. Harwood said. "Certainly it discloses nothing to which the public is entitled to be informed." [21] To the argument that the incident had been a public one Harwood replied: "One who is part of a public scene may be lawfully photographed as an incidental part of that scene in his ordinary status. Where the status he expects to occupy is changed without his volition to a status embarrassing to an ordinary person of reasonable sensitivity, then he should not be deemed to have forfeited his right to be protected from an indecent and vulgar intrusion of his right of privacy merely because misfortune overtakes him in a public place" (p. 478). While this decision certainly went against precedent, by this time the reader should not be surprised, for this is the law of privacy we are discussing.

WHEN NEWSWORTHINESS IS NOT ENOUGH

Newsmen have long been faced with the dilemma of whether or not to publish the identity of a rape victim. While it has only been in recent years that some newspapers have begun to exclude these names, the problem is not at all settled. Those who favor publication argue that if the identity of a rape victim is excluded, the identity of the victims of all crimes should be excluded, and this practice would certainly not be in the public interest. They also argue that the innocent suspect charged with the rape may conceivably be aided if the public knows who brought the charges. The victims of many "rapes" often fabricate stories in order to hurt former boyfriends or suitors, or because of unexpected and unwanted pregnancies. Those who favor exclusion of identity also correctly point out that the victim of a vicious rape carries a lifetime stigma and publicity magnifies this problem. They also argue that a victim may be reluctant to report a rape if she knows that her name will appear in the newspaper.

At least four states have taken the discretion out of the hands of the editor by prohibiting the publication of the name or identity of a rape victim.* One privacy suit resulting from the violation of one of these statutes has been reported. Patricia Nappier and Maxine Gunter were employed by the state of South Carolina in 1961 as puppeteers who traveled from school to school presenting puppet shows on health education. The pair

* The four are Florida (Florida Statutes, Sec. 794.03, 794.04), Georgia (Georgia Statutes, Sec. 26–2105), South Carolina (South Carolina Statutes, Sec. 16–81), and Wisconsin (Wisconsin Statutes, Sec. 348–412).

became known as "The Little Jack Girls" because of their puppet's name; and the words, "Little Jack, Dental Division, South Carolina State Department of Health," were printed on the door of their state-owned station wagon.

In November 1961 the two girls were attacked and raped in Kingstree, South Carolina, and their attacker fled in the station wagon. The next day the wagon was found abandoned in Florence, South Carolina. Newsmen from a local television station, WBTW, filmed the wagon—including the door—and used pictures to supplement their story about the crime on the 6:30 and 11:00 P.M. newscasts. The wagon was identified as the one used by the two rape victims, who remained unnamed.

The two girls sued for invasion of privacy, arguing that because the television station violated the South Carolina statute prohibiting the naming of rape victims, it should be liable as well for civil damages for invasion of privacy. The defendant refused to admit that the girls were identified in the news film. Federal District Judge Charles C. Wyche dismissed the suit, noting the statute specifically said that it was a misdemeanor to *name* the victim. This wording was not ambiguous, he said; it was not capable of more than one meaning. The victims were not named, therefore there was no violation of the statute and there could be no award of civil damages.[22]

The plaintiffs appealed the decision, arguing that the televising of the words on the door of the station wagon did in fact name them, since "Little Jack" was a nickname which was applied to them throughout the state. The Fourth United States Circuit Court of Appeals accepted this argument and reversed Judge Wyche's decision. Judge Albert V. Bryan said that in the context of the case the word "name" was to be read as "the equivalent of 'identity.' Since the broadcast . . . sufficiently identified the victims other than by name, it transgressed the statute and trespassed on the plaintiffs' privilege of privacy." [23]

After losing this point, the television station then asserted that even if identification was made, the crime was a newsworthy event, one of great public interest. While the statute may have been violated, the privilege of newsworthiness certainly precluded a suit for invasion of privacy. Again Judge Bryan disagreed. "The . . . statute states an exception to the exemption.

No matter the news value, South Carolina has unequivocally declared the identity of the injured person shall not be made known in press or broadcast" (p. 505).

In the seventy-nine-year history of privacy law, this is perhaps the only reported example of a successful privacy suit based on what was clearly a newsworthy item. And of course the success of the suit grew from the statute rather than the law of privacy. In the three other states with similar laws—Georgia, Florida, and Wisconsin—similar suits might also be successful. Wisconsin would likely create the most difficult problem since the state does not recognize the common law of privacy.[24] Editors in all four states, however, must be wary of this one gaping hole in the defense of newsworthiness.

NEW YORK LAW

In addition to *Time, Inc.* v. *Hill* and *Spahn* v. *Julian Messner, Inc.,*[25] to be discussed fully in the next chapter, four other important cases were tried in New York during the early sixties. While setting the stage for the landmark decisions later in the decade, each in its own way contained a lesson in the law.

INCIDENTAL ADVERTISING

During the winter of 1957–58, Shirley Booth, academy-award-winning actress and television's "Hazel," was vacationing at Round Hill resort in Jamaica. A photographer from *Holiday* magazine, who was preparing a layout on the resort, received Miss Booth's permission to photograph her on the sunny beach. The picture story on Round Hill appeared in the February 1959 issue of *Holiday*. One photograph of Miss Booth, a color picture of her standing in neck-deep water and wearing a wide-brimmed, high-crowned straw hat, was used. Four months later the same picture was used in full-page advertisements for *Holiday* magazine in the *New Yorker* and *Advertising Age*. The picture filled all but the lower one-fourth of the page and was presented as a sample of the contents of the magazine. Beneath the photo was the caption, "Shirley Booth and chapeau, from a recent issue of Holiday." This was followed by advertising copy promoting the magazine. The actress brought suit against Curtis Publishing Company in New York on the grounds that it had used her picture for purposes of trade and advertising.

Curtis argued that the republication was a logical and necessary extension of the privilege of newsworthiness: news dissemination was not possible without the sale and distribution of the medium, and the sale and distribution was not possible without resorting to advertising revenue. The plaintiff based her case on the 1959 *Flores* v. *Mosler Safe Co.* decision (see Chap. 9) in which the plaintiff was granted recovery when his name, which first appeared in a news story, later appeared in an advertisement republishing the news item. The question, then, was whether the republication was incidental to the original newsworthiness privilege, and thus protected, or whether it constituted promotion of a collateral commodity, leaving the magazine open to suit.

A trial court awarded the plaintiff $17,500, but Justice Charles D. Breitel of the appellate division of the supreme court disagreed with the lower-court verdict. "Looking . . . to the policy of the statute, the vital necessity for preserving a strong and free press, and considering the practical objections to imposing too fine a line of demarcation in an inherently fluid continuum, it is concluded that the reproductions here were not collateral but still incidental advertising, not conditionally prohibited by the statute." [26] Because the photograph was republished to illustrate the quality and content of the magazine in which it originally appeared, the statute was not violated despite the advertising use. This decision was affirmed by the court of appeals later in 1962.[27]

Three years later the appellate division dismissed a complaint made by the University of Notre Dame and its president, Father Theodore M. Hesburgh, against Twentieth Century Fox Film Corporation. Notre Dame and Father Hesburgh attempted to restrain distribution and showing of a satirical film, *John Goldfarb, Please Come Home.* The motion picture was a farcical story about the university, the United States State Department, the Central Intelligence Agency, and an oil-rich mythical Arab kingdom of Fawzia. The plaintiffs argued that the film ridiculed both Notre Dame and its president and used their names for trade purposes. Justice Bernard Botein disagreed. He noted that Hesburgh's name was mentioned twice in the book (on which the movie was based), but was not used at all in the movie. Use of the name in the book was incidental, Botein ruled, and did not violate the statute. The university, he said, could not rely on the civil rights law because only living persons were protected under the statute.[28] The film, it might be noted, enjoyed the same degree of success as the plaintiffs.

UNAUTHORIZED BIOGRAPHY

In the mid-sixties Mary Hemingway and the estate of Ernest Hemingway brought a lawsuit against Random House Publishing Company in an attempt to stop the publication of the A. E. Hotchner book, *Papa Hemingway*. Hotchner, a successful author and playwright, had been a close and intimate friend of the Hemingways prior to Ernest's death. The friendship between the author and the widow continued—until he announced plans to publish his book, a biographical study of Hemingway from 1948, when Hotchner first met him, until his death in 1961. The book was described by New York Supreme Court Justice Harry B. Frank as a "subjective presentation from the vantage of the friendship, camaraderie, and personal experiences and adventures that the younger author shared with the literary giant." [29]

The suit was based on several complaints, one of which was invasion of privacy. Mary Hemingway asserted that her name, which was mentioned in various places throughout the book, was used for trade purposes. Justice Frank ruled against the plaintiff. He said that throughout the history of the New York statute "a book of biographical import such as is here involved" had never been held to be within the meaning of the term "for trade purposes. . . . Compelling public interest in the free flow of ideas and dissemination of factual information has outweighed considerations of individual privacy in conjunction with factual publications of such type, whether authorized or not . . ." (p. 535). Frank added that Mrs. Hemingway's status as the wife and widow of the Nobel and Pulitzer prize winner thrust her into the category of a newsworthy personality who, as a figure of public interest, is not protected by the statute.

THE MAD MONK

History holds a special place for those eccentric and unusual individuals who, through their words and deeds, drive sane men to extreme measures of conduct. Grigori Efimovich Rasputin was such a man. Born in 1871 in desolate Siberia, Rasputin gained favor at the St. Petersburg court of Tsar Nicholas II by the time he was thirty-four years old. His early training was with the Russian Orthodox church, but he found orthodoxy untenable and soon constructed his own eclectic faith. Soon after joining the court of Nicholas II and Alexandra in 1905, Rasputin won the respect of the tsarina. While his actual influence upon her has remained a controversy for decades, it is known that by 1913 or 1914 he had successfully persuaded Alexandra to play a more active role in the government.

The tsar turned aside most of his wife's requests until the last days of his reign. While radicals fomented revolution, the royal government was falling to pieces. Nicholas had difficulty finding honest men to serve in government and began accepting appointees recommended by Rasputin through his wife. Russian nobility, fearful of a governmental collapse, plotted to kill the monk, whom they considered an albatross around the neck of the royal government. On 31 December 1916 the plot was carried out and Rasputin died at the hand of an assassin. His death was too late, however, to save the failing government of the tsar.

In 1927, Prince Felix Youssoupoff, a member of the former Russian royal family, wrote a book in which he asserted that he was the mastermind of the assassination. Again in 1952, from his home in Paris, Youssoupoff wrote about the conspiracy aimed at ending the life of the monk. Details of the killing and the plot were included in both volumes.

On 5 January 1963 the CBS television network broadcast a play, *If I Should Die,* the story of the last days of the royal government in St. Petersburg and the murder of Rasputin. The authors claimed the play was historically correct, based largely on Youssoupoff's books. But it was a fictional drama: imaginary dialogue was added, and other details were changed. The exact number of inaccuracies the story contained became an issue at the trial that resulted from Youssoupoff's suit against the network for invasion of privacy.

Youssoupoff first sought a summary judgment because, he said, the mere addition of imaginary dialogue and the use of actors constituted fictionalization, thus removing the play from the privilege normally granted to news and information. Justice Abraham J. Gellinoff ruled that "the use of the drama form, with an actor impersonating the plaintiff and the scenery and the dialogue the product of the author's imagination, does not of itself, as a matter of law, convert privilege from responsibility under our civil rights law into liability." [30]

The case was then tried before a jury, but before submission for a verdict the defendant sought an appeal of the trial court's refusal of a summary judgment in its favor. The argument used by the network was based on a ruling from a 1964 libel decision, *New York Times* v. *Sullivan*.[31] The *Times* decision involved an advertisement in that newspaper by a civil rights group which was critical of the conduct of some members of the Birmingham, Alabama, city government. Basic inaccuracies were found in the assertions in the advertisement, and the *Times* was found liable in an Alabama court. The United States Supreme Court, however, ruled that such communication came under the protection of the First Amendment. Speaking for the court, Justice William J. Brennan, Jr., wrote that in order for a Birmingham city official or any public official to prosecute successfully a libel suit against a publication on the basis of untruthful statements, it was necessary to demonstrate actual malice on the part of the publisher. Actual malice was defined as knowledge beforehand that the information was false, or a reckless disregard of whether it was false or not. Shortly after the *Times* decision, the Second Circuit Court of Appeals extended this ruling in its dicta to include public figures as well as public officials; that is, a public figure must also demonstrate actual malice by the publisher before he may collect damages.[32]

In their appeal the CBS attorneys argued that the *Times* malice rule should be extended to the law of privacy. The defendant argued that Youssoupoff must show actual malice before any recovery could be allowed. The plaintiff's main contention with regard to inaccuracy was that his motivation for the murder was depicted erroneously and that his relationship with Princess Irina was sensationalized to "sexualize" the play. Under the CBS argument Youssoupoff should be required to show that these errors were made deliberately, or that the network was reckless in not attempting to ascertain the truth.

But this kind of evidence was not needed, for Justice Wilfred A. Waltemade refused to accept the argument made by the television network. He pointed out that the New York *Times* decision applied only to public officials, and the plaintiff was not in that category. Even accepting the federal court ruling which extended the malice rule to public figures, Waltemade wrote, a public figure is still entitled to privacy. "This court cannot believe that it was the intention of the United States Supreme Court to subject private citizens and public figures to broadside invasion of their rights of privacy. Any requirement that such an aggrieved person must establish malice as the basis for a successful prosecution of a right of action, would be an open invitation to scandalmongers, idle gossipers and keyhole peepers to spew their reckless and sordid stories with impunity." [33] The court refused the motion for a summary judgment for CBS, noting that the plaintiff presented enough evidence of fictionalization to the jury to make a prima facie case.

Waltemade's broad statement overruling any First Amendment question in the case must be regarded as rather shortsighted, for the argument he refused to consider became law two years later.[34] While it was too late for the network to reap the fruits of its original and ingenious plea, others would.

XI

The United States Supreme Court Takes Jurisdiction

The guarantees for speech and press are not the preserve of political expression or comment upon public affairs, essential as those are to healthy government. One need only pick up any newspaper or magazine to comprehend the vast range of published matter which exposes persons to public view, both private citizens and public officials.

JUSTICE WILLIAM J. BRENNAN, JR.[1]

The story of this chapter of the growth of the law of privacy began in the early 1950s at the James J. Hill home in Whitemarsh, Pennsylvania, a small suburb of Philadelphia. In the autumn of 1952 the Hills were part of that broad, nebulous category, typical American private citizens. On 11 September, however, this status changed when their lives were interrupted by three escaped convicts who held the family—James, his wife Elizabeth, and five children—hostage for nineteen hours. The ordeal with the convicts ended on 12 September when the family was released, unharmed.

Another ordeal began almost immediately, however, as newsmen from throughout the state and nation descended upon their home. Police apprehended the convicts in a widely publicized shoot-out which resulted in the death of two of the escapees. This made the Hills' story even better front-page news, and for days the public spotlight focused on the family. In an interview with newsmen, James Hill made it quite clear that the family was scared but was not mistreated during the nineteen hours. In fact, he noted that the convicts were quite polite and treated them courteously. The Hills attempted to avoid publicity as much as possible. For example, Mr. Hill refused an offer to appear on the Ed Sullivan show. In November the family left Whitemarsh, partly for business reasons, and moved to Old Greenwich, Connecticut. And the incident was slowly forgotten.

In the spring of 1953 Random House published a novel by Joseph Hayes entitled *The Desperate Hours.* The book told the story of the four-member Hilliard family, who were held captive by three convicts in their suburban home. In the novel the Hilliards suffered violence at the hands of the escaped prisoners. The father and son were beaten and the daughter was subjected to verbal sexual abuse. Later, the book was made into a play and a motion picture. It was the play, however, that was the root of the problem.

While the drama was in tryout in Philadelphia, *Life* magazine entertainment editor Tom Prideaux, working with director Robert Montgomery and author Joseph Hayes, conceived of sending the cast to the former Hill home in Whitemarsh and preparing a photographic layout. Hayes later revealed that while the Hill incident had triggered the writing of the novel, his story was not shaped by any single incident but was based upon several similar occurrences in California, New York, and Michigan. This subject, however, was not broached at the time of the photographing session by either Hayes or Prideaux.

The photographs were taken and the layout was published in the 28 February 1955 issue of *Life.* The headline proclaimed, "True Crime Inspires Tense Play." There were several pictures accompanied by some text which began:

> Three years ago Americans all over the country read about the desperate ordeal of the James Hill family, who were held prisoners in their home outside Philadelphia by three escaped convicts. Later they read about it in Joseph Hayes' novel *The Desperate Hours,* inspired by the family's experience. Now they can see the story re-enacted in Hayes' Broadway play based on the book, and next year will see it in a movie, which has been filmed but is being held up until the play has a chance to pay off.

The layout included photographs of the son being roughed up by one of the convicts, the daughter biting the hand of a convict to make him drop a gun, and the father throwing his gun through the door after his attempt to save the family was foiled. While it was obvious the persons pictured were actors, readers were nevertheless led to believe these scenes depicted the experiences of the Hill family. How the Hayes play became so closely associated with the Hill incident in the *Life* story is somewhat of a mystery. But it is known that at the time the layout was prepared, Prideaux had in his story file several newspaper clippings on the Hill incident which revealed its nonviolent character. In addition, the magazine editor also had a clipping from *The New York Times* in which Hayes stated that the book and play and film were not based on a single incident, but on various occurrences.

Hill brought suit in New York for invasion of privacy. He argued that the inaccuracies in the *Life* story constituted fictionalization, which was forbidden under the New York privacy statute. In the initial stages of the lawsuit there were several defendants in addition to Time, Incorporated, *Life*'s publisher: Hill also brought suit against author Hayes, the play production company, Paramount Pictures, Random House, and Pocket Books, Incorporated, which published a paperback version of the novel. But during the eleven years of litigation, defendants were dropped along the way until in the end only Time, Incorporated, remained.

As the trial began, Time moved that the complaint be dismissed because it did not state a cause of action; the story did not constitute a violation of the statute because it was not published for "advertising or trade purposes."

The New York Supreme Court disagreed. Justice Henry Epstein denied the motion, ruling that "*Life* created a wholly fictitious display for commercial advertising and trade purposes, using plaintiff's name and family as the basis for a true-life thriller." Epstein said that it was amply clear from Hayes's statements that his book and play were based on many incidents—not just the events surrounding the Hill family. He added: "The use of the plaintiff's former home in Pennsylvania gave the story a verisimilitude of truth and accuracy wholly unwarranted. The parallel column display of the plaintiff's incident and the play and picture do not warrant the conclusion that defendant Time, Inc. has been sedulous in its adherence to the concept of a 'free press' news story. The result is a piece of commercial fiction. . . ." [2] Epstein said the article constituted wholesale advertising for the book, play, and motion picture.

A jury awarded Hill $75,000 in damages. On appeal the appellate division of the supreme court sustained the jury verdict of liability, but ordered a new trial regarding damages. (At a new trial the judgment was reduced to $30,000.) Justice Harold A. Stevens, in one of the most conservative privacy opinions ever written by a New York justice, ruled that the article was an advertisement, published for trade purposes. "Although the play was fictionalized, *Life*'s article portrayed it as a re-enactment of the Hills' experience. It is an inescapable conclusion that this was done to advertise and attract further attention to the play, and to increase present and future magazine circulation as well. It is evident that the article cannot be characterized as a mere dissemination of news, nor even an effort to supply legitimate newsworthy information in which the public had, or might have a proper interest." [3] To the Time argument that the members of the Hill family were public figures who lost their right of privacy when they were thrust into the public eye, Stevens answered: "The passage of time tended to dim the public interest both because of other events . . . and because plaintiffs themselves avoided capitalizing on the occurrence. In other words, the occurrence had been relegated to the outer fringe of the public consciousness" (p. 489).

The appellate division decision was remarkable in two respects in light of prior New York case law construing the statute. Stevens' argument that *Life* used the Hill article to increase circulation, hence a trade purpose, does not square with the long line of precedents regarding news publications. As early as 1908 a New York court ruled that despite the sale of newspapers and news magazines for profit, use of material within these publications did not constitute a trade purpose. [4] This ruling was adhered to for decades prior to the *Hill* case. Certainly, the fact that the story was inaccurate weakened this defense. But, and this is another remarkable feature of the opinion, there was essentially only one error—that the Hill captivity inspired the book and the play. Did this inaccuracy deserve the label of fictionalization which, in the past, was reserved for instances in which many major errors reflected badly upon the plaintiff?

If Stevens' argument was accepted on a large-scale, freedom of the press would be severely endangered. Any legitimate news story which contained an error, however harmless, could be classed as fiction and could be placed outside the protective shield of newsworthiness. The appellate division ruling stood in stark contrast to the long tradition of rulings in New York which supported the concept of an unfettered press. In his dissent Justice Bernard Botein expressed concern about these aspects of the majority opinion. "Can it be said that such flaws are of so extravagant a nature as to convert into fiction an informative presentation of legitimate news? In my opinion not; we are in a domain where the lines may not be drawn so tight as to imperil more than we protect. . . ." Botein argued that to rule that a violation of the law may be established by a showing that a newsworthy item was published solely to increase circulation injects an "unrealistic ingredient" in the complex of the right to privacy and dangerously abridges the people's right to know. "In the final analysis," he said, "the reading public, not the publisher, determines what is newsworthy, and what is newsworthy will perforce tend to increase circulation." [5]

Time appealed the ruling to the court of appeals, but lost in a five-two memorandum decision. The publishing firm then appealed again to the New York Court of Appeals, this time arguing that the statute, as applied in this case, was invalid under the First and Fourteenth Amendments to the United States Constitution. Again, Time lost. [6]

With no other avenue left, the publisher sought a hearing by the United States Supreme Court, asserting that there was a substantial federal question involved—the magazine's guaranteed right of freedom of the press. The appeal for a hearing was based on two arguments. First, it was argued that the New York courts were imposing liability on publishers merely because the articles were factually inaccurate. Second, the magazine asserted that the rules pertaining to the standard of newsworthiness had not been measured by guidelines which satisfy the First Amendment. The Supreme Court many times in the past had refused to hear privacy suits involving the mass media.[7] This time, however, it was different. On 9 January 1967 the high court reversed the New York decision and ordered the case to be retried under a new standard.

Justice William J. Brennan, Jr., wrote the opinion for the court. Justices Potter Stewart and Byron White joined Brennan, while Justices Hugo Black and William Douglas concurred in a separate opinion. Justice John Marshall Harlan concurred in part and dissented in part, and Chief Justice Earl Warren and Justice Tom Clark joined Justice Abe Fortas in a separate dissent.

Brennan, it will be recalled, was the author of the famous *New York Times* v. *Sullivan* decision of 1964, discussed in Chapter 10. In that decision the Supreme Court ruled that for a public official to prosecute successfully a civil libel suit, he must demonstrate not only that the material was false but that the publisher had knowledge of its falsity before it was printed or that he demonstrated a reckless disregard of whether the matter was false or not.

Brennan now ruled in *Time, Inc.* v. *Hill* that the same guidelines must apply to the New York standards of inaccuracy and fictionalization. That is, in order for the Hill family to prosecute successfully their invasion of privacy claim, they must demonstrate that the editors of *Life* magazine knew beforehand that the play was not based solely on the single Whitemarsh incident, or that the publishers and editors exhibited reckless disregard in attempting to determine the truth or falsity of their story. (This new standard was the argument used by CBS in the *Youssoupoff* case.) Brennan wrote: "We hold that the constitutional protections for speech and press preclude the application of the New York statute to redress false reports of matters of public interest in the absence of proof that the defendant published the report with the knowledge of its falsity or in reckless disregard of the truth."[8] The justice refused to accept the argument that the article had no legitimate public interest. "One need only pick up any newspaper or magazine to comprehend the vast range of published matter which exposes persons to public view. We have no doubt that the subject of the *Life* article, the opening of a new play linked to an actual incident, is a matter of public interest" (p. 388).

Brennan then began to present the rationale for the decision, noting that the innocent error must be protected if the freedoms of expression are to have the "breathing space" that they need in order to survive. "We create grave risk of serious impairment of the indispensable services of a free press in a free society if we saddle the press with the impossible burden of verifying to a certainty the facts associated in a news article with a person's name, picture, or portrait, particularly as related to non-defamatory matter" (p. 389). He wrote that sanctions against either the innocent error or the negligent misstatement would present a "grave hazard" of discouraging the press from exercising the constitutional guarantees. "Those guarantees are not for the benefit of the press so much as for the benefit of all of us. A broadly defined freedom of the press assures the maintenance of our political system and an open society" (p. 389). The justice added that the constitutional guarantees could, however, tolerate sanctions against the calculated falsehood without significant impairment—thus the new standard was established.

Brennan said that the New York jury had not been properly instructed and called for a new trial to measure the actions of *Life*'s editors under the standard of knowing falsity or reckless disregard. He then took a backhanded swipe at Justice Harold A. Stevens' (of the appellate division, New York Supreme Court) opinion that because the article had been published for trade purposes, it did not deserve the traditional privacy protections. "That books, newspapers, and magazines are published and sold for profit does not prevent them from being a form of expression whose liberty is safeguarded" (pp. 396–97).

How broad and far-reaching is the Brennan opinion with regard to the law of privacy? This is an important question, and difficult to answer. It obviously doesn't apply to all privacy suits, since only a small percentage involve falsity. Whether the ruling in *Time, Inc.* v. *Hill* will be extended to all of the cases falling in the so-called false light category is not really clear. It would appear, by mere analogy, that it will protect defendants in all states, whether governed by common law or statute.

But Brennan was cautious in his opinion and in at least two places tried to restrict the sweep of the court's ruling. "We find applicable here the standards of knowing or reckless falsehood . . . only upon consideration of the factors which arise *in the particular context* of the application of the New York statute in cases involving private individuals" (emphasis added) (p. 390). And, he added, "any possible difference with us as to the thrust of the constitutional command is narrowly limited in this case to the failure of the trial judge to instruct the jury that a verdict of liability could be predicated only on a finding of knowing or reckless falsity in the publication of the *Life* article" (p. 397). What is certain is that the decision is thrust at the fictionalization concept within the New York law, and henceforth all plaintiffs will be asked to bear a greater burden of proof. Since New York is responsible for about 40 percent of privacy cases, the *Time Inc.* v. *Hill* ruling will have a significant impact on the law even if courts outside the Empire State refuse to add the decision to their case law.

As noted previously, there were dissents. Justice Fortas led the way with a long, and often confusing, criticism of the majority opinion. He made three major points, but did not pursue any one of them with great vigor. Consequently, the reader is left with mixed impressions after reading the dissent. Fortas was distressed by the majority's lack of support of the right of privacy. "The Court today does not repeat the ringing words of so many of its members on so many occasions in exaltation of the right of privacy" (p. 416). While he did not completely disagree with the new standard enunciated in the Brennan opinion, Fortas insisted that it should be applied only where political personalities or issues were involved. He added that "the greatest solicitude for the First Amendment does not compel us to deny to a State the right to provide a remedy for reckless falsity in writing and publishing an article which irresponsibly and injuriously invades the privacy of a quiet family for no purpose except dramatic interest and commercial appeal" (p. 415).

Finally, he argued that the trial court had used guidelines similar to the new standard of falsity when measuring *Life* magazine's liability. "A jury instruction is not abracadabra," Fortas wrote. "At its best, it is simple, rugged communication from trial judge to a jury of ordinary people, entitled to be appraised in terms of its net effect . . ." (p. 418). He believed that if the core of the instructions was read in this perspective, it was sufficient to meet the majority's test, and the trial court's decision should be affirmed.

Fortas, who was joined in his dissent by Chief Justice Warren and Justice Clark, ably supported both virtues—the right of privacy and freedom of the press—in his opinion. The support of two conflicting rights is something which can be done in a dissent, but not in a majority opinion. But since all three of these members have left the Supreme Court, the Fortas dissent offers little aid in predicting how a future privacy case might be treated by the nation's high court.* Justice Harlan settled on a position between the Brennan and Fortas arguments. Harlan said that he believed that if the plaintiff could show negligence on the part of the defendant, rather than reckless or knowing fictionalization, the federal constitutional requirements would be met.

Time, Inc. v. *Hill* was assailed and hailed in the months after it was announced. Some writers said the decision threatened the entire law of privacy. But these authors evidently misunderstood the decision.[9] The first real test of the ruling came in New York, in December 1967, where baseball star Warren Spahn was attempting to stop the publication of his unauthorized biography.

SPAHN v. JULIAN MESSNER, INC.

The *Spahn* case began in the early sixties when author Milton J. Shapiro and publisher Julian Messner, Incorporated, announced the forthcoming publication of *The Warren Spahn Story*. Shapiro had based his biography on secondary sources, never attempting to talk to Spahn, his family, friends, or even other baseball players. There were many inaccuracies in the story, generally exaggerations of the baseball star's prowess. It made him appear to be a war hero, which he really was not; it erroneously pictured his father as the dominant figure who led Warren to baseball; and it fictionalized the impact of the elbow

---

* Justice Clark resigned in 1967, to make way for the appointment of his son, Ramsey, as United States Attorney General. Justice Fortas resigned in May 1969, after charges of improper conduct were leveled against him. Chief Justice Warren retired at the end of the 1968–69 court term.

injury (Shapiro referred to it as a shoulder injury throughout the book) on Spahn's career. Other embellishments, including many pages of fictional dialogue, seemed to place the book outside the normal protection granted to biographies.

The author and the publisher admitted that the biography was fictionalized, but argued that because the book was designed for juvenile readers, fictionalization was necessary. The case was tried before the Supreme Court ruling in *Time, Inc.* v. *Hill* was handed down, so the defendants relied upon the New York *Times* rule, arguing that the United States Constitution protected even false material published without malice. They also contended that Spahn was a public figure who enjoyed no right of privacy.[10]

As in the previously discussed *Youssoupoff* case (see Chap. 10), the New York courts refused to accept the argument based on the New York *Times* rule. Spahn, they said, was not a public official, which was the only category of plaintiff included in the libel ruling. To the assertion that Spahn was a public figure who had no right of privacy, Justice Charles D. Breitel of the New York Supreme Court's Appellate Division answered: "It is true, as it ought to be, that a public figure is subject to being exposed in a factual biography, even one which contains inadvertent or superficial inaccuracies. But surely, he should not be exposed, without his control, to biographies not limited substantially to the truth. The fact that the fictionalization is laudatory is immaterial." [11] After losing at all levels within the state, Messner and Shapiro appealed to the United States Supreme Court, and in May 1967 the New York decision was vacated and remanded to the court of appeals for further consideration in light of *Time, Inc.* v. *Hill.*[12]

On the second time around the court of appeals reached the same conclusion: Messner and Shapiro were liable for invasion of privacy, even in light of *Time, Inc.* v. *Hill.* Judge Kenneth B. Keating, who wrote the opinion, noted that "an examination of the defendant's own admission that 'in writing this biography, the author used the literary techniques of invented dialogue, imaginary incidents, and attributed thoughts and feelings' . . . clearly indicates that the test of *New York Times* v. *Sullivan* and *Time, Inc.* v. *Hill* has been met." [13] Keating said that the trial judge found gross errors in the book. Shapiro's research amounted to examination of a few secondary sources, he added, and if these interfered with the fictional story line they were ignored. "To hold that his research effort entitles the defendants to publish the kind of knowing fictionalization presented here would amount to granting a literary license which is not only unnecessary to the protection of free speech but destructive of an individual's right—albeit a limited one in the case of a public figure to be free of the commercial exploitation of his name and personality" (p. 129).

The question, on its face, seemed simple enough, especially since both author and publisher admitted fictionalization in order to capture the juvenile market. But at least one justice on the court of appeals did not accept Keating's reading of the Brennan opinion in *Time, Inc.* v. *Hill.* And in his dissent Judge Francis Bergan suggested an interpretation of the *Time* decision which, if accepted, would dramatically change a great portion of the law. After arguing that the case should have been sent back to trial court for an examination of the plaintiff's right to recover based on a showing of calculated falsehood, Judge Bergan then added: "It does not seem probable, reading Hill and New York *Times* together, that fiction alone concerning a public figure, actionable under the New York statute, is any longer actionable" (p. 131). What was the new standard? Bergan suggested: "It should be held that as to a public figure willingly playing that role, the New York privacy statute gives no protection against fictionalization not shown to hurt him and not shown designed to hurt him" (p. 131). The judge felt that the decision should be reversed.

The key word in Bergan's suggestion is "hurt." What is meant by the use of this word? Is mere commercial exploitation of the plaintiff's name—in a sense taking money out of the plaintiff's pocket—action which will "hurt" him? Or must this hurt be directed against his reputation, that is, must it lower the plaintiff in the esteem of his friends and fans? But such an action would be libel, not invasion of privacy. Or would just the publication of nondefamatory lies or untruths about the plaintiff satisfy the standard of "hurting" the plaintiff? Bergan's intention is not at all clear.

But the judge did make two things clear. In his opinion, the protection of *Time, Inc.* v. *Hill* extends only to public figures. He also asserted that any action which may "hurt" the plaintiff must be intentional action, not mere negligence. With regard to public figures and privacy, at least Judge Bergan suggests that the old tort law maxim—it is not what you aim at, but what you hit—is no longer applicable. The plaintiff must not only show that he was hit, but that he was the target as well.

Dissents provide interesting food for thought, but usually that is all. Those scholars who take great stock in dissents often forget that the caution which normally accompanies the framing of a court opinion is frequently abandoned by the dissenter. He is not writing law, he is setting no precedent, but is merely outlining his opinion, usually in bold and dramatic fashion. The dissenter is generally a free spirit and he knows that his proposals will not reverberate as a majority opinion will in courtrooms across the nation.

But for a time there was a possibility that Judge Bergan's dissent might become something more than interesting legal grist. On 14 October 1968 the United States Supreme Court agreed to hear the appeal by Messner and Shapiro that their constitutional rights had been violated by the second New York ruling. In its short memorandum opinion noting probable jurisdiction, the court asked attorneys on both sides to direct their arguments toward the question "whether the injunctive relief provided in the final judgment entered September 3, 1964, in the Supreme Court for the County of New York constitutes an unconstitutional restraint upon publication." [14]

Legal scholars interested in the orderly development of the law of privacy saw the *Spahn* suit as an opportunity for the high court to clear up some of the questions left unanswered in the earlier *Time* ruling. The notion that the high court might support the ideas of Judge Bergan (that some kind of intentional injury to the plaintiff by the defendant was now needed to sustain a privacy action) fascinated many. A decision such as that certainly would have turned the law on its head. But the new Supreme Court ruling never came forth, as the litigants settled the matter outside of court. Spahn consented to vacating the unfavorable New York judgment and the dismissal of the complaint with prejudice. Defendant Messner agreed to waive all costs. The dismissal of the appeal to the United States Supreme Court naturally followed.[15]

The further development of the law of privacy awaits, in large measure, a second ruling on the problem by the United States Supreme Court. Since the requested arguments in the Spahn appeal were to be directed toward the provisions of the New York law which grant injunctive relief, the question arises: Was the court ready to strike the injunctive process from the law of privacy, finding it in conflict with the First Amendment guarantees which prohibit prior restraint of a publication? American courts will not enjoin the publication of a libel—they never have. It is logical to argue that the same rule should apply to invasions of privacy. Such a decision would still leave plaintiffs with the opportunity to seek damages for invasions of their privacy.

Time, then, will tell. Hopefully, the nation's high court will soon have an opportunity to clarify many of the questions left after *Time, Inc.* v. *Hill* and also illuminate the reasons for its acceptance of the Spahn appeal.

OTHER ACTIONS SINCE *TIME, INC.* v. *HILL*

Several privacy cases have been reported since the *Time, Inc.* v. *Hill* ruling in 1967. Decisions in Oregon, Georgia, New York, the District of Columbia, Michigan, Massachusetts, Minnesota, Tennessee, South Carolina, and California have all cited the Supreme Court decision, confirming that its impact is being felt beyond the New York state line.[16] Courts have generally followed the interpretation given by Judge Keating in the *Spahn* case, stressing the criteria of knowing or reckless falsity. Of the decisions, a 1968 New York ruling is the most interesting, and generally represents the thrust of court opinions since *Time, Inc.* v. *Hill*.

The plaintiff in the suit was Rosemont Enterprises, Incorporated, a firm established by the close associates of Howard Hughes when it was learned that author John Keats and Random House were planning to publish an unauthorized biography of the financier. The complaint against Keats and Random House was based on the ground that Rosemont had acquired exclusive rights to "exploit commercially in any manner the name, personality, likeness or the life story or incidents in the life of Hughes." Rosemont argued that the unauthorized biography would exploit the name and likeness of the multimillionaire and would constitute an invasion of his privacy. An injunction stopping publication of the book was sought.

That the suit was built on a flimsy foundation is fairly obvious. But in his desperate attempts to remain a man of mystery, Hughes could afford the luxuries of ill-founded suits, and Keats and Random House were forced into court to defend their actions. The New York Supreme Court, however, had little patience with the plaintiffs.

Noting that the permissible limits of the right of privacy had been "clearly and decisively drawn" in the *Time* ruling, Justice Harry B. Frank ruled that a truthful account of an individual's life may not be suppressed. He pointed out that Justice Brennan, in *Time, Inc.* v. *Hill,* had also ruled "no redress is available even for material and substantial falsification in such reporting in the absence of proof that the report was published with knowledge of its falsity, or in reckless disregard of the truth. This burden upon the individual, even of false exposure, is held to be 'an essential incident of life in a society which places a primary value on freedom of speech and press.' " [17]

Frank said that there was no showing of any falsity at all in the plaintiff's complaint and the mere fact that the book would be published for profit did not constitute a trade purpose. "The publication of a newspaper, magazine, or book which imparts truthful news or other factual information to the public does not fall within 'the purposes of trade' contemplated by the New York statute, even though such publication is published and sold for a profit" (p. 128). Finally, Frank pointed out that only Howard Hughes could allege an invasion of Howard Hughes' privacy and the corporation had no standing to do so.

Two additional recent decisions deserve mention. *Holmes* v. *The Curtis Pub. Co.* shows quite graphically that lower courts are applying the same broad definition of the "public interest" in the application of the *Time, Inc.* v. *Hill* rule as they have in the past in defining public interest as an aspect of the defense of newsworthiness. The case involved a *Saturday Evening Post* feature on the control of gambling casinos in the Bahamas by crime syndicates. A group picture taken at the blackjack tables included the plaintiff, James Holmes. The caption, which did not identify Holmes, read: "High-rollers at Monte Carlo [the name of the casino] have dropped as much as $20,000 in a single night. The U.S. Department of Justice estimates that the casino grosses $20 million a year, and that one-third is skimmed off for the American mafia 'families.' " [18]

Plaintiff Holmes argued that the picture, which was taken secretly, embarrassed him by suggesting to readers he was either a heavy gambler or a syndicate man. District Judge Charles E. Simons, Jr., agreed that Holmes, an "innocent tourist whose picture was taken without his consent" (p. 526), was by no means a public figure. But, he added, the *Time, Inc.* v. *Hill* standard of falsity or reckless disregard did apply to all matters involving the public interest, and the *Post* article certainly fell within that category. The plaintiff would have to prove that the *Post* had been reckless in its inclusion of Holmes in the picture.

The second suit involved documentary film maker (*Hospital* and *Law and Order*) Frederick Wiseman. In 1965 Wiseman asked for permission to make a documentary film at the Massachusetts Correctional Institute at Bridgewater, a facility housing insane persons charged with crimes. Wiseman told Massachusetts authorities his film would be about three persons—an adult inmate, a youthful inmate, and a correctional officer—and would attempt to illustrate the various services performed (medical, punitive, rehabilitative) at the institute. Permission was granted by the state in 1966 after Wiseman agreed to protect the rights of the inmates by photographing only those who were legally competent to sign written releases. Wiseman also agreed that the film would not be released without the approval of the Massachusetts commissioner of correction, John A. Gavin, and the superintendent of the Bridgewater institute, Charles W. Gaughan.

The production, named *Titicut Follies* by Wiseman, was completed late in 1966. But the state refused to approve the film for release. Authorities complained that the film was a commercial exploitation of the lives of many persons at the institute and that it was an invasion of privacy of the many inmates who were photographed by Wiseman. Evidence presented at the trial revealed that of the sixty-two inmates identified in the film, only twelve had signed releases. Most of the others were not legally competent to do so. Also, the trial court found that many of the scenes showed inmates nude and in "situations which would be degrading to a person of normal mentality and sensitivity." [19]

Despite good "reviews" of the film after showings to groups of educators and students, the trial court granted the injunctive relief sought by the state. This action was upheld by the Massachusetts Supreme Judicial Court, even though that state has never officially recognized the existence of a legally protected right of privacy. Confronted with this argument, Justice R. Ammi Cutter ruled: "We think, in any event, that Mr. Wiseman's massive, unrestrained invasion of the intimate lives of these state patients may be prevented by properly framed injunctive relief. The Commonwealth has standing and a duty to protect reasonably, and in a manner consistent with other public interests, the inmates from any invasions of their privacy substantially greater than those inevitably arising from the very fact of confinement" (p. 615). Without recognizing a legal right of privacy in Massachusetts, the court still banned the Wiseman film on privacy grounds. Weighing heavily against the film maker was his violation of the original agreement to get valid releases from all subjects who were photographed.

Wiseman sought relief from the United States Supreme Court on First Amendment grounds, but the high court in June of 1970 refused to hear the appeal.[20] The Massachusetts court did, however, give Wiseman permission to show the film to specialized audiences of students, legislators, educators, and those who study correctional problems. The court said showing the film to persons who have a serious interest in rehabilitation would have a different effect on the inmates than showing it to satisfy the curiosity of the general public. Justice Cutter said that the value to the public interest in showing the film to specialists outweighed the harm done to the privacy of the inmates.

A CRUCIAL DECADE

The era of the 1960s has probably been the most important in the growth of the law of privacy since its inception in 1890. With United States Supreme Court recognition of the body of law which had developed during the preceding seventy-nine years, privacy truly came of age.

More important, however, was the institution of constitutional protections for the publication of truthful accounts of news and information in the public interest. For years courts throughout the land took similar steps under different guises. Material was exempt from action because it was newsworthy, because it had legitimate public interest, because it was of public concern. Throughout the years a distinct First Amendment philosophy or flavor developed in the great mass of case law on privacy. Schooled in a tradition which predates our nationhood, judges and justices generally placed freedom of the press above the individual right of privacy. That in the 1960s courts began labeling this accurately as a constitutional guarantee is a historic development in the growth of the law.

XII

Freedom and Privacy

A consideration of the limits of the right of privacy requires the exercise of a nice discrimination between the private right 'to be let alone' and the public right to news and information; there must be a weighing of the private interest as against the public interest.

JUSTICE PHILIP CONLEY [1]

In 1905 a Georgia Supreme Court justice predicted that the day would come when legal scholars would marvel that at one time eminent and able American judges refused to recognize the existence of a legal right of privacy.[2] It is appropriate to begin this summary of the law by noting that the day has not yet arrived; in fact, during the current decade, arguments have broken out within the legal profession over the necessity and worth of the right of privacy. Harry Kalven, an important legal scholar, wrote in 1966: "The lack of a legal profile and the enormity of the counterprivilege converge to raise for me the question of whether privacy is really a viable tort remedy. The mountain, I suggest, has brought forth a pretty small mouse." [3] Other writers, while perhaps not as critical as Kalven, have nevertheless expressed the same concern over the state of the law and what some individuals call the questionable need for the tort remedy.

The attempt to track this "small mouse" in the past eleven chapters surely reveals the amorphous quality of the right of privacy—even when applied only to the American press. It is difficult to extract principles from the law, principles which have remained consistent during the development of the right of privacy. The indefinitive nature of the tort is partly the result of its relative youth; compared to libel, for example, privacy is still in its developmental stages. The inconsistency also results, however, from the use by many courts of a sympathy or mores test to determine the liability of the news media. *Melvin* v. *Reid* (see Chap. 6) and *Barber* v. *Time* (see Chap. 7) are the two most famous examples of this test. A newspaper or magazine is free to report on newsworthy events or persons just as long as it does not use extremely bad taste. At that point the plaintiff gains the sympathy of the court, and doctrines and principles are pushed aside in favor of more personal considerations. This unpredictability not only confuses the layman but has given the tort a bad name among legal scholars as well.

Many persons are still uncertain why a plaintiff is compensated when his name or picture is used for trade purposes, such as in an advertisement. Is it because the individual has suffered on account of the public exposure? Or is it because he was not paid for the use of his property, that is, his name or his face, to publicize and sell a commercial item? Some leading decisions have been based on this last argument.[4]

Finally, the many hybrid varieties of invasion of privacy have added to the amorphous quality of the law. The authors of *American Jurisprudence,* a national legal encyclopedia, commented while attempting to assess the nature of the right that the kinds of cases in which privacy has been recognized "vary so widely that it might be concluded that this supposed right is nothing more than a catch-all to take care of the outer fringes of tort and contractual liability. . . ."[5]

With these problems inherent in the law of privacy, any attempt to sum up, to put the law in a meaningful perspective, is risky at best. Privacy is a perverse creature and at times defies explanation. Yet, for this study to be meaningful, some kind of general summary is required. It is with these conditions in mind that I offer this analysis.

THE HISTORICAL BACKGROUND

In many ways America in 1890 was ripe for the idea that privacy was a value worth protecting by law. The growth of the nation's urban areas and its press presented conditions that lent themselves to the development of the philosophies inherent in the right of privacy. It is surprising that the idea, presented so forcefully by Louis Brandeis and Samuel Warren, did not catch on more rapidly. But the law evolves slowly. And when a new concept, such as privacy, conflicts with other important social values, such as the free dissemination of news, a slow evolution presents the best means to evaluate the various claims involved.

It seems fairly certain now that "The Right to Privacy" was written at the urging or insistence of Samuel Warren because of his "deepseated abhorrence" of the coverage of Boston social life —especially news of social gatherings at his home—by the city's newspapers. But in their appraisal or characterization of the Boston press, Warren and Brandeis overstated their case, painting an unrealistic portrait of late nineteenth-century journalism. The attack was intemperate and at least partially ill-founded. The Boston press of 1890 deserves a better epitaph than that prepared by Warren and Brandeis.

The legal analysis presented by the two young attorneys, while impressive, was marred by their forceful condemnation of the press. Consequently, the argument was uneven. While parts were brilliant, other sections were weak, supported by assertion rather than basic case law or doctrine. Clark C. Hauighurst, editor of *Law and Contemporary Problems* in 1966, accurately noted: "Their work was thus something of a lawyer's catharsis rather than objective scholarship or judicial craftsmanship, and the law has never absorbed the privacy concept comfortably or made it altogether its own." [6]

The argument by Warren and Brandeis that the right of privacy was merely a simple extension of the common law proved fallacious as courts struggled to recognize the tort. Development of the right within the legal system was slow. Only seven states accepted the common law right of privacy in the forty years following publication of the article. The vast majority of case law in that period was the result of the New York privacy statute, which was based on some principles foreign to the Warren-Brandeis argument.

But the two attorneys were responsible for important parts of the profile of the tort. Restrictions they suggested in the application of the law remain essentially intact today. For example, they argued that privacy should not prohibit the publication of information in the public interest. While the two attorneys extended their privilege only to information about public officials and candidates for public office, and American courts have formulated a much broader standard, the public interest concept remains a key defense in a privacy action. Warren and Brandeis asserted that the law should not redress invasions of privacy by oral publication, and with a few exceptions this is good law today. Also, the pair suggested that consent was a complete defense, and in general this idea has been absorbed into the common law.

But despite these instances of shaping the tort, the basic principle suggested by Warren and Brandeis has never been successfully incorporated into the law. The kind of publication which prompted the proposal—news about the private affairs of private individuals—has rarely been used as the basis of a successful privacy action. The famous *Sidis* case (see Chap. 6), in which the boy genius was unable to stop the further investigation into his private life, presents a classic example. In this respect the impact of "The Right to Privacy" has been overestimated: its primary goal was never attained.

A great deal of adverse comment about the "yellow press" of the late nineteenth and early twentieth centuries has been published. Yet legal actions to correct these so-called evils really accomplished nothing. In 1929 law professor George Ragland wrote in the *Kentucky Law Journal:* "We might have expected that with the advent of the tabloid and similar journalism the right of privacy would have been seized upon as a much needed protection. But curiously enough this has not been the avenue of pre-eminent development. Along with the rise of this type of journalism there has come a corresponding and parallel indifference on the part of the public to its inroads on privacy." [7] The public indifference noted by Ragland in 1929 has been replaced today by concern for the right of privacy. But the press is not the villain; in fact, the press is often an ally in the fight against snooping, bugging, personality testing, and the many other devious attacks upon individual privacy.

Finally, the law of privacy has expanded to include many ideas and concepts not considered and probably not even envisioned by Warren and Brandeis. Some aspects of the right of privacy today bear no resemblance whatsoever to the principles outlined in their proposal. The concept of fictionalization, or nondefamatory falsehoods, for example, cannot be found within the pages of the Warren-Brandeis article. Yet today this is one of the most active areas of the law.

In 1929 another *Harvard Law Review* contributor asked: Has the Warren-Brandeis essay been as fruitful in its results in case law as in its contribution to legal analysis? [8] The answer is No. The right of privacy developed beyond and outside the limits set by Warren and Brandeis. Despite its deserved reputation as an important pioneer law review article, the impact of "The Right to Privacy" on the development of the law was limited.

EXPANSION OF THE LAW

The law of privacy developed slowly until the 1930s and 1940s, when several factors added impetus to the growth of the law. Some of these factors were as important in the development of the right of privacy as the original Warren-Brandeis proposal. The New York statute, approved in 1903, provided a volume of case law on privacy which enhanced expansion in other states, even though the New York litigation concerned only the state's narrow protection of the individual's right to be let alone. Up to 1930 the majority of reported cases were litigated in New York State, which still reigns as the privacy capital of the nation.*

---

* About 600 cases provided the basis for this study. Of this total, between 350 and 450 can be regarded as true invasion of privacy suits, depending upon how an invasion of privacy is defined. The remainder were actions based on copyright violations, unfair competition, libel, and other adjacent legal areas. Using the base figure of 350 privacy suits reported during the past 82 years, 149 of these were litigated in New York. Following New York, California reported 20 suits, Georgia and Kentucky each reported 15, and Pennsylvania reported 14. Again, of the 350 total, 216 involved the mass media, broadly defined to include

An increase in the number, size, and varieties of mass media also stimulated the growth of the law. In 1890 only magazines and newspapers could be used to invade an individual's privacy. The addition of motion pictures, radio, and television offered new means of committing the wrong. During the thirties the tort of privacy was officially recognized in the monumental *Restatement of the Law of Torts.*[9] This recognition undoubtedly lent respectability to the right of privacy and probably resulted in more actions. Finally, a series of law review articles, capped by Louis Nizer's review of privacy in 1940,[10] provided scholars and, more importantly, practicing attorneys with information about the law. As more persons learned of the legal right of privacy, more suits resulted.

The growth of the law accelerated, reaching what appears to be its zenith in the fifties. The number of reported actions tapered off during the sixties. Currently, the right of privacy is legally protected in thirty-three states and the District of Columbia. In four of these states—New York, Oklahoma, Utah, and Virginia—the law is governed by statute; the rest use the common law as a basis for any action. Four states—Rhode Island, Nebraska, Texas, and Wisconsin—have specifically refused to recognize the right of privacy. Courts in these states have ruled that legal recognition of the right is a task for the legislature. (See Appendix C for the status of privacy in the United States.)

Today, the form of the medium makes little difference in application of the law. Liability results solely because of what is published, not how it is published. The way in which content is used within a medium, however, is important and constitutes a basic difference between libel and privacy. Defamatory words are libelous if they appear in an advertisement or a news story. In privacy, a set of words that constitutes an invasion of privacy when published in an advertisement might not be actionable if published in a news story. Or a picture published with one story might not be an invasion of privacy whereas the same picture published with a different story would be subject to suit.

---

such media as handbills and labels on consumer products. During the first forty years of the law's growth there were only 53 suits reported. Of this number, New York recorded 32.

THE LAW OF PRIVACY

It is unusual, perhaps to be discussing a definition of invasion of privacy for the first time at this late stage. But the boundaries of the law have changed so greatly since 1890 that it is only after a thorough discussion of the development of privacy that a definition makes much sense. Also, when dealing with the common law, the most useful definition is one that reflects how the courts have defined the tortious conduct. While a definition based on legal theory or sophisticated logic might be more cohesive and well structured, it provides little guidance to the individual attempting to assess his conduct in light of the law. Consequently, the definitions and summarizations presented here represent a condensation of nearly eighty-two years of case law and statutory construction.

This condensation reveals that there are three basic kinds of mass media action or conduct that can lead to privacy suits. The first is the use of an individual's name or photograph in an advertisement without his consent. This type of action initiated the development of the law. Second, a suit can result from the publication of private information about an individual, which was the heart of the Warren-Brandeis argument. Finally, the publication of nondefamatory falsehoods about a person represents the newest kind of invasion of privacy and is the most active area of the law today.

The first action, use of a name or photograph in advertisements, almost always results in a successful suit for the plaintiff. The second action, the publication of private information, is the most difficult to predict, but is the least likely to result in success for the plaintiff. Publication of nondefamatory falsehoods, the third action, usually results in a judgment for the plaintiff, although the United States Supreme Court decision in *Time Inc.* v. *Hill* (see Chap. 11) has broadened the protection for defendants in this kind of suit.

1. USE IN ADVERTISEMENTS

The use of an individual's name or portrait for advertising or promotional gain is the oldest form of invasion of privacy by virtue of the 1903 New York statute. In the early growth of the common law of privacy, this was generally recognized as the only tortious invasion of privacy involving the mass media. It was the publication of an individual's name or photograph in an advertisement that prompted recognition of the right of privacy in Georgia, Kentucky, Missouri, and Kansas, four of the seven states to adopt the tort before 1930. The other three states, New Jersey, Louisiana, and Indiana, adopted the right in nonmedia cases. Also, statutes similar to the New York law were passed in Utah and Virginia before 1910.

Perhaps it is appropriate to digress here for a summary of the basic differences between the statutory and the common law right of privacy. While these differences often appear significant, they are really quite small. All four existing statutes narrowly define an invasion of privacy as the use of a name or picture for advertising or trade purposes without written consent. "Advertising purposes" have been defined in both Utah and New York as the use of a name to sell a collateral product.* In New York, however, "trade purposes" are not considered so restricted, but have never been specifically defined. Generally, there must be some kind of profit-making or commercial endeavor involved.

In 1908 a plaintiff in New York asserted that because a newspaper or magazine was published for profit—hence, a trade purpose—the use of a name or photograph in such a publication, even in a news story, was an invasion of privacy. The New York Supreme Court refused to accept this argument and ruled that the statute was not intended to apply to this kind of use (see *Moser* v. *Press Pub. Co.* in Chap. 4).

Other, more successful attempts to broaden the definition of trade purposes were made in 1913 in *Binns* v. *Vitagraph Co.* (see Chap. 5), and in 1932, in *Blumenthal* v. *Picture Classics* (see Chap. 6). In both cases the New York Supreme Court ruled that the addition of fictional material to an otherwise factual account created an entertainment feature, and the use of a name or picture in such a feature was a trade purpose. This interpretation has not

* The Utah statute has been construed only once, in Donahue v. Warner Bros. Pictures, 2 Utah 2d 256 (1954), while there has been no construction of either the Virginia or Oklahoma statutes. Consequently, virtually all construction of the statutory provisions is based on New York case law.

been followed in Utah, where a trade purpose is still defined as the sale of a collateral product.

The basic difference, then, between the statutory protection and the common law involves only the publication of truthful but private facts about an individual in a news story. There can be no recovery under any of the statutes for such a publication. In 1966, for example, the New York Court of Appeals ruled that "the factual reporting of newsworthy persons and events is in the public interest and protected." [11] Under the common law, however, truthful reports have been used as the basis for successful suits.

Problems in the law. While it would appear that few problems could result from the simple prohibition against the unauthorized use of names or pictures in advertisements or for trade purposes, complications do arise. There are exceptions to the prohibition. Authorized use or consent can be interpreted in various ways. Or, even the term "picture" is subject to further definition. Fortunately, litigation during the past six decades has produced some rough guidelines that aid in an understanding of the law.

The first of the three possible exceptions to the rule involves the use of a name or photograph in an advertisement which is incidental to other legitimate publication. For example, if *Look* magazine published a legitimate news article on Robert Wagner, the magazine could use Wagner's name and picture in advertisements to promote the story. Or, if Wagner's picture graced the cover of the magazine, the cover could be reproduced in an advertisement used to promote the magazine as an advertising medium.[12] The two key words are "incidental" and "collateral." The publication of a name in an advertisement incidental to a legitimate use of the name is protected; the use of a name to advertise a collateral product is not.

There are two exceptions, but both are poorly grounded and are tenuous at best. In 1948 a New York court ruled that the use of a name in a news item published in an advertisement was not prohibited. The news report was not connected with the product being promoted and was merely used to attract attention to the advertisement (see *Wallach* v. *Bacharach* in Chap. 7). In 1959, however, another New York court ruled that the use of a name in a report originally published as a news story, but republished as a part of an advertisement, was an invasion of privacy. In this case there was a connection between the story, which reported a warehouse fire in which company records, not stored in a safe, were destroyed, and the advertisement by a manufacturer of safes (see *Flores* v. *Mosler Safe Co.* in Chap. 9). Of these two cases, probably the 1959 decision, prohibiting use, is a better reflection of the law.[13]

Finally, a federal court ruled in 1942 that the use of a publicity photograph of a college football star on a calendar advertising Pabst beer was not an invasion of privacy. The picture was purchased from a university by the beer company, and there was no suggestion on the calendar that the athlete endorsed the beer. The court ruled that the football player was a public figure who sought publicity and therefore lacked a right of privacy (see *O'Brien* v. *Pabst Sales Co.* in Chap. 7).

Since this decision, however, the idea of a so-called right of publicity has emerged as a corollary to privacy. It was based on the theory that if a man has a publicity value in his name or photograph, he should enjoy the exclusive privilege of capitalizing on it. This idea was first enunciated in a court decision by Federal Circuit Judge Jerome N. Frank in 1953. The following year Frank's suggestion was explored and promoted by Melville B. Nimmer, an attorney for Paramount Pictures, in a law review article.[14] While few plaintiffs have asserted their right of publicity in the past sixteen years, the existence of such a principle would seem to neutralize the ruling in the *Pabst* case. If a similar suit arose today, it would most likely result in a judgment for the plaintiff.

The question of consent. Only the unauthorized use of a name or picture in an advertisement is prohibited, and authorization, or consent, is usually regarded as a complete defense in a privacy suit. But again, the problem is far less simple than it appears. In the four states with privacy statutes, only written consent is a defense. In common law states, while there has been no definitive litigation on the question, it would seem that written consent is the safest procedure. Oral consent, especially if given gratuitously, can be withdrawn at any time. Most advertising agencies and advertising departments have printed model releases on hand, and these should be used.

Even consent, however, does not always offer a foolproof defense, for there are at least three exceptions. The first is time lapse. Consent given today might not be valid ten years from now. In 1961 the Louisiana Supreme Court ruled that it was the responsibility of the defendant to renew the oral gratuitous consent given nine years previously (see *McAndrews* v. *Roy* in Chap. 10). Obviously, a written contract between the two parties would have stood the nine-year lapse in time. Also, if some kind of consideration—money or goods—had exchanged hands, the defendant would have been on firmer ground. The point to remember, however, is that time lapse does have an effect on consent.

Substantial and material alteration of a picture can also affect consent, even that given in a broad written agreement. The 1959 case of *Russell* v. *Marboro Books* (see Chap. 9) underscored this point. What constitutes substantial alteration? In the *Russell* case the photograph underwent major retouching that changed the context completely. In 1963 a federal court ruled that merely adding a bottle of beer and a glass to a photograph did not constitute substantial alteration (see *Sharman* v. *Schmidt & Sons* in Chap. 10). There is a wide range between the defendants' conduct in these two cases, and the actual limitations on alteration rest somewhere in the middle. More litigation will be needed to chart them.

Finally, written consent from some persons is not valid. A minor, for example, cannot give consent to the use of his or her picture in an advertisement. Such use could result in a successful privacy action, despite the existence of a signed model release (see *Semler* v. *Ultem Pubs., Inc.*, in Chap. 6). Consent should not be looked upon as a broad permission to use a picture or name in all possible ways. The publication should be consistent with the use anticipated when consent was given.

Two other considerations remain. First, what is a picture? Must it be an actual photograph of an individual, or even a close likeness? In New York since 1913 the word "picture" has meant any representation of a person (see *Binns* v. *Vitagraph Co.* in Chap. 5). This construction has been used frequently in New York and undoubtedly would constitute persuasive precedent in the common law states. The use of an actor, therefore, to portray a real individual in a commercial, or even a simple cartoon sketch of the individual, would probably constitute an invasion of privacy. Second, the inadvertent use of a name or picture offers no protection to a publisher. The fact that an error was made is not a defense in this kind of suit (see *Flake* v. *Greensboro News Co.* in Chap. 6; *Olan Mills* v. *Dodd* in Chap. 10). A mistake in the composing room never excuses the publisher in a lawsuit.

2. PUBLICATIONS ABOUT PRIVATE AFFAIRS

The original motivation behind the Warren-Brandeis proposal of legal protection for the right of privacy was irritation at press reports about a citizen's private life. Yet, strangely enough, this is the one kind of invasion of privacy to which courts have shown the most tolerance. There have been few instances in which the media have been successfully sued for publishing truthful reports about someone's private activities. Courts have granted great latitude to the press in reporting on a wide variety of subjects. If a newspaper were to report the intimate details of a private party in a private home, a suit against the publication probably would succeed. But the media usually do not report such things; too many public events occur that provide plenty of news copy. Thus the one most plausible explanation for the failure of the Warren-Brandeis argument to take hold is that the evil they sought to remedy was largely mythical. The press did not go to the extremes pictured in "The Right to Privacy." There undoubtedly have been lapses of good taste during the past eight decades, which on occasion resulted in successful privacy suits based on truthful news stories. But both this kind of publication and this kind of success occur infrequently.

The importance of the Warren-Brandeis proposal is certainly not diminished by this outcome. The existence of a means to bring a legal action because of the publication of offensive truthful reports has probably made most publishers more cautious. Legal scholar Marc Franklin noted in 1963 that if the editor is forced to anticipate a judicial analysis of his story, he will probably resolve to stay out of the borderline areas.[15] A great problem in privacy law is that few newsmen know where the borders are.

The often-quoted, but only partially correct, maxim that truth is not a defense in a privacy suit applies most appropriately to this category of the law.* This is undoubtedly an important reason why courts, in most instances, have refused to declare defendants liable in suits based on the publication of factual reports. The basic concepts of the libertarian press, the self-righting process, and the American constitutional guarantees of freedom of the press are influenced greatly by the idea that the truth should be told because the people have a right to know it. Judges, schooled in traditional civil liberties and tenets of American democracy, have been less than hospitable to the argument that a man should be held liable for publishing the truth. Consequently, this part of the tort has never been comfortably absorbed into the law.

In 1893, for example, when the widow of inventor George H. Corliss attempted to stop the publication of a biography of her husband, Federal Judge LeBaron B. Colt spoke out strongly against the idea.

Freedom of speech and of the press is secured by the constitution of the United States and the constitutions of most of the states. This constitutional privilege implies a right to freely utter and publish whatever the citizen may please, and to be protected from any responsibility for so doing, except so far as such publication, by reason of its blasphemy, obscenity, or scandalous character, may be a public offense, or by its falsehood and malice, may injuriously affect the standing, reputation, or pecuniary interests of individuals.[16]

As the development of privacy progressed, the argument that the constitutional guarantees of free speech and press blocked invasion of privacy suits was heard less often. But it was replaced with a series of defenses that were imbued with a "First Amendment philosophy. The traditional libertarian attitudes about the right of men freely to speak and write the truth played an important role in shaping the law of privacy. This can be most readily seen in the group of privacy defenses labeled newsworthiness.

The definition of newsworthiness. In every jurisdiction in which the right of privacy was protected, courts have agreed that the publication of newsworthy material was shielded from a lawsuit. While there were many different opinions about what was and what was not newsworthy, jurists have granted that Ameri-

* The maxim is only partly true, because in a suit based on the publication of a nondefamatory falsehood, the truth would serve as a strong defense.

can readers have a broad range of tastes and interests. Consequently, the press has found the defense of newsworthiness a
comfortable refuge in which to work. The concept of newsworthiness has three basic parts: public interest, public figure,
and public record. A brief look at each of these will suggest
guidelines.

If a news item or feature story has public interest, it will be
protected. Note that the phrase is *"has* public interest," not the
narrower *"in* the public interest." Courts have conceded that an
almost endless variety of topics have public interest. Stories and
pictures about women exercising in a gymnasium, divorce actions, crime, the dead and mutilated victims of criminals, and
teen-age mothers are just a few of the vast number of subjects
placed within the legitimate ambit of the American news readers'
interests. Even items not related to current affairs, such as historical accounts of people and events from earlier eras, are placed
within the protection of the public interest defense.

The public figure defense applies to the individual about whom
the story is written. If a man places himself in the public eye by
becoming a politician, an actor, a controversial personality, an
athlete, or a performer, most of the details of his life are dedicated to the public and he enjoys a very limited right of privacy.
But more important for the press is a second kind of public person, the involuntary public figure. This idea was first used to
protect the press in 1929 in Kentucky. As we have seen above,
Judge William Rogers Clay, in dismissing a complaint by a
woman who was the object of widespread publicity after she
battled assailants who had killed her husband, wrote: "There are
times . . . when one, whether willing or not, becomes an actor
in an occurrence of public or general interest. When this takes
place he emerges from his seclusion, and it is not an invasion of
his right of privacy to publish his photograph with an account of
such occurrence." [17]

The concept of the involuntary public figure provides broad
protection for the press. Almost any individual involved in a
matter of public interest finds this label attached to him. One
precaution should be noted, however. While there is no case law
on this point, it has been stated many times in judicial dicta that

the involuntary public figure loses his privacy only with regard to his involvement in the event of public interest; other aspects of his life remain shielded.

Both voluntary and involuntary public figures have attempted to defeat this defense by asserting that the passage of time restores to them the right of privacy. This argument has consistently failed when the publication involved a truthful news account of past events. The one glaring exception to the time lapse rule is the famous 1931 case of *Melvin* v. *Reid* (see Chap. 6). But this "publication" was a filmed dramatization of a reformed prostitute's early life, not a news or feature story. The *Melvin* decision represents what is clearly a minority position, a use of the sympathy test discussed earlier in the chapter, and the case has been frequently misrepresented as a leading precedent in the law of privacy.

Finally, material taken exclusively from the public record is normally immune from a privacy suit. While there are few cases on the subject, there is no reported decision to the contrary. But caution must be exercised to insure that the records quoted are indeed public records. The news media are charged with the responsibility of knowing what is and what is not a public record. A Florida newspaper, it will be recalled, was successfully sued for invasion of privacy when it quoted what it believed was a public record in a narcotic commitment case (see *Patterson* v. *Tribune Co.* in Chap. 10).

There are at least two exceptions to the defense of newsworthiness. The first involves what might be called "exceptional circumstances," when the law is given a back seat to the court's sympathy for the plaintiff. Federal Judge Charles E. Clark wrote in 1940 that some published "revelations may be so intimate and so unwarranted in view of the victim's position as to outrage the community's notions of decency." [18] There were occasions cited in earlier chapters when just such revelations seemed to defeat the argument of newsworthiness. In *Barber* v. *Time* (see Chap. 7) the public disclosure of the patient's name and illness seemed to place the case in this category. In *Daily Times Democrat* v. *Graham* (see Chap. 10) the picture of the plaintiff, a helpless victim of a carnival gimmick which raised her skirt above her head, followed along the same line. In *Bazemore* v. *Savannah Hospital* (see Chap. 5) the photograph of a deformed newborn child again seemed to exceed the limits of decency.

The determination that a truthful and accurate news story exceeds the limits of decency, or is an example of extremely bad taste, is a personal one made by judges and jurors. Consequently, it is impossible to fix a boundary line. The only rule which can be offered is that in cases involving exceptional circumstances— a high degree of embarrassment to the plaintiff coupled with a minimal public interest—newsworthiness will not succeed in defeating the suit. And the court in effect decides what is or is not news.

The other exception to the newsworthiness rule involves state statutes that modify the common law of privacy. The best example of such a statute is one prohibiting the publication of the identity of a rape victim. The *Nappier* case (see Chap. 10) suggests that a state can, with sufficient cause, exclude one kind of news from the shield of public interest or newsworthiness. The publication of the name of a rape victim, consequently, could result in a successful privacy action, despite the newsworthy aspects of the story. While only four states now have such provisions,* similar laws are likely to be enacted in other judisdictions.

Beyond newsworthiness. There is one remaining defense for the individual sued for publishing a truthful account of a plaintiff's private affairs. If the plaintiff has previously published the material, it cannot be considered private information. In *Langford* v. *Vanderbilt University* (see Chap. 8), for example, the plaintiff "published" the offensive photograph when he attached it to his pleadings in a libel suit and placed it on file at the county courthouse. It was not an invasion of privacy for the university newspaper to publish the same photograph later. But in no reported instance has this argument been the sole defense in stopping a privacy action; usually it is used in addition to another plea.

The newsman has little to fear from this kind of invasion of privacy suit as long as he sticks to his job of providing a factual

* The four are Florida, Georgia, South Carolina, and Wisconsin. See Chapter 10, page 202 for the specific statutes.

account of newsworthy events. Jurists, imbued with the belief that an informed society should take precedence over the rights of the individual, especially when there is a great public interest involved, have worked to foster the freedom of the press. The law of privacy does not provide a remedy for every annoyance that occurs in daily life. Even on the infrequent occasions when the media publish material that is in bad taste, the courts generally will support the right of the editors to decide what is newsworthy.

3. NONDEFAMATORY FALSEHOODS

The publication of a nondefamatory falsehood (a statement that is not true, but is not libelous) frequently constitutes an invasion of privacy. While it is difficult to see what this kind of publication has in common with the traditional concept of invasion of privacy, this hybrid version of the tort nevertheless has grown to be an active area of the law.

Two kinds of nondefamatory false reports have been used as the basis for invasion of privacy suits. The fictionalization of an otherwise true story has been ruled actionable numerous times, but only when the plaintiff was identified in the fictional version. For example, the story of a heroic sea rescue might be used as the basis for a television play: if the author adds the plaintiff's name to the drama, as well as imaginary dialogue between characters and other fictional embellishments, grounds would exist for a privacy suit.

The second kind of nondefamatory falsehood places the plaintiff in what some legal scholars call a "false light." [19] Using a photograph out of context could result in a false light situation. If a news photograph of a child, injured by a careless motorist, is used to illustrate a story on pedestrian carelessness, the implication that the child was at fault in the accident would constitute an invasion of privacy.

The origin of this third category of invasion of privacy can be traced to the New York privacy statute. Courts in that state ruled that through fictionalization a news item became an entertainment feature, and the use of a name or picture in an entertainment feature was a trade purpose. In one of the first decisions of this kind, the appellate division of the New York Supreme Court ruled that the use of the picture of a private citizen in a fictional travel film was an invasion of privacy (see *Blumenthal* v. *Picture Classics* in Chap. 6). The plaintiff in the case was a street vendor who was filmed as she sold bread from a sidewalk stand. As this kind of suit was not part of the Warren-Brandeis proposal for a legal right of privacy, it is another example of how the law has grown in channels foreign to the original conceptual framework.

Of all three categories of invasion of privacy, the law surrounding the publication of nondefamatory falsehoods is the least settled and most confusing. Courts seldom agree on the important questions. The number of inaccuracies necessary to constitute fictionalization of a story has not been established. The mere addition of the narrative style and imaginary dialogue to a legitimate news story may or may not create an actionable publication. In 1959 a Pennsylvania judge ruled that a narrative version of a rather innocuous news story was an invasion of privacy. In his opinion, which was discussed in Chapter 9, he wrote: "Only by reading the article can one appreciate how the author permitted his imagination to roam through the facts, and how newsworthy events are presented in a style used almost exclusively by writers of fiction." Three years later, a California judge, in dismissing a complaint based on a similar kind of publication, wrote: "We do not believe that the imagination of the writer of the article as exercised here creates a tort that would not otherwise exist." [20] This kind of contradiction runs throughout case law in this area.

There is also noticeable contradiction among decisions concerning false light. Some suggest that the false light must be an unfavorable light; that is, publishing untruthful but laudatory statements about the plaintiff would not be an invasion of privacy.[21] Other courts, however, have held that any false light is actionable. Indeed, a California court ruled that the picture of a man and his wife sitting at a confectionery stand was not an invasion of privacy when published without comment, but was actionable when it was published in an offensive context (see the *Gill* cases in Chap. 8). Newsmen should be wary of using unrelated photos to illustrate controversial articles, especially if there is any possibility the reader might view the picture in the wrong context.

There are a few simple precautions that can be taken to avoid a lawsuit for the publication of a nondefamatory falsehood. For example, if the fictional style is utilized, the use of real names should be avoided. The series of cases concerning the radio and television programs, "Big Story" and "Dragnet," demonstrates that an individual's life story can be used as the basis for a fictional drama as long as he is not identified.[22] The reverse is true as well: if the individual is going to be named, the account should be factual.

The problem of defining "identification" has resulted in several interesting lawsuits. The coincidental use of a real name in a piece of fiction is not usually an invasion of privacy. An author must use an individual's identity, which includes personal data such as his occupation, where he lives, how old he is, where he went to school. If, for example, a waiter in a novel had the name Walter Cronkite, the real Mr. Cronkite could not collect damages for invasion of privacy. But if the fictional Walter Cronkite was a New York network newscaster in his early fifties who had a burning fascination with the American space program, the real Mr. Cronkite would have a fairly good case. The simple rule is that an individual's identity—not just his name—must be appropriated before there is an invasion of privacy.

Problems such as these are primarily the concern of the scriptwriter or the novelist, not the newsman. But the new prose form of the nonfiction novel which has been used successfully by Truman Capote and others offers a fertile ground for nondefamatory falsehood suits. The law needs much more clarification and illumination before many firm guidelines will exist.

Time, Inc. v. *Hill and falsehoods.* In 1967 the United States Supreme Court gave the press additional protection in falsehood suits when it ruled that plaintiffs must prove that the errors were deliberately published, or published with careless disregard for the truth. Justice William Brennan's decision in *Time, Inc.* v. *Hill* (see Chap. 11) extended to nondefamatory falsehoods the protection given defamatory falsehoods in the 1964 *New York Times* v. *Sullivan* decision (see Chap. 10). Until June 1971 the *Times* case libel rule applied only to comments about public officials or public figures. But in *Rosenbloom* v. *Metromedia, Inc.,* the Supreme Court extended the First Amendment protection to all libelous stories which enjoy a public interest, without regard to whether persons involved are famous or anonymous.[23] In at least two recent privacy decisions by lower federal courts, the same rule was applied. That is, the fact that the story had public interest was found to be more important than whether or not the plaintiff was a public figure.[24]

With the plaintiff now being required to show that the publisher knew the material was false, or displayed reckless disregard of whether it was false or not, he will find it more difficult to succeed in this type of lawsuit. But most nondefamatory falsehood actions are instituted against publishers who are aware of their errors or inaccuracies. The fictionalization is necessary, they believe, to reach a certain market—the crime-story buffs, Hollywood fan magazine readers, or the few remaining devotees of the sensational exposé publications.

The first progeny of *Time, Inc.* v. *Hill, Spahn* v. *Julian Messner, Inc.* (see Chap. 11), is an example of the intentional fictionalization of the biography of a baseball star in an attempt to reach young readers. While it certainly appears that this is the kind of publication the United States Supreme Court has indicated can be restricted without endangering freedom of the press, the high court nevertheless agreed to hear the publisher's appeal following an adverse ruling in New York courts. However, settlement out of court denied the legal community the benefit of an additional ruling on this aspect of privacy.

Retraction statutes. Another media protection has developed in California which makes prosecution of a nondefamatory falsehood suit more difficult. In 1961 an appellate court denied compensation to a plaintiff in a falsehood suit because he failed to ask the newspaper publisher to correct the errors in the story before starting his suit. California is one of several jurisdictions that denies all but special damages in a libel suit unless the plaintiff first asks for a retraction or correction. In *Werner* v. *Times-Mirror Co.* (see Chap. 10) Justice John J. Ford ruled that the same protection must apply to the press in the case of nondefamatory falsehoods. He asserted that state policy, as declared by the legislature, was to insure the ultimate publication of the truth, and that to compensate a plaintiff for invasion of privacy because he failed to ask for a retraction and could not sue for libel would be to subvert this policy.

Many courts have found it difficult to accept the notion that nondefamatory falsehoods can serve as the basis for a lawsuit. While there have been many cases in this area of the law, courts have frequently rejected this kind of suit as being foreign to traditional Anglo-American legal principles. American judges and juries have shown great patience with the press in its efforts to present the news accurately while it is still fresh.

PRIVACY AND THE COURTS

This summation of the three basic kinds of invasion of privacy provides the newsman with most of the information needed to stay within the protection granted the press by the law. But these guidelines are not foolproof. They are general rules, and there are often exceptions to general rules. These exceptions have been pointed out in previous chapters. The newsman should also be alert to changes in the law, which occur frequently and often significantly modify existing rules.

In addition, the nature of the American judicial system requires that journalists exercise caution. This study has been based on reported cases—the law in the books. Trial courts and juries are often entities apart from the "book law." The standards they use to measure an invasion of privacy may be far broader than those enunciated by the appellate courts. The only recourse for a defendant who loses at the trial level is to appeal, and this procedure costs money, usually a great deal of money. The safest course for the newsman is to proceed well within the limits of protected conduct, not along the outer fringes. The reporter or editor will have no problem if he just sticks to his business of gathering news and presenting it as accurately as possible.

WHAT LIES AHEAD FOR PRIVACY?

A better than average crystal ball is needed to predict the future growth of the law of privacy. But certain questions and trends are suggested and a few of these deserve mention.

1. The press will probably not continue to be the center of privacy action in the years to come. More and more lawsuits today are aimed at the electronic snoopers, both private and governmental, who seek to invade the home and office of individual citizens.

2. New problems will arise with regard to mass media because of current trends both within the law and within the press. For example, clarification is needed on the status of the noncommercial advertisement—the ad that protests war or promotes a cause, such as a supermarket boycott. This kind of publication is giving more and more persons access to the media. Would the unauthorized use of a name or picture in this kind of advertisement constitute an advertising or trade purpose and therefore be an invasion of privacy under the New York statute?

3. Suggestions have been made that members of the press be forced to open their media to anyone who wishes to advertise. If the press thus loses control over its choice of advertisers, who will be responsible for invasions of privacy? Will the publisher be given an immunity from suits?

4. State retraction statutes will probably be applied to nondefamatory falsehood privacy suits as well as libel suits. This change will occur gradually, probably on a state by state, case by case basis.

5. The greatest amount of legal action involving the mass media will center around the nondefamatory falsehood suits, rather than actions involving advertising or the publication of truthful accounts. This is still the most confusing area of the law and much more judicial surveying is needed before boundaries will be clearly marked.

While other problems and trends will emerge in the years ahead, the five outlined above seem the most apparent today.

FREEDOM AND PRIVACY

While the future poses many questions, some inquiries into the past remain unanswered or unanswerable. Was the legal concept of a right of privacy really needed? Certainly, citizens needed and deserved a remedy to stop the unauthorized use of their names and pictures in advertisements. Also, the publication of purposeful nondefamatory falsehoods serves no overriding social function and should be restricted. But the answer is not as clear when truthful news stories are considered. Today, the privilege or defense against such suits is so large that the remedy has little potency. And this is perhaps the way it should be.

Spawned as a theoretical argument rather than a neatly packaged legal principle, the law of privacy has encountered difficulty from the beginning in establishing itself as a part of the American legal code. The development of privacy as a legal concept presents a textbook example of the classic struggle within a democracy between the rights of the society and the rights of the individual. In almost every case the problem before the court could be reduced to this simple question: Which is more important, the protection of society by a free and unfettered press, or the individual's claim to personal solitude? When the publication has involved commercial or false material, the court usually has sided with the individual. In this case the public interest involved was not great enough. When the publication has been a truthful or factual account of even private or personal affairs, the court usually has sided with the press. Here society's interest in a free press took precedence.

Man needs his privacy in order to survive the din and roar of this crowded world. As United States Supreme Court Justice William O. Douglas once wrote, "The right to be let alone is indeed the beginning of all freedom." [25] But man has also found that his society is served best by an unfettered press. The law of privacy today is a result of the careful weighing and measuring of these two interests during the past eighty years. While at times the result has been complex and confusing, it nevertheless represents a desirable compromise.

Appendix A

IMPORTANT CASES AND EVENTS IN THE DEVELOPMENT OF THE LAW OF PRIVACY

1. The first important event was the publication in 1890 of "The Right to Privacy" by Samuel Warren and Louis Brandeis, proposing a legally protected right of privacy.

2. *Corliss* v. *Walker,* 57 Fed. Rep. 434 (1893); 64 Fed. Rep. 280 (1894). Federal Judge LeBaron B. Colt refused to recognize the right of privacy on grounds that it restricted freedom of the press.

3. Passage of the New York privacy statute in 1903. The nation's first privacy law prohibited the unauthorized use of an individual's name or picture for advertising or trade purposes.

4. *Pavesich* v. *New England Life Ins. Co.,* 122 Ga. 190 (1905). Georgia became the first state to provide legal protection for the right of privacy throughout the common law.

5. *Moser* v. *Press Pub. Co.,* 109 N.Y.S. 963 (1908). A New York court ruled that the sale of a newspaper or magazine did not constitute a "trade purpose" within the meaning of the statute. Hence, publication of an individual's name in the news columns of a newspaper was not an invasion of privacy.

6. *Binns* v. *Vitagraph Co.,* 147 App. Div. 783 (1911), aff'd. 210 N.Y. 51 (1913); and *Blumenthal* v. *Picture Classics,* 235 App. Div. 570 (1932), aff'd. 261 N.Y. 504 (1933). New York courts ruled that fictionalization of a news item created an entertainment feature, the sale of which was a trade purpose. This broadened the New York statute to include false material as well as advertisements.

7. *Jones* v. *Herald Post Co.,* 230 Ky. 227 (1929). A Kentucky court ruled that when an individual became involved in a newsworthy event he took on the status of a public figure and consequently lost much of his right to privacy.

8. *Sidis* v. *F-R Publishing Corp.,* 113 F. 2d 806 (1940). In the fiftieth year after the publication of the Warren-Brandeis proposal a

federal judge ruled that a former child prodigy could not stop the publication of truthful reports about his private life.

9. *Gautier* v. *Pro-Football, Inc.,* 99 N.Y.S. 2d 812; rev'd. 278 App. Div. 431 (1951), aff'd. 304 N.Y. 354 (1952). A New York court ruled that despite the fact that television programs are sponsored, the use of a name or a picture in a truthful report on a television program did not constitute a trade purpose.

10. *Time, Inc.* v. *Hill,* 385 U.S. 374 (1967). The United States Supreme Court, acting for the first time in a privacy suit involving the mass media, ruled that the First Amendment in some instances prohibited state courts from imposing liability upon a publication for an invasion of privacy.

Appendix B

IMPORTANT PRIVACY DECISIONS

The following is a list of court decisions which were important in the growth of the law of privacy. Most of them involve the mass media, but some do not. Those cases decided prior to 1890 were not privacy decisions, but have been considered by many legal scholars as the roots of the law. Federal court cases are included within the state listing in which the case originated.

Great Britain—Before 1890

Cherrington v. Abney, 2 Vernon 645 (1709)
Pope v. Curl, 2 Atk. 341 (1741)
Duke of Queensbury v. Shebbeare, 2 Eden 329 (1758)
Millar v. Taylor, 4 Burrow's Rep. 2303 (1769)
Thompson v. Stanhope, Ambler 737 (1774)
Cotteral v. Griffiths, 4 Esp. 69 (1801)
Chandler v. Thompson, 3 Camp. 80 (1811)
Perceval v. Phipps, 2 Ves. & Beam. 19 (1813)
Gee v. Pritchard, 2 Swanst. 402 (1818)
Yovatt v. Winyard, 1 J. & W. 394 (1820)
Cross v. Lewis, 2 B. & C. 686 (1824)
Abernathy v. Hutchinson, 3 L.J. Ch. 209 (1825)
Murray v. Heath, 1 B. & Ad. 804 (1831)
Tipping v. Clarke, 2 Hare 383 (1843)
Prince Albert v. Strange, 1 MacN. & G. 25 (1849)
Morison v. Moat, 9 Hare 241 (1851)
Turner v. Spooner, 30 L.J. Ch. 801 (1861)
Mayhall v. Higbey, 1 Hurl. & G. 148 (1862)
Tapling v. Jones, 11 H.L.C. 290 (1865)
Duke of Buccleuch v. Metro Bd. of Works, L.R. (5 Eng. App.) 418 (1872)
Nicols v. Pitman, 53 L.J. Ch. (N.S.) 552 (1884)

Tuck & Sons v. Priester, L.R. 19 Q.B.D. 629 (1887)
Caird v. Sime, 57 L.J.P.C. 2 (1887)
Pollard v. The Photographic Co., 58 L.J. Ch. (N.S.) 251 (1888)

Alabama

Smith v. Doss, 251 Ala. 250 (1948)
Abernathy v. Thornton, 263 Ala. 496 (1955)
Bell v. Birmingham Broadcasting Corp., 259 Ala. 656; 263 Ala. 355
    (1955); 266 Ala. 266 (1957)
Daily Times Democrat v. Graham, 162 So. 2d 474 (1962)

Alaska

Smith v. Suratt, 7 Alas. Rep. 416 (1926)

Arizona

Reed v. Real Detective Pub. Co., 63 Ariz. 294 (1945)

Arkansas

Olan Mills v. Dodd, 353 S.W. 2d 22 (1962)

California

Melvin v. Reid, 112 Cal. App. 285 (1931)
Lillie v. Warner Bros. Pictures, 139 Cal. App. 724 (1934)
Metter v. Los Angeles Examiner, 35 Cal. App. 2d 304 (1939)
Mau v. Rio Grande Oil, Inc., 28 F. Supp. 845 (1939)
Kerby v. Hal Roach Studios, Inc., 53 Cal. App. 2d 207 (1942)
Cohen v. Marx, 94 Cal. App. 2d 704 (1949)
Stryker v. Republic Pictures, 108 Cal. App. 2d 191 (1951)
Coverstone v. Davies, 38 Cal. 2d 315 (1952)
Gill v. Curtis Pub. Co., 231 P. 2d 565 (1951); 239 P. 2d 630 (1952)
Gill v. Hearst Pub. Co., 231 P. 2d 570 (1951); 239 P. 2d 636 (1952);
    253 P. 2d 441 (1953)
Samuel v. Curtis Pub. Co., 122 F. Supp. 327 (1954)
Fairfield v. American Photocopy Equip. Co., 138 Cal. App. 2d 82
    (1955)
Smith v. NBC, 292 P. 2d 600 (1956)
Strickler v. NBC, 167 F. Supp. 68 (1958)
James v. Screen Gems, 174 Cal. App. 2d 650 (1959)
Werner v. Times-Mirror Co., 193 Cal. App. 2d 111 (1961)
Carlisle v. Fawcett Pub. Inc., 201 Cal. App. 2d 733 (1962)
York v. Story, 324 F. 2d 450 (1963)

Varnish v. Best Medium Pub. Co., 405 F. 2d 608 (1968)
Kapellas v. Kofman, 459 P. 2d 912 (1969)

Colorado

Fitzsimmons v. Olinger Mortuary Assoc., 91 Colo. 544 (1932)
McCreery v. Miller's Grocerteria, 99 Colo. 499 (1937)

Connecticut

O'Connell v. The Hartford Times, 15 Conn. Supp. 85 (1947)
Hazlitt v. Fawcett Pub., 116 F. Supp. 538 (1953)
Korn v. Rennison, 21 Conn. Supp. 400 (1959)
Travers v. Paton, 261 F. Supp. 110 (1966)

Delaware

Miller v. NBC, 157 F. Supp. 240 (1957)
Reardon v. News Journal Pub. Co., 164 A. 2d 263 (1960)
Barbieri v. News Journal Pub. Co., 189 A. 2d 773 (1963)

District of Columbia

Peed v. Washington Times Co., 55 Wash. L. Rep. 182 (1927)
Elmhurst v. Shoreham Hotel, 58 F. Supp. 484 (1945); aff'd. 153 F. 2d
   467 (1946)
Peay v. Curtis Pub. Co., 78 F. Supp. 305 (1948)
Bernstein v. NBC, 129 F. Supp. 817, aff'd. 232 F. 2d 369 (1955)
Klein v. McGraw-Hill, Inc., 263 F. Supp. 919 (1966)
Afro-American v. Jaffe, 366 F. 2d (1966)
Liberty Lobby v. Drew Pearson, 390 F. 2d 491 (1968)
Pearson v. Dodd, 410 F. 2d 701 (1969)

Florida

Cason v. Baskin, 155 Fla. 198 (1944); 159 Fla. 31 (1947)
Jacova v. Southern Radio-Television Co., 83 So. 2d 34 (1955)
Patterson v. Tribune Co., 146 So. 2d 623 (1962)

Georgia

Pavesich v. New England Mutual Life Ins. Co., 122 Ga. 190 (1905)
Candler v. Byfield, 160 Ga. 732 (1925)
Bazemore v. Savannah Hospital, 171 Ga. 257 (1930)
McDaniels v. Atlanta Coca-Cola Bottling Co., 60 Ga. App. 92 (1939)
Stanley v. Warner Bros. Pictures, 64 Ga. App. 228 (1940)
Colgate-Palmolive Co. v. Tullos, 219 F. 2d 617 (1955)

Waters v. Fleetwood, 212 Ga. 161 (1956)
Cabanis v. Hipsley, 151 S.E. 2d 496 (1966)
McQueen v. Wilson, 117 Ga. App. 488 (1968)

Idaho

Peterson v. Idaho First Nat'l. Bank, 83 Idaho 578 (1961)

Illinois

Estill v. Hearst Pub. Co., 186 F. 2d 1017 (1951)
Eick v. Perk Dog Food Co., 347 Ill. App. 293 (1952)
Branson v. Fawcett Pub., 124 F. Supp. 429 (1954)
Rohzon v. Triangle Publications, 230 F. 2d 359 (1956)
Annerino v. Dell Pub. Co., 17 Ill. App. 2d 205 (1958)
Bradley v. Cowles Magazines, 26 Ill. App. 2d 331 (1960)
Buzanski v. Do-All, 31 Ill. App. 2d 191 (1961)
Wagner v. Fawcett Pub., 307 F. 2d 409 (1962)
Maritote v. Desilu Productions, 345 F. 2d 418 (1965)

Indiana

Pritchett v. Knox County Board of Commissioners, 42 Ind. App. 3
    (1908)
Continental Optical Co. v. Reed, 119 Ind. App. 643 (1949)

Iowa

Bremmer v. Journal-Tribune Pub. Co., 247 Iowa 817 (1956)

Kansas

Kunz v. Allen & Bayne, 102 Kan. 883 (1918)
Johnson v. Boeing Airplane Co., 175 Kan. 275 (1953)

Kentucky

Grigsby v. Breckenridge, 65 Ky. (2 Bush) 480 (1867)
Foster-Milburn Co. v. Chinn, 134 Ky. 424 (1909)
Douglas v. Stokes, 149 Ky. 506 (1912)
Brents v. Morgan, 221 Ky. 765 (1927)
Jones v. Herald Post Co., 230 Ky. 227 (1929)
Rhodes v. Graham, 238 Ky. 225 (1931)
Trammell v. Citizens News Co., 285 Ky. 529 (1941)
Bell v. Courier-Journal and Louisville Times, 402 S.W. 2d 84 (1966)

Louisiana

Denis v. Leclerc, 1 Mart. (O.S.) 297 (1811)
Schulman v. Whitaker, 117 La. 704 (1906)

Itzkovitch v. Whitaker, 117 La. 798 (1906)
McAndrews v. Roy, 131 So. 2d 256 (1961)
Mahaffey v. Official Detective Stories, Inc., 210 F. Supp. 251 (1962)

Maryland

Ex parte Sturm, 152 Md. 114 (1927)
Graham v. Baltimore Post Co., 22 Ky. L.J. 108 (1933)
Carr v. Watkins, 227 Md. 578 (1962)

Massachusetts

Corliss v. E. W. Walker Co., 57 Fed. Rep. 434 (1893); 64 Fed. Rep.
  280 (1894)
Thayer v. Worcester Post Co., 284 Mass. 160 (1933)
Uproar v. NBC, 8 F. Supp. 358 (1934); aff'd. as mod. 81 F. 2d 373
  (1936)
Marek v. Zanol Products, 298 Mass. 1 (1937)
Themo v. New England Newspaper Pub. Co., 306 Mass. 54 (1940)
Wright v. RKO Radio Pictures, Inc., 55 F. Supp. 639 (1944)
Kelley v. Post Publishing Co., 327 Mass. 275 (1951)
Brauer v. Globe Newspapers Co., 217 N.E. 2d 736 (1966)
Commonwealth v. Wiseman, 249 N.E. 2d 610 (1969)
DeSalvo v. 20th Century Fox Film Corp., 300 F. Supp. 742 (1969)

Michigan

Demay v. Roberts, 46 Mich. 160 (1881)
Atkinson v. Doherty, 121 Mich. 372 (1899)
Pallas v. Crowley-Milner Co., 322 Mich. 411 (1948); 334 Mich. 282
  (1952)
Weeren v. Evening News Association, 152 N.W. 2d 676 (1967)

Minnesota

Moore v. Rugg, 44 Minn. 28 (1890)
Berg v. Minneapolis Star and Tribune Co., 79 F. Supp. 957 (1948)
Hurley v. Northwest Publications, Inc., 273 F. Supp. 967 (1967);
  aff'd. 398 F. 2d 346 (1969)

Mississippi

Martin v. Dorton, 210 Miss. 668 (1951)

Missouri

Munden v. Harris, 153 Mo. App. 652 (1911)
Vassar v. Loose-Wiles Biscuit Co., 197 Fed. 982 (1912)
Barber v. Time, 348 Mo. 1199 (1942)

Montana

Bennett v. Gusdorf, 101 Mont. 39 (1935)
Welsh v. Roehm, 125 Mont. 517 (1952)

Nebraska

Brunson v. Ranks Army Store, 161 Neb. 519 (1955)

Nevada

Norman v. City of Las Vegas, 64 Nev. 38 (1947)

New Hampshire

Hamberger v. Eastman, 206 A. 2d 239 (1964)

New Jersey

Vanderbilt v. Mitchell, 72 N.J. Eq. 910 (1907)
Edison v. Edison Mfg. Co., 73 N.J. Eq. 136 (1907)

New Mexico

Hubbard v. Journal Publishing Co., 69 N.M. 473 (1962)

New York

Brandreth v. Lance, 8 Paige 23 (1839)
Wetmore v. Scovell, 3 Edw. Ch. 543 (1842)
Hoyt v. MacKenzie, 3 Barb. Ch. 320 (1848)
Woolsey v. Judd, 11 N.Y. Sup. Ct. 379 (1855)
Eyre v. Higbee, 35 Barb. 502 (1861)
Manola v. Stevens, see *New York Times*, 15, 18, 21 June 1890
MacKenzie v. Soden Mineral Springs Company, 18 N.Y.S. 240 (1891)
Schuyler v. Curtis, 19 N.Y.S. 264 (1892); 147 N.Y. 434 (1895)
Marks v. Jaffa, 26 N.Y. Supp. 908 (1893)
Murray v. Gast Lithographic and Engraving Co., 28 N.Y. Supp. 271 (1894)
Roberson v. Rochester Folding Box Co., 171 N.Y. 538 (1902)
Moser v. Press Pub. Co., 109 N.Y.S. 963 (1908)
Wyatt v. James McCreery Co., 126 App. Div. 650 (1908)
Rhodes v. Sperry and Hutchinson, 193 N.Y. 223 (1908); aff'd. 220 U.S. 502 (1910)
Eliot v. Jones, 120 N.Y.S. 989 (1910)
Jeffries v. New York Evening Journal Pub. Co., 124 N.Y.S. 780 (1910)
Wendell v. Conduit Mach. Co., 133 N.Y.S. 758 (1911)

Wyatt v. Hall's Portrait Studio, 128 N.Y.S. 247 (1911)

Binns v. Vitagraph Co., 147 App. Div. 783 (1911); aff'd. 210 N.Y. 51 (1913)

D'Altomonte v. New York Herald Co., 154 App. Div. 453 (1913); 208 N.Y. 596 (1913).

Colyer v. Richard K. Fox Pub. Co., 162 App. Div. 297 (1914)

Merle v. Sociological Research Film Corp., 166 App. Div. 376 (1915)

Humiston v. Universal Film Manufacturing Co., 189 App. Div. 467 (1919)

Loftus v. Greenwich Lithographing Co., Inc., 192 App. Div. 251 (1920)

Feeney v. Young, 191 App. Div. 501 (1920)

Fairbanks v. Winik, 198 N.Y.S. 299 (1922)

Damron v. Doubleday, Doran & Co., 231 N.Y.S. 444 (1928); aff'd. 226 App. Div. 796 (1929)

McNulty v. Press Pub. Co., 241 N.Y.S. 29 (1930)

Martin v. New Metropolitan Fiction, 248 N.Y.S. 359 (1931); rev'd. 237 App. Div. 863 (1932)

Blumenthal v. Picture Classics, 235 App. Div. 570 (1932); aff'd. 261 N.Y. 504 (1933)

Swacker v. Wright, 277 N.Y.S. 296 (1935)

Davis v. RKO Radio Pictures, 16 F. Supp. 195 (1936)

Sweenek v. Pathé News, Inc., 16 F. Supp. 746 (1936)

People v. Robert McBride & Co., 288 N.Y.S. 501 (1936)

Gardella v. Log Cabin Products Co., 89 F. 2d 891 (1937)

Middleton v. News Syndicate Co., 295 N.Y.S. 120 (1937)

Sarat Lahiri v. Daily Mirror, 295 N.Y.S. 382 (1937)

Semler v. Ultem Pubs., Inc., 9 N.Y.S. 2d 319 (1938)

Krieger v. Popular Publications, 3 N.Y.S. 2d 480 (1938)

Redmond v. Columbia Pictures Corp., 253 App. Div. 708 (1937); aff'd. 277 N.Y. 707 (1938)

Jackson v. Consumer Publications, 10 N.Y.S. 2d (1939)

Banks v. King Features Syndicate, 30 F. Supp. 352 (1939)

Kline v. Robt. McBride & Co., 11 N.Y.S. 2d 674 (1939)

Lane v. F. W. Woolworth Co., 11 N.Y.S. 2d 199 (1939)

Griffin v. Medical Society, 11 N.Y.S. 2d 109 (1939)

Sidis v. F-R Publishing Corp., 113 F. 2d 806 (1940)

Young v. Greneker Studios, 26 N.Y.S. 2d 357 (1941)

Nebb v. Bell Syndicate, 41 F. Supp. 929 (1941)

Miller v. Madison Square Garden Corp., 28 N.Y.S. 2d 811 (1941)

Levey v. Warner Bros. Pictures, 57 F. Supp. 40 (1944)

Lawrence v. Ylla, 55 N.Y.S. 2d 343 (1945)

Molony v. Boy Comics Publishers, 65 N.Y.S. 2d 173 (1946)

Toscani v. Hersey, 271 App. Div. 445 (1946)

Koussevitzky v. Allen, Towne & Heath, 68 N.Y.S. 2d 779 (1947); aff'd. 272 App. Div. 759 (1947)

Wallach v. Bacharach, 80 N.Y.S. 2d 37, aff'd. 84 N.Y.S. 2d 894 (1948)

Orsini v. Eastern Wine Corp., 73 N.Y.S. 2d 426 (1947); aff'd. 273 App. Div. 947 (1948)

Sutton v. Hearst Pub. Co., 98 N.Y.S. 2d 233 (1950)

Thompson v. Close-Up, Inc., 99 N.Y.S. 2d 864 (1950)

Sharkey v. NBC, 93 F. Supp. 986 (1950)

Callas v. Whisper, Inc., 101 N.Y.S. 2d 532 (1950); aff'd. 278 App. Div. 974 (1951)

Garner v. Triangle Publications, 97 F. Supp. 546 (1951)

Gautier v. Pro-Football, Inc., 99 N.Y.S. 2d 812, rev'd. 278 App. Div. 431 (1951); aff'd. 304 N.Y. 354 (1952)

Jansen v. Hilo Packing Co., 118 N.Y.S. 2d 162 (1952)

Haelan Labs Inc. v. Topps Chewing Gum, 202 F. 2d 866 (1953)

Oma v. Hillman Periodicals, 281 App. Div. 240 (1953)

People v. Scribner's Sons, 130 N.Y.S. 2d 514 (1954)

Metzger v. Dell, 136 N.Y.S. 2d 888 (1955)

Roberts v. Conde Nast Pub., Inc., 286 App. Div. 729 (1955)

Stillman v. Paramount Pictures, 147 N.Y.S. 2d 504; aff'd. 2 App. Div. 2d 18 (1956)

Time, Inc. v. Hill, 155 N.Y.S. 2d 234 (1956); 207 N.Y.S. 2d 901 (1960); aff'd. 18 App. Div. 2d 485 (1963); aff'd. 15 N.Y. 2d 986 (1965); rev'd. 385 U.S. 374 (1967)

Myers v. U.S. Camera Pub. Corp., 167 N.Y.S. 2d 771 (1957)

Dallesandro v. Henry Holt & Co., 4 App. Div. 2d 470 (1957)

Goelet v. Confidential, 5 App. Div. 2d 226 (1958)

Flores v. Mosler Safe Co., 7 N.Y. 2d 276 (1959)

Russell v. Marboro Books, 183 N.Y.S. 2d 8 (1959)

Goldberg v. Ideal Pub., 210 N.Y.S. 2d 928 (1960)

Rosenthal v. Kotler, 208 N.Y.S. 2d 167 (1960)

Durgom v. CBS, 214 N.Y.S. 2d 752 (1961)

Schneiderman v. New York Post, 220 N.Y.S. 2d 1008 (1961)

Moglen v. Varsity Pajamas, Inc., 13 App. Div. 2d 114 (1961)

Booth v. Curtis Pub. Co., 15 App. Div. 2d 343, 11 N.Y. 2d 907 (1962)

Selsman v. Universal Photo Books, 18 App. Div. 2d 151 (1963)

Thompson v. G. P. Putnam & Sons, 243 N.Y.S. 2d 652 (1963)

Spahn v. Julian Messner, Inc., 250 N.Y.S. 2d 529 (1964); aff'd. 23 App.

Div. 2d 216 (1965); aff'd. 18 N.Y. 2d 324 (1966); judgment vacated, remanded to court of appeals, 387 U.S. 239 (1967); 21 N.Y. 2d 124 (1967); probable jurisdiction noted, 89 S. Ct. 80 (1968)

University of Notre Dame v. 20th Century Fox, 22 App. Div. 2d 452, 15 N.Y. 2d 940 (1965)

Youssoupoff v. CBS, 244 N.Y.S. 2d 701, 265 N.Y.S. 2d 754 (1965)

Fignole v. Curtis Pub. Co., 247 F. Supp. 595 (1965)

Estate of Hemingway v. Random House, 268 N.Y.S. 2d 531, 25 App. Div. 2d 719 (1966)

Cullen v. Grove Press, 276 F. Supp. 727 (1967)

Rosemont Enterprises, Inc. v. Random House, Inc., 294 N.Y.S. 2d 122 (1968)

Paulsen v. Personality Posters, Inc., 59 Misc. 2d 444 (1968)

Pagan v. New York Herald Tribune, Inc., 301 N.Y.S. 2d 120 (1969)

Rand v. The Hearst Corp., 298 N.Y.S. 2d 405, 31 A.D. 2d 206 (1969)

North Carolina

Flake v. Greensboro News Co., 212 N.C. 780 (1938)

Ohio

Martin v. F.I.Y. Theatre Co., 10 Ohio Ops. 338 (1938)

Johnson v. Scripps Pub. Co., 18 Ohio Ops. 372 (1940)

Friedman v. Restaurant Employees, 20 Ohio Ops. 473 (1941)

Oklahoma

Paramount Pictures v. Leader Press, 24 F. Supp. 1004 (1938); rev'd. on other grounds, 106 F. 2d 229 (1939)

Oregon

Hinish v. Meier & Frank Co., 166 Ore. 482 (1941)

Hamilton v. Crown Life Ins., 246 Ore. 4 (1967)

Pennsylvania

Widdemer v. Hubbard, 19 Phil. (Pa.) 263 (1887)

Harlow v. Buno, 36 Pa. D.&C. 101 (1939)

Clayman v. Bernstein, 38 Pa. D.&C. 543 (1940)

Leverton v. Curtis Pub. Co., 97 F. Supp. 181, aff'd. 192 F. 2d 974 (1951)

Schnabel v. Meredith, 378 Pa. 609 (1954)

Ettore v. Philco Television Broadcasting Co., 229 F. 2d 481 (1956)

Hull v. Curtis Pub. Co., 182 Pa. Super. 86, 126 A. 2d 644 (1956)

Jenkins v. Dell Pub. Co., 251 F. 2d 447 (1958)
Aquino v. Bulletin Company, 190 Pa. Super. 528 (1959)
Raynor v. ABC, 222 F. Supp. 795 (1963)
Sharman v. Schmidt & Sons, 216 F. Supp. 401 (1963)

Rhode Island

Henry v. Cherry and Webb, 30 R.I. 13 (1909)

South Carolina

Holoman v. Life Ins. Co. of Va., 192 S.C. 454 (1940)
Meetze v. AP, 95 S.E. 2d 606 (1956)
Frith v. AP, 176 F. Supp. 671 (1959)
Nappier v. Jefferson Standard Life Ins. Co., 213 F. Supp. 174; rev'd.
    322 F. 2d 502 (1963)
Holmes v. The Curtis Pub. Co., 303 F. Supp. 522 (1969)

South Dakota

Truxes v. Kenco Enterprises, 119 N.W. 2d 914 (1963)

Tennessee

Langford v. Vanderbilt University, 199 Tenn. 389 (1956)
Cordell v. Detective Publications, Inc., 307 F. Supp. 1212 (1968)

Texas

O'Brien v. Pabst Sales Co., 124 F. 2d 167 (1942)
Milner v. Red River Valley Pub. Co., 249 S.W. 2d 227 (1952)

Utah

Donahue v. Warner Bros. Pictures, 194 F. 2d 6 (1952); 2 Utah 2d
    256 (1954)

Vermont

Newell v. Witcher, 53 Vt. 589 (1880)

Washington

Hillman v. Star Pub. Co., 64 Wash. 691 (1911)
Hodgeman v. Olsen, 86 Wash. 615 (1915)
State ex rel. La Follette v. Hinkle, 131 Wash. 86 (1924)
Lewis v. Physicians Credit, 27 Wash. 2d 267 (1947)

West Virginia

Roach v. Harper, 143 W. Va. 869 (1958)

Wisconsin

Judevine v. Benzies-Montanye Fuel & Warehouse Co., 222 Wis. 512
  (1936)
State v. Evjue, 253 Wis. 146 (1948)
Yoeckel v. Samonig, 272 Wis. 430 (1956)

Appendix C

STATUS OF THE LAW OF PRIVACY IN THE FIFTY STATES AND THE DISTRICT OF COLUMBIA

Alabama: Recognized, Smith v. Doss, 251 Ala. 250 (1948)

Alaska: Recognized, Smith v. Suratt, 7 Alas. Rep. 416 (1926)

Arizona: Recognized, Reed v. Real Detective Pub. Co., 63 Ariz. 294 (1945)

Arkansas: Recognized, Olan Mills v. Dodd, 353 S.W. 2d 22 (1962)

California: Recognized, Melvin v. Reid, 112 Cal. App. 285 (1931)

Colorado: Reported cases, but decided on other grounds

Connecticut: Recognized, Korn v. Rennison, 21 Conn. Supp. 400 (1959)

Delaware: Recognized, Barbieri v. News Journal Pub. Co., 189 A. 2d 773 (1963)

Florida: Recognized, Cason v. Baskin, 155 Fla. 198 (1944)

Georgia: Recognized, Pavesich v. New England Mutual Life Ins. Co., 122 Ga. 190 (1905)

Hawaii: No reported cases found

Idaho: Reported cases, but decided on other grounds

Illinois: Recognized, Eick v. Perk Dog Food Co., 347 Ill. App. 293 (1952)

Indiana: Recognized, Pritchett v. Knox County Board of Commissioners, 42 Ind. App. 3 (1908)

Iowa: Recognized, Bremmer v. Journal-Tribune Pub. Co., 247 Iowa 817 (1956)

Kansas: Recognized, Kunz v. Allen & Bayne, 120 Kan. 883 (1918)

Kentucky: Recognized, Foster-Milburn Co. v. Chinn, 134 Ky. 424 (1909)

Louisiana: Recognized, Schulman v. Whitaker, 117 La. 704 (1906)

Maine: No reported cases found

Maryland: Recognized, Carr v. Watkins, 227 Md. 578 (1962)

Massachusetts: Reported cases, privacy neither recognized nor rejected

Michigan: Recognized, Pallas v. Crowley-Milner Co., 322 Mich. 411 (1948)

Minnesota: Reported cases, privacy neither recognized nor rejected

Mississippi: Recognized, Martin v. Dorton, 210 Miss. 668 (1951)

Missouri: Recognized, Munden v. Harris, 153 Mo. App. 652 (1911)

Montana: Recognized, Welsh v. Roehm, 125 Mont. 517 (1952)

Nebraska: Rejected, Brunson v. Ranks Army Store, 161 Neb. 519 (1955)

Nevada: Reported cases, privacy neither recognized nor rejected

New Hampshire: Recognized, Hamberger v. Eastman, 206 A. 2d 239 (1964)

New Jersey: Recognized, Vanderbilt v. Mitchell, 72 N.J. Eq. 910 (1907)

New Mexico: Reported cases, privacy neither recognized nor rejected

New York: Recognized, 1903, Secs. 50 and 51, New York Civil Rights Law

North Carolina: Recognized, Flake v. Greensboro News Co., 212 N.C. 780 (1938)

North Dakota: No reported cases found

Ohio: Recognized, Martin v. F.I.Y. Theatre Co., 10 Ohio Ops. 338 (1938)

Oklahoma: Recognized, 1955, Okla. Stats. Title 21, Secs. 839.1, 839.2, and 839.3

Oregon: Recognized, Hinish v. Meier & Frank Co., 166 Ore. 482 (1941)

Pennsylvania: Recognized, Harlow v. Buno Co., 36 Pa. D.&C. 101 (1939)

Rhode Island: Rejected, Henry v. Cherry and Webb, 30 R.I. 13 (1909)

South Carolina: Recognized, Holloman v. Life Ins. Co. of Va., 192 S.C. 454 (1940)

South Dakota: Recognized, Truxes v. Kenco Enterprises, 119 N.W. 2d 914 (1963)

Tennessee: Reported cases, privacy neither recognized nor rejected

Texas: Rejected, Milner v. Red River Valley Pub. Co., 249 S.W. 2d 227 (1952)

Utah: Recognized, 1909, Utah Code Annotated, Secs. 76–4–8 and 76–4–9

Vermont: No reported cases found

Virginia: Recognized, 1904, Virginia Code Annotated, Sec. 8–650

Washington: Reported cases, privacy neither recognized nor rejected

West Virginia: Recognized, Roach v. Harper, 143 W. Va. 869 (1958)

Wisconsin: Rejected, Judevine v. Benzies-Montanye Fuel & Warehouse Co., 222 Wis. 512 (1936)

Wyoming: No reported cases found

District of Columbia: Recognized, Peay v. Curtis Pub. Co., 78 F. Supp. 305 (1948)

Appendix D

TEXTS OF EXISTING PRIVACY STATUTES

1. NEW YORK STATE *
Civil Rights Law
Article 5—Right of Privacy

Sec. 50. Right of privacy

A person, firm or corporation that uses for advertising purposes, or for the purpose of trade, the name, portrait or picture of any living person without having first obtained the written consent of such person, or if a minor of his or her parent or guardian, is guilty of a misdemeanor.

Sec. 51. Action for injunction and for damages

Any person whose name, portrait or picture is used within this state for advertising purposes or for the purposes of trade without the written consent first obtained as above provided may maintain an equitable action in the supreme court of this state against the person, firm or corporation so using his name, portrait or picture, to prevent and restrain the use thereof; and may also sue and recover damages for any injuries sustained by reason of such use and if the defendant shall have knowingly used such person's name, portrait or picture in such manner as is forbidden or declared to be unlawful by the last section, the jury, in its discretion, may award exemplary damages.
[The following was added in 1921.] But nothing contained in this act shall be so construed as to prevent any person, firm or corporation, practicing the profession of photography, from exhibiting in or about his or its establishment specimens of the work of such establishment, unless the same is continued by such person, firm or corporation after written notice objecting thereto has been given by the person portrayed; and nothing contained in this act shall be so construed as to

* McKinney's Consolidated Laws of New York Annotated.

prevent any person, firm or corporation from using the name, portrait or picture of any manufacturer or dealer in connection with the goods, wares and merchandise manufactured, produced or dealt in by him which he has sold or disposed of with such name, portrait or picture used in connection therewith; or from using the name, portrait or picture of any author, composer or artist in connection with his literary, musical or artistic productions which he has sold or disposed of with such name, portrait or picture used in connection therewith. As amended L.1911, c. 226; L.1921, c. 501, eff. May 3, 1921.

2. VIRGINIA *
Civil Remedies and Procedures

Sec. 8–650. Unauthorized use of the name or picture of any person. —A person, firm, or corporation that knowingly uses for advertising purposes, or for the purposes of trade, the name, portrait, or picture of any person resident in the State, without having first obtained the written consent of such person, or if dead, of his surviving consort, or if none, his next of kin, or if a minor, of his or her parent or guardian, as well as that of such minor, shall be deemed guilty of a misdemeanor and be fined not less than fifty nor more than one thousand dollars. Any person whose name, portrait, or picture is used within this State for advertising purposes or for the purposes of trade, without such written consent first obtained, or the surviving consort or next of kin, as the case may be, may maintain a suit in equity against the person, firm, or corporation so using such person's name, portrait, or picture to prevent and restrain the use thereof; and may also sue and recover damages for any injuries sustained by reason of such use. And if the defendant shall have knowingly used such person's name, portrait, or picture in such manner as is forbidden or declared to be unlawful by this chapter, the jury, in its discretion, may award exemplary damages. (Code 1919, Sec. 5782.)

3. UTAH †
Advertising Offenses

Sec. 76–4–8. Use of name or picture of individual.—Any person who uses for advertising purposes or for purposes of trade, or upon any postal card, the name, portrait or picture of any person, if such

---

* Code of Virginia, 1950.
† Utah Code Annotated 1953.

person is living, without first having obtained the written consent of such person or, if a minor, of his parent or guardian, or, if such person is dead, without the written consent of his heirs or personal representatives, is guilty of a misdemeanor.

Sec. 76–4–9. [As revised 1963.] Civil liability.—Any living person, or the heirs or personal representatives of any deceased person, whose name, portrait or picture is used within this state for advertising purposes or for the purposes of trade, without the written consent first obtained as provided in the next preceding section and, any person or corporation may maintain an action against a violator of any other section of this chapter defining advertising offenses. If in such actions the court shall find that the defendant is violating or has violated any of the provisions of this act, it shall enjoin the defendant from a continuance thereof. It shall not be necessary that actual damages to the plaintiff be alleged or proved, but if damages are alleged and proved, the plaintiff in said action shall be entitled to recover from the defendant the actual damages, if any, sustained in addition to injunctive relief and a reasonable attorney's fee. And in the case of a violation of 76–4–8, if the defendant shall have knowingly used such person's name, portrait or picture in such manner as is declared to be unlawful, the jury or court, if tried without a jury, in its discretion may award exemplary damages.

4. OKLAHOMA *
Title 21
Chapter 30.—Miscellaneous Offenses Against
the Person
Right of Privacy
[As Revised 1965]

Sec. 839.1 Right of privacy—Use of name or picture for advertising without consent—Misdemeanor

Any person, firm or corporation that uses for the purpose of advertising for the sale of any goods, wares or merchandise, or for the solicitation of patronage by any business enterprise, the name, portrait or picture of any person, without having obtained, prior or subsequent to such use, the consent of such person, or, if such person is a minor, the consent of a parent or guardian, and, if such person is deceased, without the consent of the surviving spouse, personal repre-

* Oklahoma Statutes Annotated.

sentatives, or that of a majority of the deceased's adult heirs, is guilty of a misdemeanor. Laws 1965, c. 431, Sec. 1.

Sec. 839.2 Right of action—Damages

Any person whose right of privacy, as created in Section 1 hereof, is violated or the surviving spouse, personal representatives or a majority of the adult heirs of a deceased person whose name, portrait, or picture is used in violation of Section 1 hereof, may obtain an action against the person, firm or corporation so using such person's name, portrait or picture to prevent and restrain the use thereof, and may in the same action recover damages for any injuries sustained, and if the defendant in such action shall have knowingly used such person's name, portrait or picture in such manner as is declared to be unlawful, the jury or court, if tried without a jury, in its discretion may award exemplary damages. Laws 1965, c. 431, Sec. 2.

Sec. 839.3 Right of photographer to exhibit specimens of work— Other uses excepted

Nothing contained in this act shall be so construed as to prevent any person, firm or corporation, practicing the profession of photography, from exhibiting in or about his or its establishment specimens of the work of such establishment, unless the same is continued by such person, firm or corporation after written notice objecting thereto has been given by the person portrayed; and nothing contained in this act shall be so construed as to prevent any person, firm or corporation from using the name, portrait or picture of any manufacturer or dealer in connection with the goods, wares and merchandise manufactured, produced or dealt in by him which he has sold or disposed of with such name, portrait or picture used in connection therewith; or from using the name, portrait or picture of any author, composer or artist in connection with his literary, musical or artistic productions which he has sold or disposed of with such name, portrait or picture used in connection therewith. Provided that this act shall not prevent the continued use of names of such persons by business establishments using such names and displaying such names at the effective date of this act. Laws 1965, c. 431, Sec. 3.

Notes

PREFACE

1. Edward Hall, *The Hidden Dimension* (Garden City, N.Y.: Doubleday, 1966).

2. Alan Westin, *Privacy and Freedom* (New York: Atheneum, 1967); Vance Packard, *The Naked Society* (New York: David McKay, 1964); Myron Brenton, *The Privacy Invaders* (New York: Coward-McCann, 1964).

3. Samuel Hofstader and George Horowitz, *Right of Privacy* (New York: Central Book Co., 1964).

CHAPTER 1

1. William M. Beaney, "The Right of Privacy and American Law," *Law and Contemporay Problems* 31, no. 2 (1966):255.

2. Henry Steele Commager, *The American Mind* (21st ed.; New Haven, Conn.: Yale University Press, 1950), p. 41.

3. Jacques Barzun and Henry F. Graff, *The Modern Researcher* (Harbinger ed.; New York: Harcourt, Brace and World, 1962), p. 149.

4. William Bradford, *Of Plymouth Plantation, 1620–1647*, ed. Samuel E. Morrison (New York: Alfred A. Knopf, 1952), pp. 149–53.

5. The idea of great homogeneity in rural colonial American villages and its impact upon individual liberty is best explored in John P. Roche, "American Liberty: An Examination of the Tradition of Freedom," *Shadow and Substance* (New York: Macmillan, 1964), pp. 3–38. Population figures are taken from U.S. Department of Commerce, Bureau of the Census, *Historical Statistics of the United States: Colonial Times to 1957* (Washington, D.C.: U.S. Government Printing Office, 1960), p. 9. These reports counted as urban dwellers anyone living in an incorporated place with a population of 2,500.

6. Alfred McClung Lee, *The Daily Newspaper in America* (New York: Macmillan, 1937), p. 715.

7. Henry Adams, *The Education of Henry Adams: An Autobi-*

ography (Boston: Houghton Mifflin, 1918), p. 237. Arthur M. Schlesinger's *Rise of the City, 1878–1898* (New York: Macmillan, 1933) is still one of the best sources for a description of the monumental movement from the farm to the city.

8. Bureau of the Census, *Historical Statistics,* pp. 56–57.

9. Thomas H. O'Connor, "The Right to Privacy in Historical Perspective," *Massachusetts Law Quarterly* 53 (June 1968):108–9.

10. Edward Shils, "Privacy: Its Constitution and Its Vicissitudes," *Law and Contemporary Problems* 31, no. 2 (1966): 288, 299. Granville Hicks, "The Invasion of Privacy: The Limits of Privacy," *American Scholar,* Spring 1959, p. 185.

11. Shils, "Privacy," pp. 291–92.

12. Lee, *Daily Newspaper,* p. 722. Bureau of the Census, *Historical Statistics,* p. 499.

13. Bureau of the Census, *Historical Statistics,* p. 500. Lee, *Daily Newspaper,* p. 732.

14. Sidney Kobre, *The Yellow Press and Gilded Age Journalism* (Tallahassee: Florida State University, 1964), p. 7.

15. Edwin Emery, *The Press and America* (2nd ed.; Englewood Cliffs, N.J.: Prentice-Hall, 1962), p. 398.

16. Ibid., p. 346.

17. Schlesinger, *Rise of the City,* p. 153; Emery, *The Press,* p. 352.

18. Statistics on the growth of American education during the period can be found in Bureau of the Census, *Historical Statistics,* pp. 207–9.

19. Kobre, *Yellow Press,* p. 2.

20. Louis Nizer, "The Right of Privacy: A Half-Century's Development," *Michigan Law Review* 39 (February 1941):526. Edward N. Doan, "The Newspaper and the Right of Privacy," *The Journal of the Bar Association of the State of Kansas* 5 (February 1937):214.

21. "The Profession of Journalism," *Nation,* 17 July 1873, p. 37.

22. As reported in "Newspaper Espionage," *Forum,* August 1886, p. 533.

23. E. L. Godkin, "The Rights of the Citizen, IV: To His Own Reputation," *Scribner's Magazine,* July 1890, p. 67.

24. Schlesinger, *Rise of the City,* p. 194. Elbridge L. Adams, "The Right of Privacy and Its Relation to the Law of Libel," *American Law Review* 39 (January–February 1905):37. Frank Luther Mott, *American Journalism* (New York: Macmillan, 1941), p. 444.

25. Joseph E. Chamberlain, *The Boston Transcript* (Cambridge, Mass.: Riverside Press, 1930), p. 158.

26. Edward J. Bloustein, "Privacy as an Aspect of Human Dignity: An Answer to Dean Prosser," *New York University Law Review* 39 (December 1964):984.

CHAPTER 2

1. Samuel D. Warren and Louis D. Brandeis, "The Right to Privacy," *Harvard Law Review* 4 (December 1890):220.

2. "Table Gossip," *Boston Globe,* 7 December 1890, p. 13.

3. Alpheus T. Mason, *Brandeis: A Free Man's Life* (New York: Viking Press, 1946), p. 70.

4. Marc A. Franklin, "A Constitutional Problem in Privacy Protection: Legal Inhibitions on Reporting of Fact," *Stanford Law Review* 16 (December 1963):112, n. 28.

5. William L. Prosser, "Privacy," *California Law Review* 40 (August 1960):383.

6. Godkin, "Rights of the Citizen," p. 67.

7. Adams, "The Right of Privacy," p. 37. Louis D. Brandeis to Samuel D. Warren, 8 April 1905, Brandeis Papers, University of Louisville Law School Library, Louisville, Ky. Samuel Warren IV to the author, 25 July 1968.

8. Mason, *Brandeis,* p. 70.

9. Warren and Brandeis, "The Right to Privacy," p. 195.

10. See, for example, Pope v. Curl, 2 Atk. 341 (1741); Duke of Queenberry v. Shebbeare, 2 Eden 329 (1758); Millar v. Taylor, 4 Burrow's Rep. 2302 (1769); Perceval v. Phipps, 2 Ves. & Beam. 19 (1813); Prince Albert v. Strange, 1 MacN. & G. 25 (1849).

11. Gee v. Pritchard, 2 Swanst. 402 (1818); Woolsey v. Judd, 4 Duer 379 (1851).

12. Lectures: Abernathy v. Hutchinson, 3 L.J. Ch. 209 (1825). Etchings: Prince Albert v. Strange, 1 MacN. and G. 25 (1849). Photograph: Pollard v. The Photographic Co., 58 L.J. Ch. (N.S.) 251 (1888).

13. Warren and Brandeis, "The Right to Privacy," p. 219, n. 3.

14. Olmstead v. United States, 277 U.S. 438 (1928), at 478.

15. Harry Kalven, Jr., "Privacy in Tort Law—Were Warren and Brandeis Wrong?" *Law and Contemporary Problems* 31, no. 2 (1966):328.

CHAPTER 3

1. 25 May 1890, p. 1.

2. Hyde v. U.S., 225 U.S. 347, at 391.

3. The most thorough challenge to the Warren-Brandeis position was published in 1894. See Herbert Spencer Hadley, "The Right to Privacy," *Northwestern Law Review* 3 (October 1894):1–21. This publication, which is not to be confused with the *Northwestern*

University Law Review, is difficult to find, and the Hadley piece has gone largely unnoticed.

4. Warren and Brandeis, "The Right to Privacy," p. 196.

5. *American Newspaper Annual* (Philadelphia: N. W. Ayer and Sons, 1891), pp. 298–304; Mott, *American Journalism*, p. 452; Kobre, *Yellow Press*, p. 120.

6. Edwin M. Bacon, *Dictionary of Boston* (Boston, 1886), cited in Chamberlain, *The Boston Transcript*, p. 159.

7. Chamberlain, *The Boston Transcript*, p. 158.

8. The statements in this section are based upon an extensive analysis of the Boston press for the year 1890. All editions of four of the city's eight daily newspapers published during the year provided the basic source material for the analysis.

9. *Boston Evening Journal*, 24 February 1890, p. 2.

10. *Boston Morning Journal*, 9 April 1890, p. 2.

11. *Boston Daily Advertiser*, 13 March 1890, p. 4; *Boston Evening Transcript*, 6 January 1890, p. 4.

12. Of the eight daily newspapers published in Boston in 1890, only these four are available on microfilm. I inspected all editions of the *Journal*, the *Daily Advertiser*, the *Globe*, and the *Evening Transcript*. The four other newspapers—the *Herald*, the *Evening Record*, the *Post*, and the *Traveller*—are not readily available. Two important qualifications, therefore, must be noted about analysis. First, I saw only half of the daily papers. And second, these might represent the four best newspapers, as libraries are prone to collect only good examples of an era's culture. Today, for example, most libraries keep copies of *The New York Times* and the *Washington Post*, but few bother to save the less respectable journals, such as the Hearst newspapers, the underground press, or the sensational weeklies like the *National Enquirer*. However, secondary sources such as Emery, *The Press*, Mott, *American Journalism*, and Chamberlain, *The Boston Transcript*, do not suggest that any of the four unexamined newspapers were sensational or especially irresponsible. Indeed, there is nothing to suggest that they differed in any substantial way from the four newspapers in the analysis.

13. *Boston Globe*, 8 June 1890, p. 13.

14. Warren and Brandeis, "The Right to Privacy," p. 196.

15. The only known source is the Harvard College Library, whose holding includes issues from 1890.

16. *Boston Daily Advertiser*, 17 June 1890, p. 1; *Boston Globe*, 22 June 1890, p. 13; *Boston Evening Transcript*, 18 June 1890, p. 3.

17. Nizer, "The Right of Privacy," p. 527.

18. Winsmore v. Greenbank, Willes 577 (1745).

19. 2 Vernon 645 (1709).

20. See Cotteral v. Griffiths, 4 Esp. 69 (1801); Chandler v. Thompson, 3 Camp. 80 (1811); Cross v. Lewis, 2 B. & C. 686 (1824); Tur-

ner v. Spooner, 30 L.J. Ch. 801 (1861); Tapling v. Jones, 11 H.L.C. 290 (1865).

21. Chandler v. Thompson, p. 81.

22. Pope v. Curl, 2 Atk. 341 (1741).

23. Duke of Queensbury v. Shebbeare, 2 Eden 329 (1758).

24. Millar v. Taylor, 4 Burrow's Rep. 2303 (1769).

25. 2 Ves. & Beam. 19 (1813). Plumer, by the way, was not without his critics—even before his ruling in the *Perceval* case. Sir Samuel Romilly, a contemporary, wrote this comment about Plumer in his diary: "A worse appointment than that of Plumer to be vice-chancellor, could hardly have been made. He knows nothing of the law of real property, nothing of the law of bankruptcy, and nothing of the doctrines peculiar to courts of equity." Extract from the private diary of Sir Samuel Romilly, 9 April 1813, from *Memoirs of the Life of Sir Samuel Romilly,* 2:310, as quoted in Woolsey v. Judd, 11 N.Y. Sup. Ct. 379 (1855), at 395.

26. 2 Swanst. 402 (1818). See "A Re-interpretation of Gee v. Pritchard," *Michigan Law Review* 25 (June 1927):889–91, for quotation (p. 890) and a more complete discussion of this point.

27. 1 MacN. & G. 25 (1849).

28. Prince Albert v. Strange, 2 DeGex. & Sm. 650 (1849), at 695.

29. 1 MacN. & G. 25 (1849), at 36; Hadley, "The Right to Privacy," p. 2.

30. 1 Hurl. & G. 148 (1862).

31. Denis v. Leclerc, 1 Mart. (O.S.) 297 (La. 1811).

32. 8 Paige 23 (1839).

33. 3 Edw. Ch. 543 (1842).

34. 3 Barb. Ch. 320 (1848), at 324.

35. 4 Duer 379 (1855).

36. See Folsom v. Marsh, 2 Story 100 (1842); Eyre v. Higbee, 35 Barb. 502 (1861); Grigsby v. Breckenridge, 65 Ky. (2 Bush) 480 (1867); Parton v. Prang, 3 Clifford 537 (1872); and Widdemer v. Hubbard, 19 Phil. (Pa.) 263 (1887).

37. Warren and Brandeis, "The Right to Privacy," p. 205.

38. See, for example, Yovatt v. Winyard, 1 J. & W. 394 (1820); Abernathy v. Hutchinson, 3 L.J. Ch. 209 (1825); Nicols v. Pitman, 53 L.J. Ch. (N.S.) 552 (1884); Morison v. Moat, 9 Hare 241 (1851); Tuck & Sons v. Priester, L.R. 19 Q.B.D. 629 (1887); Caird v. Sime, 57 L.J.P.C. 2 (1887); Pollard v. The Photographic Co., 40 Ch. Div. 345 (1888); and Moore v. Rugg, 44 Minn. 28 (1890).

39. Yovatt v. Winyard; Abernathy v. Hutchinson; Nicols v. Pitman.

40. 58 L.J. Ch. (N.S.) 251 (1888).

41. Warren and Brandeis, "The Right to Privacy," pp. 211, 213.

42. Winsmore v. Greenbank.

43. See Bedford v. McKowl, 3 Esp. 119 (1800); Martin v. Payne, 9 Johns 387 (1812); Andrews v. Askey, 8 C. & P. 7 (1837); Phelin v.

Kinderline, 20 Pa. St. 354 (1853); and Lavery v. Crooke, 52 Wisc. 612 (1881).

44. 4 Gray 568 (1855), at 571.

45. Newell v. Whitcher, 53 Vt. 589 (1880), at 589, 591.

46. Canning v. Williamstown, 1 Cush. 451 (1848).

47. Black v. Carrolton, 10 La. Ann. 33 (1855); Covington Street Railway Co. v. Packer, 9 Bush 455 (1872), at 456.

48. As an example, see Roberson v. Rochester Folding Box Co., 171 N.Y. 538 (1902).

49. Kalven, "Privacy in Tort Law," p. 329.

50. 46 Mich. 160 (1881).

51. See *The New York Times*, 15 June 1890, p. 2; 18 June 1890, p. 3; 21 June 1890, p. 2.

52. Brandeis to Warren, 8 April 1905, Brandeis Papers.

53. Kalven, "Privacy in Tort Law," p. 328.

54. See Stig Stromholm, *Right of Privacy and Rights of the Personality* (Stockholm: P. A. Norstedt and Soners Forlag, 1967) for a broad comparative survey of the right of privacy in Europe and the United States. With regard to England, Stromholm says: "As far as courts are concerned, it is enough to state that there is no decision where a right of privacy has been acknowledged and an action sustained merely on the ground that the defendant's conduct constituted an invasion of privacy." In 1961 a broad right of privacy bill was introduced in the House of Lords by Lord Mancroft. It was withdrawn, however, allegedly because of lack of government support.

CHAPTER 4

1. Frederick Davis, "What Do We Mean by 'Right to Privacy'?" *South Dakota Law Review* 4 (Spring 1959):6.

2. Beaney, "The Right to Privacy," p. 257.

3. Schuyler v. Curtis, 19 N.Y.S. 264 (1892), at 265.

4. 147 N.Y. 434 (1895), at 447.

5. See, for example, Metter v. Los Angeles Examiner, 35 Cal. App. 2d 304 (1939).

6. Marks v. Jaffa, 26 N.Y. Supp. 908 (1893), at 909.

7. Murray v. Gast Lithographic and Engraving Co., 28 N.Y. Supp. 271 (1894).

8. Corliss v. E. W. Walker Co., 57 Fed. Rep. 434 (1893), at 435.

9. Corliss v. E. W. Walker Co., 64 Fed. Rep. 280 (1894), at 282.

10. Atkinson v. Doherty, 121 Mich. 372 (1899), at 373.

11. 65 N.Y.S. 1109 (demurrer overruled, Sup. Ct., Monroe County, 1900).

12. 71 N.Y.S. 876 (1901).

13. 171 N.Y. 538 (1902), at 556.

14. Denis O'Brien, "The Right of Privacy," *Columbia Law Review* 2 (November 1902):443, 445, 446–47.

15. See Appendix D for the complete text of the measure, Secs. 50 and 51, New York Civil Rights Law.

16. 126 App. Div. 650 (1908).

17. Rhodes v. Sperry and Hutchinson, 193 N.Y. 223 (1908); aff'd. Sperry and Hutchinson Co. v. Rhodes, 220 U.S. 502 (1910).

18. MacKenzie v. Soden Mineral Springs Company, 18 N.Y.S. 240 (1891).

19. Moser v. Press Pub. Co., 109 N.Y.S. 963 (1908), at 965. Unfortunately, the facts in this case remain sketchy. Information about the news story, why it was printed, and why Moser believed it was offensive was not included in the court's opinion.

20. Jeffries v. New York Evening Journal Pub. Co., 124 N.Y.S. 780 (1910), at 780.

21. See Time, Inc. v. Hill, 385 U.S. 374 (1967).

22. Pavesich v. New England Mutual Life Ins. Co., 122 Ga. 190 (1905).

23. Brandeis to Cobb, 17 April 1905, Brandeis Papers.

24. 42 Ind. App. 3 (1908).

25. Foster-Milburn Co. v. Chinn, 134 Ky. 424 (1909), at 432.

26. Schulman v. Whitaker, 117 La. 704 (1906); Itzkovitch v. Whitaker, 117 La. 708 (1906).

27. Vanderbilt v. Mitchell, 72 N.J. Eq. 910 (1907).

28. 30 R.I. 13 (1909), at 25.

29. Act of May 12, 1903, P.L. 349.

30. Laws of Pennsylvania, Session of 1903, p. 352; Act of May 1, 1907, P.L. 124.

31. See Appendix D, Virginia Code Annotated, Sec. 8–650 (1950).

32. 11 Va. L. Reg. (1905).

33. Utah Code Annotated, Secs. 76–4–8 and 76–4–9 (1953); Donahue v. Warner Bros. Pictures, 2 Utah 2d 256 (1954).

34. Warren and Brandeis, "The Right to Privacy," p. 215.

35. Time, Inc. v. Hill, 385 U.S. 374 (1967).

CHAPTER 5

1. Zechariah Chafee, Jr., *Government and Mass Communications* (Chicago: University of Chicago, 1947; reprint ed.; Hamden, Conn.: Archon Books, 1965), p. 138.

2. For examples of the debate over the existence of the right, see Roy Moreland, "The Right of Privacy Today," *Kentucky Law Journal* 19 (January 1931):101; Rufus Lisle, "The Right of Privacy (A Contra View)," *Kentucky Law Journal* 19 (January 1931):137. Francis H.

Bohlen, "Fifty Years of Torts," *Harvard Law Review* 50 (March 1937):431.

3. Munden v. Harris, 153 Mo. App. 652 (1911), at 655.

4. Kunz v. Allen & Bayne, 102 Kan. 883 (1918).

5. 7 Alas. Rep. 416 (1926), at 423.

6. See Judge Jerome Frank's decision in Haelan Labs Inc. v. Topps Chewing Gum, 202 F. 2d 866 (1953).

7. *Seattle Star*, 26 August 1910, as quoted in Hillman v. Star Pub. Co., 64 Wash. 691 (1911), at 693.

8. *State ex rel.* La Follette v. Hinkle, 131 Wash. 86 (1924), at 94.

9. Peed v. Washington Times Co., 55 Wash. L. Rep. 182 (1927); Peay v. Curtis Pub. Co., 78 F. Supp. 305 (1948).

10. Binns v. Vitagraph Co., 147 App. Div. 783 (1911); 210 N.Y. 51 (1913).

11. Merle v. Sociological Research Film Corp., 166 App. Div. 376 (1915).

12. Humiston v. Universal Film Manufacturing Co., 189 App. Div. 467 (1919), at 474, 476.

13. Colyer v. Richard K. Fox Pub. Co., 162 App. Div. 297 (1914), at 299.

14. Damron v. Doubleday, Doran & Co., 231 N.Y.S. 444 (1928), at 445, 446.

15. McNulty v. Press Pub. Co., 241 N.Y.S. 29 (1930).

16. Wyatt v. Hall's Portrait Studio, 128 N.Y.S. 247 (1911); Loftus v. Greenwich Lithographing Co., 192 App. Div. 251 (1920), at 256.

17. Jones v. Herald Post Co., 230 Ky. 227 (1929).

18. Bazemore v. Savannah Hospital, 171 Ga. 257 (1930).

19. Douglas v. Stokes, 149 Ky. 506 (1912).

20. Vassar v. Loose-Wiles Biscuit Co., 197 Fed. 982 (1912).

21. *Ex parte* Sturm, 153 Md. 114 (1927).

22. Carr v. Watkins, 227 Md. 578 (1962).

CHAPTER 6

1. Richard A. Snyder, "The Right of Privacy: 50 Years After," *Temple University Law Quarterly* 15, no. 1 (November 1940):155.

2. Melvin v. Reid, 112 Cal. App. 285 (1931); Sidis v. F-R Publishing Corp., 113 F. 2d 806 (1940).

3. Melvin v. Reid, p. 286.

4. Stanley G. Pearson, "Torts: The Right to Privacy and the Pursuit of Happiness," *California Law Review* 20 (November 1931):101.

5. Mau v. Rio Grande Oil, Inc., 28 F. Supp. 845 (1939).

6. Metter v. Los Angeles Examiner, 35 Cal. App. 2d 304 (1939), at 311–12.

7. See T. M. Leovy, Jr., "Torts: The Right of Privacy," *Southern California Law Review* 13 (November 1939):81–91.

8. Ibid., p. 90.

9. Martin v. F.I.Y. Theatre Co., 10 Ohio Ops. 338 (1938), at 340.

10. Johnson v. Scripps Pub. Co., 18 Ohio Ops. 372 (1940).

11. Flake v. Greensboro News Co., 22 N.C. 780 (1938), at 793.

12. Harlow v. Buno Co., 36 Pa. D.&C. 101 (1939), at 104, 105.

13. Clayman v. Bernstein, 38 Pa. D.&C. 543 (1940).

14. Holloman v. Life Ins. Co. of Va., 192 S.C. 454 (1940).

15. Judevine v. Benzies–Montanye Fuel & Warehouse Co., 222 Wis. 512 (1936), at 572.

16. Fitzsimmons v. Olinger Mortuary Assoc., 91 Col. 544 (1932); McCreery v. Miller's Grocerteria, 99 Col. 499 (1937).

17. Thayer v. Worcester Post Co., 284 Mass. 160 (1933), at 161.

18. Themo v. New England Newspaper Pub. Co., 306 Mass. 54 (1940).

19. Bennett v. Gusdorf, 101 Mont. 39 (1935).

20. Durkin v. Colgate-Palmolive-Peet Co. (1937), unreported, but noted in "Radio Broadcasting, Invasion of Privacy, Broadcast of Current News Events," *AIR Law Review* 11 (January 1940):86.

21. Paramount Pictures v. Leader Press, 24 F. Supp. 1004 (1938). For the law, see Oklahoma Statutes Annotated, Title 21, Secs. 839.1, 839.2, 839.3.

22. Martin v. New Metropolitan Fiction, 248 N.Y.S. 359 (1931).

23. 237 App. Div. 863 (1932).

24. Swacker v. Wright, 277 N.Y.S. 296 (1935), p. 298.

25. Krieger v. Popular Publications, 3 N.Y.S. 2d 480 (1938).

26. Davis v. RKO Radio Pictures, 16 F. Supp. 195 (1936).

27. Gardella v. Log Cabin Products Co., 89 F. 2d 891 (1937).

28. Blumenthal v. Picture Classics, 235 App. Div. 570 (1932), p. 574.

29. Chafee, *Government and Mass Communications,* pp. 136–37.

30. Sarat Lahiri v. Daily Mirror, 295 N.Y.S. 382 (1937), at 388.

31. Schley v. New York Journal, 99 N.Y.L.J. 3107:2 (28 June 1938), as quoted in Nizer, "The Right of Privacy," p. 542.

32. Sweenek v. Pathé News, Inc., 16 F. Supp. 746 (1936), at 747–48.

33. People v. Robert McBride & Co., 288 N.Y.S. 501 (1936), at 508, 509.

34. Kline v. Robt. McBride & Co., 11 N.Y.S. 2d 674 (1939), at 683.

35. Middleton v. News Syndicate Co., 295 N.Y.S. 120 (1937).

36. Semler v. Ultem Pubs., 9 N.Y.S. 2d 319 (1938).

37. Jackson v. Consumer Publications, 10 N.Y.S. 2d 691 (1939).

38. Banks v. King Features Syndicate, 30 F. Supp. 352 (1939).

39. Jared Manley, "April Fool," *New Yorker,* 14 August 1937, p. 23.

40. Ibid.

41. Ibid., p. 26.

42. Sidis v. F-R Publishing Co., pp. 808, 809.

CHAPTER 7

1. Nizer, "The Right of Privacy," p. 529.
2. Hinish v. Meier & Frank Co., 166 Ore. 482 (1941), p. 503.
3. Florida Constitution, Declaration of Rights, Sec. 4, as quoted in Cason v. Baskin, 155 Fla. 198 (1944), at 212.
4. Justice Brown's description, Cason v. Baskin, pp. 205–6.
5. 159 Fla. 31 (1947).
6. Reed v. Real Detective Pub. Co., 63 Ariz. 294 (1945).
7. Smith v. Doss, 251 Ala. 250 (1948).
8. Pallas v. Crowley-Milner and Co., 322 Mich. 411 (1948); 334 Mich. 282 (1952).
9. Peay v. Curtis Pub. Co., 78 F. Supp. 305 (1948).
10. James J. Brennan, "Never Give a Passenger a Break," *Saturday Evening Post*, 28 February 1948, p. 34.
11. See, for example, Gill v. Curtis Pub. Co., 239 P. 2d 630 (1952); Leverton v. Curtis Pub. Co., 97 F. Supp. 181, 192 F. 2d 974 (1951); and Hull v. Curtis Pub. Co., 126 A. 2d 644 (1956).
12. William L. Prosser, *Handbook of the Law of Torts* (St. Paul, Minn.: West Publishing, 1964), p. 837.
13. See, for example, Hull v. Curtis.
14. Pritchett v. Knox County Board of Commissioners, 42 Ind. App. 3 (1908).
15. Continental Optical Co. v. Reed, 119 Ind. App. 643 (1949).
16. Norman v. City of Las Vegas, 64 Nev. 38 (1947).
17. See Prosser, *Handbook of the Law of Torts*, p. 831; and Hofstader and Horowitz, *Right of Privacy*, p. 20.
18. Berg v. Minneapolis Star and Tribune Co., 79 F. Supp. 957 (1948), at 960.
19. Reprint of the *Time* magazine story as quoted in Barber v. Time, 348 Mo. 1199 (1942), at 1203.
20. 65 N.Y.S. 2d 173 (1946); rev'd. 272 App. Div. 166 (1950).
21. 272 App. Div. 166 (1950), at 171.
22. Reprint of the story in New York *Daily Mirror* in Sutton v. Hearst Pub. Co., 98 N.Y.S. 2d 233 (1950), at 234, 235.
23. Sutton v. Hearst Pub. Co., 277 App. Div. 155 (1950).
24. Lawrence v. Ylla, 55 N.Y.S. 2d 343 (1945), at 345.
25. Koussevitzky v. Allen, Town & Heath, 68 N.Y.S. 2d 779 (1947), aff'd. 272 App. Div. 759 (1947).
26. 68 N.Y.S. 2d 779 (1947), at 783.
27. Nebb v. Bell Syndicate, 41 F. Supp. 929 (1941).
28. Kerby v. Hal Roach Studios, Inc., 53 Cal. App. 2d 207 (1942).
29. Wright v. RKO Radio Pictures, Inc., 55 F. Supp. 639 (1944).
30. Levey v. Warner Bros. Pictures, 57 F. Supp. 40 (1944).

31. Toscani v. Hersey, 271 App. Div. 445 (1946).

32. Wright v. RKO Radio Pictures, p. 640.

33. Levey v. Warner Bros., p. 41.

34. Toscani v. Hersey, p. 448.

35. O'Brien v. Pabst Sales Co., 124 F. 2d 167 (1942).

36. Wallach v. Bacharach, 80 N.Y.S. 2d 37 (1948), p. 39.

CHAPTER 8

1. Leon R. Yankwich, "The Right of Privacy: Its Development, Scope and Limitations," *Notre Dame Lawyer* 27, no. 4 (1952): 525–26.

2. Martin v. Dorton, 210 Miss. 668 (1951), at 673.

3. Eick v. Perk Dog Food Co., 347 Ill. App. 293 (1952), at 306.

4. Welsh v. Roehm, 125 Mont. 517 (1952), at 521, 524.

5. Bremmer v. Journal-Tribune Pub. Co., 247 Iowa 817 (1956), at 827, 828.

6. Roach v. Harper, 143 W. Va. 869 (1958), at 875–76.

7. O'Connell v. The Hartford Times, 15 Conn. Supp. 85 (1947).

8. Korn v. Rennison, 21 Conn. Supp. 400 (1959), at 403.

9. Langford v. Vanderbilt University, 199 Tenn. 389 (1956), at 403–4.

10. See Prosser, *Handbook of the Law of Torts,* p. 837, and Hofstader and Horowitz, *Right of Privacy,* p. 20, for support of the notion that the *Langford* case constituted recognition. Relying heavily on Prosser, Judge Frank W. Wilson, in Cordell v. Detective Publications, Inc., 307 F. Supp. 1212 (1968), ruled that he believed there was a legally protected right of privacy in Tennessee. However, the judge found Mrs. Cordell's complaint without a cause of action, and so there still has been no successful suit for invasion of privacy in Tennessee.

11. Oklahoma Statutes, Title 21, Sections 839 and 840.

12. Paramount Pictures v. Leader Press, 24 F. Supp. 1004 (1938), rev'd. on other grounds, 106 F. 2d 229 (1939); and McKinzie v. Huckaby, 112 F. Supp. 642 (1953).

13. Oklahoma Statutes, Title 21, Sections 839.1, 839.2, and 839.3.

14. Donahue v. Warner Bros. Pictures, 194 F. 2d 6 (1952), at 12.

15. 2 Utah 2d 256 (1954), at 260.

16. Richard L. Dewsnup, "Utah Right of Privacy Statute Covers Only Advertisements for Sale of Collateral Product," *Utah Law Review* 4 (Fall 1954):279.

17. Milner v. Red River Valley Pub. Co., 249 S.W. 2d 227 (1952), at 229.

18. Reprinted in the court opinion, Brunson v. Ranks Army Store, 161 Neb. 519 (1955), at 520.

19. Yoeckel v. Samonig, 272 Wis. 430 (1956), at 434.

20. Gill v. Curtis Pub. Co., 231 P. 2d 565 (1951), 239 P. 2d 630

(1952); Gill v. Hearst Pub., 231 P. 2d 570 (1951), 239 P. 2d 636 (1952), 253 P. 2d 441 (1953).

21. Gill v. Curtis, 231 P. 2d 565 (1951), at 568.
22. Gill v. Curtis, 239 P. 2d 630 (1952), at 632.
23. Gill v. Hearst, 239 P. 2d 636 (1952), at 638.
24. Gill v. Hearst, 253 P. 2d 441 (1953), at 443, 444, 445.
25. William Prosser, "Privacy," *California Law Review* 48 (August 1960):389.
26. Leon R. Yankwich, "Trends in the Law Affecting Media of Communication," *Federal Rules Decision* 15 (1954):326.
27. Kelley v. Post Publishing Co., 327 Mass. 275 (1951), at 277–78.
28. Abernathy v. Thornton, 263 Ala. 496 (1955), at 498.
29. Jacova v. Southern Radio-Television Co., 83 So. 2d 34 (1955), at 36.
30. Meetze v. AP, 95 S.E. 2d 606 (1956), at 609.
31. Frith v. AP, 176 F. Supp. 671 (1959).
32. Estill v. Hearst Pub. Co., 186 F. 2d 1017 (1951), at 1019.
33. Samuel v. Curtis Pub. Co., 122 F. Supp. 327 (1954), at 329.

CHAPTER 9

1. Smith v. NBC, 292 P. 2d 600 (1956), at 604.
2. Oma v. Hillman Periodicals, 281 App. Div. 240 (1953).
3. Goelet v. Confidential, 5 App. Div. 2d 226 (1958), at 229–30.
4. Time, Inc. v. Hill, 385 U.S. 374 (1967).
5. People v. Scribner's Sons, 130 N.Y.S. 2d 514 (1954).
6. Flores v. Mosler Safe Co., 7 N.Y. 2d 276 (1959).
7. 202 F. 2d 866 (1953), at 868.
8. Russell v. Marboro Books, 183 N.Y.S. 2d 8 (1959), at 18.
9. Leverton v. Curtis Pub. Co., 97 F. Supp. 181 (1951).
10. Leverton v. Curtis Pub. Co., 192 F. 2d 974 (1951), at 978.
11. Hull v. Curtis Pub. Co., 182 Pa. Super. 86 (1956), at 87.
12. Schnabel v. Meredith, 378 Pa. 609 (1954), at 610.
13. Aquino v. Bulletin Company, 190 Pa. Super. 528 (1959), at 531.
14. Gautier v. Pro-Football, Inc., 99 N.Y.S. 2d 812 (1951).
15. Gautier v. Pro-Football, Inc., 278 App. Div. 431 (1951), at 434–35.
16. Gautier v. Pro-Football, Inc., 304 N.Y. 354 (1952), at 358.
17. Bernstein v. NBC, 129 F. Supp. 817 (1955), at 828.
18. Smith v. NBC, 292 P. 2d 600 (1956).
19. Miller v. NBC, 157 F. Supp. 240 (1957), at 243.
20. Strickler v. NBC, 167 F. Supp. 68 (1958).
21. Garner v. Triangle Publications, 97 F. Supp. 546 (1951).
22. Hazlitt v. Fawcett Pub., 116 F. Supp. 538 (1953), at 545; Annerino v. Dell Pub. Co., 17 Ill. App. 2d 205 (1958), at 210.
23. 230 F. 2d 359 (1956); 251 F. 2d 447 (1958).
24. Jenkins v. Dell, p. 451.

CHAPTER 10

1. From his dissent in Olmstead v. United States, 277 U.S. 438 (1928), at 472–73, quoting Justice Joseph McKenna, Weems v. United States, 217 U.S. 349 (1910), at 373.

2. 385 U.S. 374 (1967).

3. Such a case arose in Spahn v. Julian Messner, Inc., 21 N.Y. 2d 124 (1967); probable jurisdiction noted, 89 S. Ct. 80 (1968). The suit was dismissed, however, when the litigants settled the matter out of court.

4. Olan Mills v. Dodd, 353 S.W. 2d 22 (1962).

5. See *Kentucky Law Journal* 22, no. 1 (1933):108–21 for a report of the decision.

6. Ibid., p. 121.

7. Carr v. Watkins, 227 Md. 578 (1962), at 588.

8. Reardon v. News Journal Pub. Co., 164 A. 2d 263 (1960), at 266–67.

9. Barbieri v. News Journal Pub. Co., 189 A. 2d 773 (1963), at 775.

10. Truxes v. Kenco Enterprises, 119 N.W. 2d 914 (1963), at 919.

11. Hamberger v. Eastman, 206 A. 2d 239 (1964), at 242.

12. Peterson v. Idaho First Nat'l Bank, 83 Idaho 578 (1961), at 585.

13. Hubbard v. Journal Publishing Co., 69 N.M. 473 (1962).

14. Schneiderman v. New York Post, 220 N.Y.S. 2d 1008 (1961), at 1009.

15. Durgom v. CBS, 214 N.Y.S. 2d 752 (1961), at 754.

16. McAndrews v. Roy, 131 So. 2d 256 (1961), at 259.

17. Sharman v. Schmidt & Sons, 216 F. Supp. 401 (1963), at 407.

18. Werner v. Times-Mirror Co., 193 Cal. App. 2d 111 (1961), at 119.

19. Carlisle v. Fawcett Pub., Inc., 201 Cal. App. 2d 733 (1962), at 747.

20. Patterson v. Tribune Co., 146 So. 2d 623 (1962), at 624.

21. Daily Times Democrat v. Graham, 162 So. 2d 474 (1962), at 476.

22. Nappier v. Jefferson Standard Life Ins. Co., 213 F. Supp. 174 (1963).

23. Nappier v. Jefferson Standard Life Ins. Co., 322 F. 2d 502 (1963), at 503.

24. There has been a criminal action based on the Wisconsin statute. See State v. Evjue, 253 Wis. 146 (1948), 254 Wis. 581 (1949). However, no invasion of privacy action was brought by the rape victim in this case.

25. Time, Inc. v. Hill, 18 App. Div. 485 (1963), 15 N.Y. 2d 986 (1965), 385 U.S. 374 (1967); Spahn v. Julian Messner, Inc., 250 N.Y.S. 2d 529 (1964), 23 App. Div. 216 (1965), 18 N.Y. 2d 324 (1966), 387 U.S. 239 (1967), 21 N.Y. 2d 124 (1967).

26. Booth v. Curtis Pub. Co., 15 App. Div. 2d 343 (1962), at 349.

27. 11 N.Y. 2d 907 (1962).

28. University of Notre Dame v. 20th Century Fox, 22 App. Div. 2d 452 (1965), at 454.

29. Estate of Hemingway v. Random House, 268 N.Y.S. 2d 531 (1966), at 534. Aff'd. 23 N.Y. 2d 341 (1968).

30. Youssoupoff v. CBS, 244 N.Y.S. 2d 701 (1965), at 706.

31. 376 U.S. 254 (1964).

32. Pauling v. News Syndicate Co., 335 F. 2d 659 (1964).

33. Youssoupoff v. CBS, 265 N.Y.S. 2d 754 (1965), at 758.

34. Time, Inc. v. Hill, 385 U.S. 374 (1967).

CHAPTER 11

1. Time, Inc. v. Hill, 385 U.S. 374 (1967), at 387.

2. Hill v. Hayes, 207 N.Y.S. 2d 901 (1960), at 903.

3. Hill v. Hayes, 18 App. Div. 2d 485 (1963), at 489.

4. Moser v. Press Pub. Co., 109 N.Y.S. 963 (1908).

5. Hill v. Hayes, 18 App. Div. 2d 485, p. 493.

6. 15 N.Y. 2d 986 (1965); 16 N.Y. 2d 658 (1965).

7. See, for example, Curtis Publishing Co. v. Neyland, 290 U.S. 661 (1933), and Wagner v. Fawcett Publications, Inc., 372 U.S. 909 (1963).

8. Time, Inc. v. Hill, 385 U.S. 374 (1967), at 387–88.

9. See, for example, Marshall S. Shapo, "Media Injuries to Personality: An Essay on Legal Regulation of Public Communication," *Texas Law Review* 46 (April 1968):657, where the author suggests that powerful members of the media will now attack "defenseless individuals who lack effective reply or remedy."

10. Spahn v. Julian Messner, Inc., 250 N.Y.S. 2d 529 (1964); 23 App. Div. 2d 216 (1965); 18 N.Y. 2d 324 (1966).

11. 23 App. Div. 2d 216 (1965), at 221.

12. 387 U.S. 239 (1967).

13. 21 N.Y. 2d 124 (1967), at 127.

14. 89 S. Ct. 80 (1968).

15. Letter from Selig J. Levitan, attorney for the defendant, 10 September 1970.

16. Oregon: Hamilton v. Crown Life Ins., 246 Ore. 4 (1967). Georgia: McQueen v. Wilson, 117 Ga. App. 488 (1968). New York: Rosemont Enterprises, Inc. v. Random House, Inc., 294 N.Y.S. 2d 122 (1968); Cullen v. Grove Press, Inc., 276 F. Supp. 727 (D.C.N.Y. 1967); Paulsen v. Personality Posters, Inc., 59 Misc. 2d 444 (1968); Pagan v. New York Herald Tribune, Inc., 301 N.Y.S. 2d 120 (1969); Rand v. The Hearst Corp., 298 N.Y.S. 2d 405 (1969). District of Columbia: Liberty Lobby v. Drew Pearson, 390 F. 2d 491 (1968); Pearson v. Dodd, 410 F. 2d 701 (1969), cert. den. 89 S. Ct. 2021 (1969). Michigan: Weeren v. Evening News Association, 152 N.W. 2d 676 (1967). Massachusetts: Commonwealth v. Wiseman, 249 N.E.

2d 610 (1969); DeSalvo v. 20th Century Fox Film Corp., 300 F. Supp. 742 (1969). Minnesota: Hurley v. Northwest Publications, Inc., 273 F. Supp. 967 (1967); aff'd. 398 F. 2d 346 (1969). Tennessee: Cordell v. Detective Publications, Inc., 307 F. Supp. 1212 (1968). South Carolina: Holmes v. The Curtis Pub. Co., 303 F. Supp. 522 (1969). California: Kapellas v. Kofman, 459 P. 2d 912 (1969); Varnish v. Best Medium Pub. Co., 405 F. 2d 608 (1968).

17. Rosemont v. Random House, p. 127.

18. Holmes v. Curtis, p. 523.

19. Commonwealth v. Wiseman, p. 615.

20. "Massachusetts Ban on Prison Life Film Upheld as Supreme Court Refuses to Hear Appeal," *FOI Digest* 12 (July–August 1970):8.

CHAPTER 12

1. Carlisle v. Fawcett Pub., Inc., 201 Cal. App. 2d 733 (1962), at 745.

2. Justice Andrew J. Cobb, Pavesich v. New England Mutual Life Ins. Co., 122 Ga. 190 (1905), at 220.

3. Kalven, "Privacy in Tort Law," p. 337.

4. Flake v. Greensboro News Co., 212 N.C. 780 (1938); Munden v. Harris, 153 Mo. App. 652 (1911).

5. 41 Am. Jur. 925, n. 11.

6. Clark C. Hauighurst, "Foreword, Privacy Symposium," *Law and Contemporary Problems* 31, no. 2 (1966):251.

7. George Ragland, Jr., "The Right of Privacy," *Kentucky Law Journal* 17 (January 1929):87.

8. "The Right of Privacy Today," *Harvard Law Review* 43 (December 1929):297–302.

9. *Restatement of the Law of Torts* (St. Paul, Minn.: American Law Institute Publishers, 1939), 4:398–402.

10. Nizer, "The Right of Privacy," pp. 526–60. This article was cited frequently in judicial opinions after its publication.

11. Spahn v. Julian Messner, Inc., 18 N.Y. 2d 324 (1966).

12. See Humiston v. Universal Film Manufacturing Co., 178 N.Y.S. 752 (1918); Booth v. Curtis Pub. Co., 15 App. Div. 2d 343 (1962).

13. See also the recent Rand v. The Hearst Corp., 31 A.D. 2d 206 (1969).

14. Haelan Labs Inc. v. Topps Chewing Gum, 202 F. 2d 866 (1953); Melville B. Nimmer, "The Right of Publicity," *Law and Contemporary Problems* 19 (Spring 1954):203–23.

15. Franklin, "A Constitutional Problem in Privacy Protection," p. 140.

16. Corliss v. E. W. Walker Co., 57 Fed. Rep. 434 (1893), at 435.

17. Jones v. Herald Post Co., 230 Ky. 227 (1929), at 229.

18. Sidis v. F-R Publishing Co., 113 F. 2d 806 (1940), at 809.

19. See, for example, Prosser, *Handbook of the Law of Torts,* p. 837.

20. Aquino v. Bulletin Company, 190 Pa. Super. 528 (1959); Carlisle v. Fawcett Pub., Inc., 201 Cal App. 733 (1962).

21. See, for example, Moloney v. Boy Comics, 272 App. Div. 166 (1950); Hull v. Curtis Pub. Co., 182 Pa. Super. 86 (1956).

22. See Bernstein v. NBC, 129 F. Supp. 817 (1955); Smith v. NBC, 292 P. 2d 600 (1956); Miller v. NBC, 157 F. Supp. 240 (1957).

23. 401 U.S. —, 91 S. Ct. 1811 (1971).

24. See Holmes v. The Curtis Pub. Co., 303 F. Supp. 522 (1969); Rosenbloom v. Metromedia, 415 F. 2d 892 (1969).

25. Public Utilities Commission v. Pollak, 343 U.S. 451 (1952), at 467.

Selected Bibliography

Among the published material available in most larger libraries to the reader inclined to pursue the subject, the following have been found useful in the preparation of this work:

BOOKS

American Newspaper Annual. Philadelphia: N. W. Ayer and Sons, 1891.

Brenton, Myron, *The Privacy Invaders.* New York: Coward-McCann, 1964.

Chamberlain, Joseph E. *The Boston Transcript.* Cambridge, Mass.: Riverside Press, 1930.

Commager, Henry Steele. *The American Mind.* 21st ed. New Haven, Conn.: Yale University Press, 1950.

Cooley, Thomas M. *A Treatise on the Law of Torts.* 2nd ed. Chicago: Callaghan, 1888.

Emery, Edwin. *The Press and America.* 2nd ed. Englewood Cliffs, N.J.: Prentice-Hall, 1962.

Hachten, William A. *The Supreme Court on Freedom of the Press.* Ames, Iowa: Iowa State Press, 1968.

Hofstader, Samuel, and Horowitz, George. *Right of Privacy.* New York: Central Book Co., 1964.

Holmes, Oliver W. *The Common Law.* Boston: Little, Brown, 1881.

Hurst, James Willard. *Law and Social Process in United States History.* Ann Arbor: University of Michigan Law School, 1960.

Kalven, Harry, Jr. "The *New York Times* Case: A Note on 'The Central Meaning of the First Amendment.'" In *The Supreme Court Review, 1964,* edited by Philip B. Kurland. Chicago: University of Chicago Press, 1964.

————. "The Reasonable Man and the First Amendment: Hill, Butts, and Walker." In *The Supreme Court Review, 1967,* edited by Philip B. Kurland. Chicago: University of Chicago Press, 1967.

Kobre, Sidney. *The Yellow Press and Gilded Age Journalism.* Tallahassee: Florida State University, 1964.

Lee, Alfred McClung. *The Daily Newspaper in America.* New York: Macmillan, 1937.

Lee, James M. *History of American Journalism.* New York: Houghton Mifflin, 1917.

Mason, Alpheus T. *Brandeis: A Free Man's Life.* New York: Viking Press, 1946.

Mott, Frank L. *American Journalism.* New York: Macmillan, 1941.

Packard, Vance. *The Naked Society.* New York: David McKay, 1964.

Prosser, William L. *Handbook of the Law of Torts.* St. Paul, Minn.: West Publishing, 1964.

Schlesinger, Arthur M. *The Rise of the City, 1878–1898.* History of American Life, vol. 10. New York: Macmillan, 1933.

Stromholm, Stig. *Right of Privacy and Rights of Personality.* Stockholm: P. A. Norstedt and Soners Forlag, 1967.

Todd, A. L. *Justice on Trial: The Case of Louis D. Brandeis.* New York: McGraw-Hill, 1964.

U.S. Department of Commerce, Bureau of the Census. *Historical Statistics of the United States, Colonial Times to 1957.* Washington, D.C.: U.S. Government Printing Office, 1960.

Westin, Alan. *Privacy and Freedom.* New York: Atheneum, 1967.

PERIODICALS

Adams, Elbridge L. "The Right of Privacy and Its Relation to the Law of Libel." *American Law Review* 39 (January–February 1905): 37–58.

Beaney, William M. "The Right of Privacy and American Law." *Law and Contemporary Problems* 31, no. 2 (1966): 253–71.

Bloustein, Edward J. "Privacy as an Aspect of Human Dignity: An Answer to Dean Prosser." *New York University Law Review* 39 (December 1964): 962–1007.

———. "Privacy, Tort Law, and the Constitution: Is Warren and Brandeis Tort Petty and Unconstitutional as Well?" *Texas Law Review* 46 (April 1968): 611–29.

Bohlen, Francis H. "Fifty Years of Torts." *Harvard Law Review* 50 (March 1937): 425–48.

Clemons, L. S. "The Right of Publicity in Relation to the Publication of Photographs." *Marquette Law Review* 14 (June 1930): 193–98.

Davis, Frederick. "What Do We Mean by 'Right to Privacy'?" *South Dakota Law Review* 4 (Spring 1959): 1–24.

Dewsnup, Richard L. "Utah Right of Privacy Statute Covers Only Advertisements for Sale of Collateral Product." *Utah Law Review* 4 (Fall 1954): 276–79.

Dickler, Gerald. "The Right of Privacy: A Proposed Redefinition." *United States Law Review,* 70 (August 1936): 435–36.

Doan, Edward N. "The Newspaper and the Right of Privacy." *The*

Journal of the Bar Association of the State of Kansas 5 (February 1937): 203–14.

Edwards, Percy L. "Right of Privacy and Equity Relief." *Central Law Journal* 55 (August 1902): 123–27.

Fitzpatrick, John R. "The Unauthorized Publication of Photographs." *Georgetown Law Journal* 20 (January 1932): 134–59.

Franklin, Marc A. "A Constitutional Problem in Privacy Protection: Legal Inhibitions on Reporting of Fact." *Stanford Law Review* 16 (December 1963): 107–48.

Godkin, E. L. "The Rights of the Citizen, IV: To His Own Reputation." *Scribner's Magazine*, July 1890, pp. 58–67.

Gordon, William S. "The Right of Privacy." *The Canadian Law Times* 22 (August 1902): 281–91.

Green, Leon. "Continuing the Privacy Discussion: A Response to Judge Wright and President Bloustein." *Texas Law Review* 46 (April 1968): 750–56.

———. "The Right of Privacy." *Boston University Law Review* 12 (June 1932): 353–95.

Hadley, Herbert Spencer. "The Right to Privacy." *Northwestern Law Review* 3 (October 1894): 1–21.

Hand, Augustus N. "Schuyler against Curtis and the Right to Privacy." *The American Law Register and Review* 36 (December 1895): 745–59.

Handler, Earl. "The Right of Privacy and Some of Its Recent Developments." *Dickinson Law Review* 44 (October 1939): 39–48.

Hauighurst, Clark C. "Foreword, Privacy Symposium." *Law and Contemporary Problems* 31, no. 2 (1966): 251.

Hicks, Granville, "The Invasion of Privacy: The Limits of Privacy." *American Scholar*, Spring 1959, pp. 185–96.

Kacedan, Basil W. "The Right of Privacy." *Boston University Law Review* 27 (November 1932): 237–60.

Kalven, Harry, Jr. "Privacy in Tort Law—Were Warren and Brandeis Wrong?" *Law and Contemporary Problems* 31, no. 2 (1966): 326–41.

Konvitz, Milton R. "Privacy and the Law: A Philosophical Prelude." *Law and Contemporary Problems* 31 (1966): 272–80.

Larremore, Wilbur. "The Law of Privacy." *Columbia Law Review* 12 (December 1912): 693–708.

Leovy, T. M., Jr. "Torts: The Right of Privacy." *Southern California Law Review* 13 (November 1939): 81–91.

Lisle, Rufus. "The Right of Privacy (A Contra View)." *Kentucky Law Journal* 19 (January 1931): 137–44.

Ludwig, Frederick J. "Peace of Mind in 48 Pieces vs. Uniform Right of Privacy." *Minnesota Law Review* 32 (June 1948): 734–65.

McCarthy, Francis J. "Privacy: Burgeoning Rights and Remedies." *Connecticut Bar Journal* 38 (December 1964): 555–624.

McClean, W. Archibald. "The Right of Privacy." *The Green Bag* 15 (1903): 494–98.

Moreland, Roy. "The Right of Privacy Today." *Kentucky Law Journal* 19 (January 1931): 101–36.

Mosburg, Marjorie P. "Torts: Effects of Statute in Oklahoma." *Oklahoma Law Review* 10 (August 1957): 353–56.

Nimmer, Melville B. "The Right of Publicity." *Law and Contemporary Problems* 19 (Spring 1954): 203–23.

Nizer, Louis. "The Right of Privacy: A Half-Century's Development." *Michigan Law Review* 39 (February 1941): 526–60.

O'Brien, Denis. "The Right of Privacy." *Southern California Law Review* 13 (November 1939): 81–91.

O'Connor, Thomas H. "The Right to Privacy in Historical Perspective." *Massachusetts Law Quarterly* 53 (June 1968): 101–15.

Oglesby, Dwayne L. "Freedom of the Press v. the Rights of the Individual—A Continuing Controversy." *Oregon Law Review* 47 (February 1968): 132–45.

Overton, Nelson T. "The Virginia 'Right of Privacy' Statute." *Virginia Law Review* 38 (January 1952): 117–25.

Patterson, Marion D. "Privacy—A Summary of the Past and Present." *Pennsylvania Bar Association Quarterly* 35 (October 1963): 52–64.

Pearson, Stanley G. "Torts: The Right to Privacy and the Pursuit of Happiness." *California Law Review* 20 (November 1931): 100–102.

Pember, Don R. "Privacy and the Press: The Defense of Newsworthiness." *Journalism Quarterly* 45 (Spring 1968): 14–24.

Pound, Roscoe. "The Fourteenth Amendment and the Right of Privacy." *Western Reserve Law Review* 13 (December 1961): 34–35.

———. "Interests of Personality." *Harvard Law Review* 28 (February 1915): 343–65.

"Privacy, Defamation and the First Amendment: The Implications of Time, Inc. v. Hill." *Columbia Law Review* 67 (May 1967): 926–52.

Ragland, George, Jr. "The Right of Privacy." *Kentucky Law Review* 17 (January 1929): 85–122.

"A Re-interpretation of Gee v. Pritchard." *Michigan Law Review* 25 (June 1927): 889–91.

"The Right of Privacy." *The Albany Law Journal* 64 (December 1902): 428–29.

"The Right of Privacy." *Michigan Law Review* 3 (1902): 559–63.

"The Right of Privacy Today." *Harvard Law Review* 43 (December 1929): 297–302.

"Right of Privacy vs. Free Press: Suggested Resolution of Conflicting Values." *Indiana Law Journal* 28 (Winter 1953): 179–94.

Rubenhausen, Oscar M., and Brim, Orville G., Jr. "Privacy and Behavioral Research." *Columbia Law Review* 65 (November 1965): 1184–1211.

Shaheen, Joseph. "Right of Privacy—A Re-evaluation of Theoretical Bases Underlying the Right." *University of Detroit Law Review* 16 (January 1953): 79–88.

Shapo, Marshall S. "Media Injuries to Personality: An Essay on Legal Regulation of Public Communication." *Texas Law Review,* 46 (April 1968): 650–67.

Sheinman, Martin L. "Torts: Invasion of Right of Privacy: Libel." *University of Pittsburgh Law Review* 13 (Winter 1952): 435–38.

Silver, Isadore. "Privacy and the First Amendment." *Fordham Law Review* 34 (May 1966): 553–68.

Snyder, Richard A. "The Right of Privacy: 50 Years After." *Temple University Law Quarterly* 15, no. 1 (November 1940): 148–55.

Wade, John W. "Defamation and the Right of Privacy." *Vanderbilt Law Review* 15 (October 1962): 1093–1125.

Warren, Samuel D., and Brandeis, Louis D. "The Right to Privacy." *Harvard Law Review* 4 (December 1890): 193–220.

Winfield, Percy L. "Privacy." *The Law Quarterly Review,* 47 (January 1931): 23–42.

Wright, J. Skelly. "Defamation, Privacy, and the Public's Right to Know: A National Problem and a New Approach." *Law and Contemporary Problems* 31 (1966): 272–80.

Yankwich, Leon R. "The Right of Privacy: Its Development, Scope and Limitations." *Notre Dame Lawyer* 27, no. 4 (1952): 499–528.

———. "Trends in the Law Affecting Media of Communication." *Federal Rules Decision* 15 (1954): 291–331.

NEWSPAPERS

Boston Daily Advertiser, 1 January 1890–31 December 1890.
Boston Evening Transcript, 1 January 1890–31 December 1890.
Boston Globe, 1 January 1890–31 December 1890.
Boston Journal, 1 January 1890–31 December 1890.

Index